CHARLES WILLSON PEALE

and His World

EDGAR P. RICHARDSON

BROOKE HINDLE

LILLIAN B. MILLER

with a Foreword by

Charles Coleman Sellers

A BARRA FOUNDATION BOOK

CHARLES WILLSON PEALE

and His World

HARRY N. ABRAMS, INC., *Publishers, New York*

Frontispiece: Self-Portrait. 1821

Peale normally painted directly without preliminary studies; but for his very important autobiographi-
cal picture *The Artist in His Museum* (see No. 75),
with its subtle problems of indirect lighting and its
large size, he made one of his rare preparatory
studies, perhaps unique and showing how much importance he attached to this painting. (*Private collection*)

Supervising Editor: Regina Ryan

Editor: Joanne Greenspun

Designer: Philip Grushkin

Library of Congress Cataloging in Publication Data
Peale, Charles Willson, 1741–1827.
   Charles Willson Peale and his world.

   "A Barra Foundation book."
   Includes bibliography and index.
   1. Peale, Charles Willson, 1741–1827. 2. Painters—
United States—Biography.   I. Richardson, Edgar Preston,
1902–   .   II. Hindle, Brooke.   III. Miller, Lillian B.
IV. Title.
ND237.P27A4 1983   759.13 [B]   82-8838
ISBN 0–8109–1478–6   AACR2

FIRST EDITION

Printed and bound in Japan

CONTENTS

ACKNOWLEDGMENTS

THE APPEARANCE OF *Charles Willson Peale and His World* marks the culmination of years of effort and collaboration among many people who believed that the life and achievements of the extraordinary Mr. Peale had been generally underestimated. His life had been seen only in part; the full range of his interests and achievements had not been recognized. It was time for a reappraisal. Through the most comprehensive and compelling means possible—a book and an exhibition displaying his accomplishments both in art and in natural science—the modern American public would have an opportunity to learn about Mr. Peale and his world.

From start to finish, both this book and the concurrent exhibition have been guided by the vision of Edgar P. Richardson. Charles Coleman Sellers, until his death in 1980, also made vital contributions to the entire project. The National Portrait Gallery, the Amon Carter Museum, and the Metropolitan Museum of Art join in expressing our gratitude to Dr. Richardson and our regret that Dr. Sellers is not with us to share in the delights and accomplishments of a job well done.

Special thanks are due to the Barra Foundation and their Publication Consultant, Regina Ryan. The Barra Foundation developed the concept behind this book, arranged for its publication, and saw it through to completion. We would also like to express our appreciation to Brooke Hindle and Lillian Miller for sharing in these pages their unique insights into Peale's character and achievements.

A planning grant awarded to the Metropolitan Museum by the National Endowment for the Humanities helped establish the framework of the exhibit; a generous gift from Lawrence and Barbara Fleischman made the exhibition a reality.

The staff of each of the participating institutions contributed substantially to the book and exhibition. John K. Howat, Chairman of the Departments of American Art at the Metropolitan Museum, conceived the project and initiated the involvement of Drs. Richardson and Sellers. Doreen B. Burke of the Metropolitan staff made significant contributions to all phases of the exhibition. Her research of the natural history specimens was invaluable, and she undertook, as well, the difficult task of coordinating the exhibition at the Metropolitan. We are also grateful to the Metropolitan's conservation staff, particularly Dianne Dwyer, for work done on restoring objects to be exhibited in the show. Harold F. Pfister, as then Acting Director of the National Portrait Gallery, worked closely with the Barra Foundation in developing the book and overseeing the formation of the exhibit during its early stages. We are particularly grateful to Beverly Cox, Curator of Exhibitions, National Portrait Gallery. She and her staff not only undertook the complicated task of arranging the loans for the exhibition, but also did much to assemble and organize the text and illustrations for the book. The staffs of the Charles Willson Peale Papers and the Catalogue of American Portraits, both at the National Portrait Gallery, provided essential research assistance and deserve our special thanks for their thoroughness and efficiency. Carol Clark, Curator of Paintings at the Amon Carter Museum, served as coordinator for that institution, an all-important role.

We were very pleased to have the excellent professional advice of Robert Peck, Acting Vice-President, Museum of the Academy of Natural Sciences, Philadelphia, and Charlotte Porter, Assistant Curator at the Florida State Museum. After the death of Charles Coleman Sellers, these two consultants helped in the identification and cataloging of natural history and ethnographical objects from Peale's Museum.

The American Philosophical Society is the repository of the Peale-Sellers Collection; without the society's cooperation and willingness to share the many objects in their collection, neither the exhibit nor the book would have been possible. Dr. Edmund Carter, Murphy Smith, and Stephen Catlett of that institution were most generous with their time and good will. We were also very fortunate that the Peabody Museum of Archaeology and Ethnology, holder of a number of artifacts that were originally part of Peale's Philadelphia Museum, was able to contribute to this project. We particularly owe thanks to Fran Silverman, Director/Collections Sharing, for negotiating the many details involved. Most of Peale's "Gallery of Distinguished Americans" is now at Independence National Historical Park in Philadelphia. We especially appreciate the generous loans made by this institution with the indispensable help of John Milley, Chief of Museum Operations.

It is always difficult to find words sufficient to express the debt we owe to all the lenders whose names are listed in the back of this publication. We trust, however, that they know they have our deepest gratitude.

ALAN FERN
Director, National Portrait Gallery

JAN KEENE MUHLERT
Director, Amon Carter Museum

PHILIPPE DE MONTEBELLO
Director, The Metropolitan Museum of Art

LIST OF
ILLUSTRATIONS

ABOUT THE BOOK

I CANNOT LET THIS BOOK GO OUT without a word of affection and respect for Charles Coleman Sellers.

In 1974, John Howat, then Curator of American painting at the Metropolitan Museum of Art, suggested an exhibition of the paintings of Charles Willson Peale, the only major figure of the period of the Revolution and early republic who lacked a proper one-man exhibition. Would I be interested? I was interested: but no one had ever done justice to the many-sided achievement of that fascinating, remarkable, and delightful figure. Might I bring in Charles Sellers to work on Peale the natural scientist and museum man?

Charles Sellers was a descendant of Peale. He had written two admirable biographies of the artist. He knew Peale's world so intimately that at dinner he was as apt to tell an amusing anecdote of something that happened in 1790 as a story of something yesterday. He was at work on the story of Peale's Museum. It would be absurd, almost indecent, to do an exhibition of Peale without Charles Sellers. He agreed to do the museum, I the painter. Most of the information on the museum's collections in this book came from his knowledge. But he, alas, is gone, his great store of information, his lively wit, his charm, vanished with him in 1980.

We, his friends, the survivors, think of this book as a memorial to him, a great scholar and a delightful human being.

E.P.R.
May, 1982

FOREWORD: THE UNITY
OF A DIVERSE CAREER
by Charles Coleman Sellers

In 1815, at the end of a long, hard winter, Thomas Jefferson, the farmer at Monticello, and Charles Willson Peale, the farmer at "Belfield," were looking forward to busy days. Jefferson wrote to his friend of a new way to plant corn, of an improvement in his plow, his straw-cutter, his hominy-beater, and his sawmill. Peale replied that he had the Jefferson plow at work and the clover-seed machine as well. His greenhouse was in full flower, his garden planted, his watermill throbbed with the power of the April rains, and he had invented a windmill which would stand proof against the high winds of any coming storm.

But Peale had also a doubt to confess. He, an artist, had too long neglected brush and palette for a multitude of other interests. "A steady habit to any one object perhaps would have been more advantageous," he wrote. "I can reconcile this conduct to myself, because it has constituted much of my happiness—but the judicious and prudent will condemn me!"

Later critics of the Peale career would indeed deplore its many digressions. Yet one must expect among artists an itch for mechanical experiment and a love of nature. Both were as much a part of this painter's life as were his delight in art, music, poetry, and love. His life, for all its turns and variations, was nonetheless an integral whole, every new aspect allied to what had come before. Thus the farm, though at first a radical departure from his previous endeavors, soon evolved into a vast garden with winding paths, moral and patriotic monuments, replete with mechanical innovations and dedicated to a reverential study of nature. It became a flowering offshoot of that museum of natural history to which so many of his years had been given.

The Philadelphia Museum, in turn, had evolved from the painting-room gallery which every established artist of the eighteenth century maintained. Earlier, during the war for independence, he had begun to expand the gallery into a hall of fame for Revolutionary heroes. By war's end it held a long array of full-length and bust-size portraits. In this tall skylighted chamber the museum enterprise began, with the portraits high on the walls representing the primates, while the lower forms of life filled the cases and the floor below. Every exhibit was, in effect, a work of art using new techniques and constructed both for attractive and accurate representation, and the whole display composed to give an appealing sense of the harmony of all natural life. Old skills and new went into the museum's making, and he was well aware that to succeed as a "School of Wisdom" it must be interesting, authentic, and beautiful.

The museum idea, conceived in 1784, had behind it, in turn, the long years of the Revolutionary struggle in which Peale had both marched with Washington's army and joined in the political campaigns for a wider and more direct democracy. The peace found him in financial straits, while at the same time on fire, as were so many others, to see the new nation set an example of freedom and enlightenment for all the world. A museum could be the answer. Natural science must be brought to all America's people in an institution of such pervasive influence and importance that it would receive a national endowment.

Look back to the very beginning of this career, and you will find a poor boy, son of an impoverished gentleman. The child was bound apprentice to a saddler, and from those years under a hard-driving master had come a lifelong emotional need constantly to be active. Out of this too came a passionate conviction that freedom is the need and right of all rational beings.

From saddler's apprentice to painter to soldier to museum man and naturalist— even in his interval as gentleman farmer—all had been united in the urge to ceaseless activity, the drive for freedom, the search for beauty, health, and improvements of every sort. The experiments, the failures and successes, year after year, were all part of one man's enjoyment of his life.

IMPORTANT DATES IN THE LIFE OF CHARLES WILLSON PEALE

1741   APRIL 15: Born in Queen Anne's County, Maryland.

1750   NOVEMBER: Death of father, Charles Peale.

1751   Family moves to Annapolis.

1754   Apprenticed to Nathan Waters, saddler.

1761   DECEMBER: Released from apprenticeship; establishes shop in Annapolis.

1762   JANUARY 12: Marries Rachel Brewer (1744–1790). Develops interest in painting and buys first paints.

1763   Studies painting briefly with John Hesselius.

1764   Joins Sons of Freedom in opposition to Maryland's court party.

1765   Sails to Boston and Newburyport.

 JULY 14: Arrives in Boston.

 JULY 31–OCTOBER: in Newburyport.

 c. OCTOBER–JANUARY: Meets John Singleton Copley and briefly studies in his studio.

1766   SPRING: Returns to Accomac, Virginia.

 OCTOBER: Returns to Annapolis.

 DECEMBER: Leaves for England to study with Benjamin West.

1767   FEBRUARY: Arrives in London.

1768   Sends full-length portrait of Lord Chatham (William Pitt) to Virginia and makes his first engraving from it.

 APRIL 28: Exhibits in ninth exhibition of Society of Artists of Great Britain.

 FALL: Exhibits in special exhibition of Society of Artists of Great Britain.

1769 JUNE: Returns to Annapolis; paints in Maryland and Philadelphia.

1772 Paints first portrait of Washington as colonel.

1774 FEBRUARY 17: Raphaelle Peale, first surviving child, born Annapolis (d. 1825).

1775 DECEMBER 22: Angelica Kauffman Peale (Robinson) born Charlestown, Maryland (d. 1853).

1776 Moves family to Philadelphia. Enlists in city militia as private; elected first lieutenant in December. Joins "Furious Whigs." Participates in battles of Trenton and Princeton. Paints three-quarter-length portrait of Washington.

1777 MARCH: Serves as chairman of Whig Society.

JUNE 17: Commissioned captain of the Fourth Battalion or Regiment of Foot.

1778 FEBRUARY 22: Rembrandt Peale born Bucks County, Pennsylvania (d. 1860).

SPRING: Evacuation of Philadelphia by British. Active in Philadelphia politics; serves as agent for confiscated estates.

1779 JANUARY 8: Commissioned by Supreme Executive Council of Pennsylvania to paint portrait of Washington.

SPRING: Serves as chairman of Constitutional Society. Elected representative from Philadelphia to General Assembly of Pennsylvania.

1780 Purchases house at Third and Lombard streets, Philadelphia.

AUGUST 1: Titian Ramsay Peale I born Philadelphia (d. 1798).

OCTOBER: Loses re-election to Assembly.

1781 SUMMER: Builds painting room.

1782 NOVEMBER: Adds long room for exhibition of portraits; opens "portrait gallery."

1784 JANUARY: The Triumphal Arch erected and burns; re-created May 10.

MAY 4: Rubens Peale born Philadelphia (d. 1865).

1785 MAY 20: Opens exhibition of moving pictures.

1786 APRIL 24: Sophonisba Angusciola Peale (Sellers) born Philadelphia (d. 1859).

JULY 18: Opening of the Philadelphia Museum (Peale's Museum).

1787 Makes mezzotint prints from his collection of portraits of illustrious personages.

1790 APRIL 12: Rachel Brewer Peale dies.

1791 MAY 30: Marries Elizabeth DePeyster (1765–1804).

1794 MARCH 20: Charles Linnaeus Peale born Philadelphia (d. 1832).

JUNE–JULY: Moves Peale's Museum to Philosophical Hall.

DECEMBER 29: Founding of Columbianum, or American Academy of the Fine Arts.

1795 MAY 22: First exhibition of the Columbianum Society.

SEPTEMBER: Paints portrait of Washington.

OCTOBER 15: Benjamin Franklin Peale born Philadelphia (d. 1870).

1797 MARCH: Publishes *An Essay on Building Wooden Bridges*. Develops the patent fireplace.

OCTOBER 28: Sybilla Miriam Peale (Summers) born Philadelphia (d. 1856).

1798 SEPTEMBER 19: Titian Ramsay Peale I dies.

1799 NOVEMBER 2: Titian Ramsay Peale II born Philadelphia (d. 1885).

NOVEMBER 16: Publishes first lecture, *Introduction to a Course of Lectures on Natural History Delivered in the University of Pennsylvania . . .*

1800 NOVEMBER 8: Publishes *Discourse Introductory* to second series of lectures.

1801 JUNE: Purchases mastodon bones.

JULY–SEPTEMBER: Organizes expedition to exhume the mastodon.

DECEMBER 24: Exhibits assembled mastodon.

1802 APRIL 16: Elizabeth DePeyster Peale (Patterson) born Philadelphia (d. 1857).

Introduces physiognotrace for taking profiles.

1802–3 Improves and introduces the polygraph.

1803 FEBRUARY: Publishes *An Epistle to a Friend*.

1804 Publishes *Guide to the Philadelphia Museum*.

FEBRUARY 19: Elizabeth DePeyster Peale dies.

MAY 29: Accompanies Baron von Humboldt to Washington, D.C.

1805 JUNE: Helps to found the Pennsylvania Academy of the Fine Arts.

AUGUST 12: Marries Hannah Moore (1755–1821).

1810 JANUARY 1: Retires to "Belfield"; deeds museum to Rubens.

1812 FEBRUARY: Publishes *An Essay to Promote Domestic Happiness*.

1816 Publishes *Address to The Corporation and Citizens of Philadelphia*.

1818 NOVEMBER–FEBRUARY 1819: In Washington, D.C.

1821 FEBRUARY 1: Incorporates Philadelphia Museum Company.

OCTOBER 10: Hannah Moore Peale dies.

1822 Resumes management of museum.

SUMMER: Begins experiments with the manufacture of porcelain teeth.

1825 Raphaelle Peale dies.

1827 FEBRUARY 22: Dies in Philadelphia.

CHARLES WILLSON PEALE

and His World

Charles Willson Peale

AND HIS WORLD

———

EDGAR P. RICHARDSON

I

PEALE'S PORTRAITS arc works of art which give a picture of that time in America un-matched in historical interest. He was an observer of genius who, as a young man, painted the elegance of life in the colonial plantations of Chesapeake Bay. He saw the war for independence and the creation of our republic from the midst of the action, painting its chief actors before time had wrapped a veil of idealization about them, and turned them into patriarchs and mythical heroes. He lived long enough to paint Andrew Jackson, Henry Clay, and John Quincy Adams, leaders of a republic in which the old colonial life and even the war for independence were fading from memory.

He was both an artist and a naturalist, and an inventor, like his elder contemporary Benjamin Franklin, whom he knew in London and Philadelphia. We think of Franklin primarily as philosopher-scientist, yet he was an artist in prose, whose lucid, witty, persuasive writing made him the first American writer to enjoy an international audience. We think of Peale primarily as an artist, yet he turned both to natural science and invention. A soldier in the war for independence, he was also an effective propagandist, creating parades, floats, and illuminations to rouse public feeling or celebrate victory. An eighteenth-century Deist, like Franklin, he found nature "a bewitching study," whether in painting a landscape or creating a museum of natural history.

Like many other early American painters, Peale began as a self-taught amateur. His true career as an artist commenced in London in the late 1760s. Aiming to be a portrait painter, he created his own version of the English conversation piece—the portrait of a man or woman in his or her own domestic setting—adapting it to the needs and wishes of Maryland planters and Philadelphia gentry. He next developed his own form of the neoclassic portrait: clearly lighted figures, drawn with great precision and grasp of character, the color and light decorative but subordinate. In his final phase he began to experiment with light as his central artistic theme.

Primarily he was a draftsman, color playing a subordinate role as in all neoclassic painting; yet independent drawings by him are very rare. His likenesses were drawn directly upon the canvas and his drawings disappeared beneath his paint: but it is his sure, accurate drawing that gave his portraits their strength of character. His painter son, Rembrandt Peale, was an excellent critic when he observed, "As a painter, his likenesses were strong but never flattered; his execution spirited and natural."[1] His method of work was rapid—a day or two sufficed for a three-quarter-length portrait. This was advantageous for a painter in the sparsely settled country of the Chesapeake, who often made long journeys from house to house on the eastern shore to paint portraits.

THE GREAT BAY OF CHESAPEAKE

". . . No Country in the World can be more curiously watered"

(SEVENTEENTH-CENTURY TRAVELER)

In the eighteenth century, Virginia and Maryland were the most populous and richest of the American colonies; yet their people were scattered over widely spaced plantations rather than gathered in towns. In a century when water provided the best form of transportation, the rivers, creeks, and streams of the Great Bay were a high road on which the planter could ship his tobacco from his own wharf to London more cheaply than he could carry it a dozen miles on land. He could buy his clothes, materials for his wife's dresses, his children's shoe buckles, his books, every article of quality from London as easily as, or more easily than, in the bay towns of Norfolk, Williamsburg, Annapolis, and Chestertown.

Peale was born in 1741 in Queen Anne's County, Maryland, on the eastern shore of the bay. A year later, in 1742, his father became master of the Kent County School at Chestertown, then a thriving seaport near the head of the bay on the eastern shore. In 1750, when Peale was nine, his father died, leaving his widow with five small children. A kindly graduate of the school, John Beale Bordley, helped her to move across the bay to Annapolis.

Annapolis, on the Severn River, was small but it was the capital of the province of Maryland, and a widow might hope to earn a living there as a needlewoman. The Reverend Andrew Burnaby, an English traveler who passed through it in 1756, thought Annapolis a poor, straggling village.

But the little capital had its moment of glory in Peale's time. It was the center of the official and fashionable life of the province. The great landowners who came to take their seats in the Assembly or on the Governor's Council during the "public times," the lawyers and officeholders, built town houses there which are among the handsomest of our colonial heritage. Others came for the social life of the place, especially during the race meetings. One may catch a glimpse of that gay little society in George Washington's diary. When he spent a few days there in 1771, he lost £8 at the races, went four times to the theater, and danced at three balls. Again, in 1772, between Sunday and Friday, he went four times to the theater, to one ball, lost £5.6 at cards but won £13.7 at the races. The merchants, stimulated by the presence of such custom, tried to make

Annapolis an entrepôt of foreign goods, as Charleston was in Carolina; but geography was against them. By 1790, Baltimore, which controlled the wheat, iron, and timber from higher up the Susquehanna, had become the great port of Maryland.

The widow Peale had no part in this prosperity. She was glad to apprentice her son Charles, a nine-year-old, bright, curious boy, skillful with his hands, to a saddler. In Maryland the horse was a major part of life; and the skilled craftsman who made saddles and harnesses, if diligent and sober, would thrive. "NATHAN WATERS, From PHILADEL-PHIA, at the House of Mr. *Charles Wallace*, Staymaker, opposite to Mr. *James Mac-cubbin's* Store, in *Church Street, Annapolis*" taught the boy to work in leather and metal, to do wood carving and joining, and to make saddles.

THE IDEA OF MAKING PICTURES

Those who were born to be artists in the colonies discovered their art in various ways. Benjamin West as a child met a Welsh painter, William Williams, in Philadelphia, who lent him books on art; in his teens West was taken up by Provost Smith of the College of Philadelphia, who introduced him to the brightest, most powerful people in the province, who became his friends and sponsors. In Boston John Singleton Copley's step-father, Peter Pelham, was a well-born engraver and painter, in whose home the boy grew up among books, pictures, prints, music, and genteel behavior. The Pelhams knew all the people of quality in Boston. Peale had no such entré to the gentry of Annapolis; he started in life with nothing but his own inquiring mind and skilled hands. He was twenty-one in 1762, married, and an independent saddlemaker before he ever saw a painting. He had gone down the bay to purchase leather in Norfolk. There, in the house of a Scottish merchant, he saw for the first time "several landscapes and one Portrait, with which he had decorated his rooms. They were miserably done," said Peale, "had they been better, perhaps they would not have led Peale to the Idea of attempting anything in that way."[2]

The idea of making pictures took possession of his mind. He had taught himself to make and repair watches, why not try making pictures? He began by doing portraits of himself, his wife, brothers, sisters, and best friend, to their delight and admiration. When a neighboring gentleman paid him £10 to paint his and his lady's portraits, Peale considered that this might be a more profitable skill than saddlemaking or mending watches. But how to proceed? He had never seen a palette or an easel, knew nothing of the painter's technique. Undismayed, he set off for the big city, Philadelphia. Christopher Marshall, "At the Sign of the Golden Ball, in Chestnut street," sold "oils and colours for painting, London crown glass, clock faces, etc." Peale did not even know the names of colors, except of the most common kind. He went around the corner to Rivington's bookstore, at Front and Market streets, and found a book called *The Handmaid to the Arts*—published in London in 1752 by the newly organized Society for the encouragement of Arts, Manufactures and Commerce (now the Royal Society of Arts). This eighteenth-century how-to-do-it book contained instructions for every kind of art and artistic craft. Peale bought it, studied in his lodgings for four days, learned what supplies he would

Fig. a. John Hesselius, Jr.
Mrs. Richard Galloway, Jr.
1764. Oil on canvas.
The Metropolitan Museum of Art,
New York City

need, spent what money he possessed at Christopher Marshall's shop, and returned to Annapolis.

There was one other means of learning to paint. At a plantation called "Primrose Hill" near Annapolis lived the painter John Hesselius, son of an artist who had migrated in 1711 from Sweden to Philadelphia. Shortly after 1750 the younger Hesselius moved to Maryland, where he painted portraits and eventually married a widow, owner of a plantation on the Severn. Hesselius could show Peale the solid portrait formula that was the heritage of the late baroque—an upright figure, more costume than personality, but constructed with knowing skill and decorative effect.

Peale offered Hesselius one of his best saddles and fittings to be allowed to watch him paint a picture. Hesselius painted one half of a face, leaving the other half to be painted by Peale, then allowed him to watch the painting of two portraits. One of these may have been the portrait, *Mrs. Richard Galloway, Jr.*, in the Metropolitan Museum of Art, the only surviving portrait by Hesselius of that year, 1764 (Fig. a). It was not a bad introduction to the painter's craft, and timely, for troubles suddenly crowded upon

Peale. His partner in his saddle- and chaise-making business "decamped" with their money, leaving Peale in debt for their materials. He sold many of his leather supplies and saddles cheaply in order to get some money to pay off his debts, and turned optimistically to watchmaking and silversmithing while continuing to make saddles. Almost immediately, however, he became involved in the Maryland election of 1764, a move that caused the bottom to drop out of his career.

Maryland was a Proprietary colony and, as a recent historian observed, "At no time in the eighteenth century, from the restoration of the proprietary government [to the Lords Baltimore in 1715] to the Revolution, was there even an interval of real political peace in Maryland."[3] The colony was divided into a "court" party and a "country" party. The country party opposed the court party and the governors appointed by Lord Baltimore on issues of control of the revenue and taxation of the Proprietor's estates. In the election of 1764 the candidate of the court party for Annapolis's seat in the Assembly, Dr. George Steuart, mayor of the town and a standard-bearer of the party, was opposed by a hotheaded young lawyer, Samuel Chase.[4] Chase was a newcomer but had the backing of Charles Carroll, called Barrister, to distinguish him from three other living Charles Carrolls.[5] Carroll was a man who was to play a large part in Peale's life. Peale admired him as "possessing every manly virtue"; and with heedless idealism he threw himself into the campaign. Chase won by 89 votes to 59; but angry members of the court party to whom Peale owed money had four writs for debt served upon him. He took refuge on the eastern shore, from which he was driven by a fifth writ, and boarded a vessel about to sail for New England with a cargo of corn.

. . . A Great Feast

The shipmaster, Peale's brother-in-law Robert Polk, sold his corn in Newburyport, Massachusetts, where Peale went ashore to try his fortune. He painted a few portraits and banners to be carried in a parade protesting the Stamp Act, joined in picnics on Plum Island, but finding himself without work, went to Boston. There he visited the old painting room of John Smibert, the first professional portrait painter to emigrate to the colonies from England, now dead some fourteen years. The room was hung with Smibert's copies after Italian masters ("a great feast," Peale said). He made some purchases in Smibert's color shop, now run by his nephew, John Moffatt. Peale called upon John Singleton Copley, who received him kindly, showing Peale his painting room full of portraits and lending him a "candle light"—a head painted by candlelight—to copy as a test of skill. Peale acquired some prints after Sir Joshua Reynolds. But he could see that there was no future for him in Boston. When he received a letter telling him that his wife had given birth to a son, he took ship for the eastern shore of Virginia.

Up until this time he had made only a few naive portraits. Now, he made copies after the prints he had bought in Boston and sent one of these—after a print of Reynolds—across the bay to Charles Carroll, Barrister, at Annapolis. Carroll was impressed and helped Peale's brother, St. George Peale, to arrange an accommodation between Charles Willson Peale and his creditors so that he could return home.

"Something must and shall be done for Charles"

Peale sent another picture to the home of Miss Elizabeth Bordley at Annapolis, where her brother, John Beale Bordley, was staying while he attended a meeting of the Governor's Council. Bordley had once been a student of Peale's father and a helpful friend to the Peale family. Peale wrote in his autobiography: "When he [Bordley] rose in the morning he went into a cold room where the picture was put, before he had gathered up his stockings, and staid there viewing it near 2 hours, and when he came out he said to his sister, 'Something must and shall be done for Charles.'"[6]

Bordley organized a subscription to send Peale to study painting in London. He himself subscribed ten guineas; Charles Carroll, Barrister, twenty-five guineas; Governor Sharpe, eight pounds sterling; Daniel Dulany, ten guineas; Robert Lloyd, five guineas; Benjamin Tasker, three guineas; Thomas Ringgold, three guineas; Benjamin Calvert, five guineas; Thomas Sprigg, five guineas; Daniel of St. Thomas Jennifer, three guineas; Charles Carroll of Carrollton, five guineas. The list represents both court and country parties of the province. The Barrister gave him passage on one of his ships for London. The *Brandon* sailed in December, 1766, carrying Peale and the unused revenue stamps for the Stamp Act, which had never been allowed on shore.

Fig. b. THE PEALE FAMILY (detail).
c. 1770–73 and 1808

In the background of *The Peale Family* (No. 146) are shown three portrait busts (all unlocated): a self-portrait in the center, Benjamin West at the left, and Edmund Jenings on the right. Jenings, born in Virginia and reared in Maryland, spent most of his life in London. He was Peale's warm friend and patron during the artist's student years. (*The New-York Historical Society*)

1. Charles Carroll, Barrister. c. 1770–71

Charles Carroll, one of the most powerful members of the Maryland aristocracy, lived the life of a merchant prince on his Baltimore estate, "Mount Clare." In 1764, Peale and Carroll worked together for the election to the provincial assembly of the Sons of Freedom candidate, Samuel Chase. A feeling of mutual respect and admiration grew between saddler and lawyer, and when Carroll was approached by John Beale Bordley to subscribe to the fund for sending Peale to London, the Barrister readily agreed.

Carroll advised the young artist against becoming a miniature painter. "I would have you Consider whether [miniature painting] . . . may suit so much with the Taste of the People with us as Larger Portrait Painting which I think would . . . Turn out the Greater Profit here," he wrote. "But," he added, "after all Consult and be guided by the best of your own Genius and Study that Branch to which your Disposition Leads you. . . . You had better be a Good Painter in Miniature than an Indifferent one in Either of the other Branches." Despite his doubts, the Barrister was one of the first to order an ivory from Peale, shown here actual size. (*Private collection*)

LONDON, 1767–1769

"... *being an American was recommendation enough*"

When Peale presented himself to Benjamin West bearing a letter from Chief Justice William Allen of Pennsylvania, who had been West's first great benefactor, the artist observed that it was the best reference he could have brought but that being an American was recommendation enough. West found him lodgings, gave him a place to work in his studio, and, when Peale's money began to run out, arranged to have him take his meals with the West family so that he might stay longer in London. West was then twenty-nine and had been in London a little less than four years: his star was rising but his own future was not yet secure and his kindness to the young man from Maryland was most generous. Peale was in the studio on the day that West, summoned by the king to show his picture of *Agrippina Landing at Brundisium with the Ashes of Germanicus*, went off in a hired coach to Windsor wearing court dress and a sword.

A born experimenter, Peale "was not contented with knowing how to paint in one way, but he engaged in the whole circle of the arts, except painting in enamel. And also at Modeling, and casting in plaster of Paris. He made some essays in Mezzotinto scraping."[7] From an Italian assistant of the English sculptor Joseph Wilton, he learned to model busts, producing a self-portrait, a bust of West, and a bust of a Virginia-born lawyer living in London named Edmund Jenings, who now enters the story to become another generous and helpful friend (Fig. b). Part of his living expenses in London Peale earned by painting miniatures. By an arrangement with a jeweler in Ludgate Hill, country clients came to Peale for portraits in miniature, the jeweler making his profit by mounting the ivories. Peale enjoyed small, precise, delicate work. He wrote to Charles Carroll, Barrister, in Maryland that he hoped to devote himself to miniature painting (No. 1). Carroll replied that he doubted this would do in Maryland; but he sent some more money, saying that he hoped Peale would stay as long as needed.[8]

2. MATTHIAS AND
THOMAS BORDLEY. 1767

While in London, Peale became a
member of the Society of Artists,
and entered three miniatures in its
1768 exhibition, including this
double portrait of John Beale
Bordley's sons. Thomas and
Matthias had just arrived in England on their way to study at Eton,
and are seen dutifully improving
themselves with the classics. They
stand between a bust of Minerva,
goddess of wisdom, and the dome
of St. Paul's, symbol of religious
faith. (*National Museum of American Art, Smithsonian Institution*)

3. WILLIAM PITT. 1768

Edmund Jenings, a Maryland lawyer living in
London, gave Peale his first major commission
when he engaged the artist to produce a full-
length portrait of William Pitt, the famous
defender of American resistance to the Stamp
Act, as a gift for the gentlemen of Westmoreland County in Virginia. Since Pitt was unable
to sit for the portrait, Peale used as his model a
statue, recently carved by Joseph Wilton, that
depicted Pitt as a Roman orator. Peale's portrait was a message to England and the world
that America's freedom must not be trifled
with. He engraved this mezzotint from the
painting in the hope of profiting from the sale
of prints when he returned to Maryland.
(*The Pennsylvania Academy of the Fine Arts*)

A DESCRIPTION OF THE PICTURE AND MEZZOTINTO OF MR. PITT,

DONE BY CHARLES WILLSON PEALE, OF MARYLAND.

THE Principal Figure is that of Mr. PITT, in a Confular Habit, fpeaking in Defence of the Claims of the American Colonies, on the Principles of the British Conftitution.

With MAGNA CHARTA in one Hand, he points with the other, to the Statue of British *Liberty*, trampling under Foot the Petition of the Congress at New-York.—— Some have thought it not quite proper to reprefent Liberty as guilty of an Action fo contrary to her genuine Spirit; for that, conducting herfelf in ftrict Propriety of Character, fhe ought not to violate, or treat with Contempt, the Rights of any one. To this it may be fufficient to fay, the Painter principally intended to allude to the Obfervation which hath been made by Hiftorians, and Writers on Government, that the *States which enjoy the higheft Degree of Liberty are apt to be oppreffive of thofe who are fubordinate, and in Subjection to them.* Montesquieu, fpeaking of the Conftitution of Rome, and the Government of the Roman Provinces, fays, " *La Liberté croit,* " *dans le Centre et la Tyrannie aux Extrimetés:*" And again, " *La Ville ne fentoit point la Tyrannie,* " *qui ne s' exercoit que fur les Nations Affujettis.*" And fuppofing Mr. PITT, in his Oration, to point, as he does, at the Statue, it makes a Figure of Rhetoric ftrongly and juftly farcaftic on the prefent faint Genius of British Liberty ; in which Light, Gentlemen of Reading and Tafte have been pleafed to commend it. The Fact is, that the Petition of the Congrefs at New-York, againft Acts of meer Power, adverfe to American Rights, was rejected by the Houfe of Commons, the Guardians, the Genius, of *that* Liberty, languifhing as it *is*.

An Indian is placed on the Pedeftal, in an *erect* Pofture, with an attentive Countenance, watching, as America has done for Five Years paft, the extraordinary Motions of the British Senate——He liftens to the Orator, and has a Bow in his Hand, and a Dog by his Side, to fhew the natural *Faithfulnefs and Firmnefs* of America.

It was advifed by fome, to have had the Indian drawn in a dejected and melancholy Pofture : And, confidering the apparent Weaknefs of the Colonies, and the Power of the Parent Country, it might not, perhaps, have been improper to have executed it in that Manner ; but in Truth the Americans, being well founded in their Principles, and animated with a facred Love for their Country, have never difponded.

An Altar, with a Flame is placed in the Foreground, to fhew that the Caufe of Liberty is facred, and, that therefore, they who maintain it, not only difcharge their Duty to their King and themfelves, but to GOD. It is decorated with the Heads of Sidney and Hampden, who, with undaunted Courage, fpoke, wrote, and died in Defence of the true Principles of Liberty, and of thofe Rights and Bleffings which Great-Britain now enjoys : For, as the Banner placed between them expreffes it,

Sanctus Amor Patriæ dat Animum.

A Civic Crown is laid on the Altar, as confecrated to *that* Man who preferved his Fellow-Citizens and Subjects from Deftruction !

The View of W——h—— is introduced in the Back Ground, not meerly as an elegant Piece of Architecture, but as it was the Place where ———— fuffered, for attempting to invade the Rights of the British Kingdoms : And it is obfervable, that the Statue and Altar of British Liberty are erected near the Spot where that great *Sacrifice* was made, through fad Neceffity, to the Honour, Happinefs, Virtue, and in one Word, to the Liberty of the British People.

The Petition of the Congrefs at New-York, and the Reprefentation of W——h—— point out the Time, and almoft the Place, where the Speech was delivered.

The chief Object of this Defign will be anfwered, if it manifefts, in the leaft, the Gratitude of America to his Lordfhip. It will, with Tradition, unprejudiced by the Writings of *Hirelings*, who are made to glide in with the courtly Streams of Falfhood, be the faithful Conveyance to Pofterity of the Knowledge of thofe Great Things which we, who are not to be impofed on by " the bufy Doings and Undoings" of the envious Great, have feen.

4. Broadside describing the William Pitt portrait. 1768

Perhaps fearing that his American audience would not be familiar with the traditional images of liberty he had incorporated in the William Pitt portrait, Peale spelled out their meaning in this broadside, prepared to accompany the mezzotint. Some of the symbolism appears in later works, such as the portraits of John Beale Bordley and Conrad-Alexandre Gérard (Nos. 5, 28). (*Library of Congress*)

Edmund Jenings, of a wealthy and prominent Maryland family, educated at Eton and Cambridge and settled in London as a lawyer, now gave him a number of portrait commissions. One was for the miniature of the two young sons of John Beale Bordley (No. 2) who had been sent in Jenings's care to be educated at Eton. Jenings followed this by a still more important commission: a portrait of William Pitt. It came about in this way. A group of gentlemen of Westmoreland County, the "northern neck" of Virginia, had tried to order from West a portrait of Lord Camden, one of the Parliamentary leaders who was opposed to the Stamp Act. Camden was unwilling to sit. Jenings then intervened, ordering from Peale a full-length portrait of Pitt, the other hero of American Whigs, to be his gift to the gentlemen of Virginia, filled with allusions to British liberty and past struggles for it. Pitt was unable to sit, so Peale copied a statue of him, recently carved by Joseph Wilton. Peale made from his portrait a mezzotint (No. 3), which he hoped (unsuccessfully as it turned out) to sell in America.

THE COLONIES AND BRITAIN DRAW APART

An aristocratic government is the least fitted of all others to extensive empire ... The House of Commons, which ought to be the representative of the people, is become the instrument of the people to raise money from the subjects
(CHARLES CARROLL OF CARROLLTON TO EDMUND JENINGS, AUGUST 9, 1771)

I wish you may not be put off from your affection for your own country by growing prejudices &c. You went away young; don't forget you are a Buckskin; I hope you are an improved one; which is better than to be a spoiled Englishman
(JOHN BEALE BORDLEY, FROM WYE ISLAND, TO HIS SON AT ETON, 1772)

Benjamin West had been sent abroad at the age of twenty-two in 1760. He never lost his fondness for the land of his birth; but his art was his true country. He never felt the anguish of choice confronting Americans at home, such as Copley, who had married into a great Loyalist family and was driven from Boston by fear of revolutionary mob violence. Peale also felt no anguish of choice. The issue for him was very simple: America was right, Britain was wrong. "From the time in which G. Britain first attempted to lay a tax on America," he said in his autobiography, "he was a zealous advocate for the liberties of his Country."

During the first months of Peale's stay in London, early in the summer of 1767, Parliament passed Charles Townshend's bill to impose its will upon the Assembly of the province of New York. The dispute was over who should pay for the quartering of British troops in the province. Parliament declared all acts of the New York Assembly null until it obeyed the directions of the Parliament at London. Peale then resolved that "he would never pull off his hat as the King passed by and ... determined he would do all in his power to render his Country independent."[9]

THE WORLD OF ART

In London two groups of artists presented exhibitions in the 1760s, before the founding of the Royal Academy. The stronger group was the Society of Artists of Great Britain, who exhibited in "the Great Room in Spring-Garden, Charing Cross." West and Peale showed their work with this group. The other was "The Free Society of Artists associated for the Relief of their Distressed and Decayed Brethren, their widows and children" who exhibited at "the Two New Great Exhibitions Rooms in Pall-Mall, next to the bottom of the Hay-Market." Peale undoubtedly studied the work shown by both societies.

In the spring exhibition of the Society of British Artists he was represented by one canvas and three miniatures:

No. 117, Portrait of a young gentleman, three quarters.
No. 118, Ditto of a lady in miniature.
No. 119, Ditto of two young gentlemen, ditto (No. 2).
No. 120, Ditto of two ladies, ditto.

The society again held an exhibition in September in honor of the visiting king of Denmark; Peale showed:

No. 84, A portrait of a girl.

The young provincial, who had hardly been painting more than five years, now saw his work hanging on a wall with some of the great British pictures of the eighteenth century. In the spring exhibition he saw two of Gainsborough's most splendid full-lengths, *The Honorable Thomas Needham* (Ascott, The National Trust) and a naval portrait, *Captain Augustus John Harvey, Third Earl of Bristol* (Ickworth, The National Trust); in the autumn exhibit was one of Richard Wilson's great Italian landscapes, *A View of Rome from the Villa Madama* (Fig. c), a grand and solemn picture showing the full impact of the Italian tradition of landscape upon English painting. Peale was to remember these pictures. When a decade later, he was asked to paint Washington as victorious general (No. 26), his mind seems to have gone back to the pose of Gainsborough's *Captain Harvey* (Fig. d). Gainsborough's rich coloristic style did not help Peale, who was to become one of the earliest painters in a neoclassic style; but the pose of a figure, leaning against a great ship's anchor (in the cross-legged pose that then symbolized elegance and ease), with a captured battle flag lying at his feet, offered suggestions Peale gladly used.

He had come a long way from his saddle shop in Annapolis. Many people had liked and helped him. In the portrait West painted of him at this time (Fig. e) one sees a

Fig. c. Richard Wilson. A VIEW OF ROME FROM THE VILLA MADAMA. 1753. Oil on canvas. Yale Center for British Art, New Haven, Connecticut. Paul Mellon Collection

spirited, sensitive, intelligent face. Peale was enthusiastic, affectionate, eager to please, never jealous of the success of others, ingenious, and incessantly active. Memories of West's studio tell us of his activity. One comes from John Trumbull. Visitors to West's studio were surprised by the sound of hammering in another room. "Oh," explained West, "that is our young countryman, Mr. Peale, who when he is not painting, amuses himself repairing my locks and bells."[10] Charles Leslie remembered that "Mr. West painted to the last with a palette which Peale had most ingeniously mended for him, after he [West] had thrown it aside as useless. It was a small palette; but he never used any other for his largest pictures."[11]

In the spring of 1769, homesick for his wife and child, and out of money after two years in London, Peale sailed for home on one of Mr. Jenings's ships. In June he was at Annapolis. The Chesapeake country at last had a painter of its own.

Fig. d. Thomas Gainsborough. CAPTAIN AUGUSTUS JOHN HARVEY. c. 1769. Oil on canvas. Ickworth, The National Trust, England

PAINTING FOR MARYLAND

The young portrait painter who sailed from London to Annapolis in 1769 exchanged a luxurious metropolitan city for a country village. When Rochambeau's army marched through Annapolis years later on the way to Yorktown, an abbé attached to the Auxonne (artillery) regiment observed that the streets were unpaved but the town had "a few fine houses."[12] Peale's wife and child were there: he owed money at six percent interest, which he felt bound to pay. Were there portraits to be painted? Except in the "public times" Annapolis was not populous. Carl Bridenbaugh, in *Cities in Revolt*, estimated the size of colonial cities in 1760: Philadelphia had 23,750 people; New York, 18,000; Boston, 15,631; Charleston, 8,000; Newport, 7,500. Annapolis had fewer than 5,000. A portrait painter might well starve.

Yet the shores of the Chesapeake and its tributary rivers were dotted by plantation houses in which many people lived in comfort and even luxury. Planters bought their clothes and household goods in London, and sent their sons to English schools (or in the case of Roman Catholic families to schools on the Continent). They were trained for the law at the Inns of Court in London. Merchants often lived for a time in London. Planters in Maryland maintained family relations with relatives in England, and their ideal of life was similar to that in country houses of English gentry. Family portraits were part of this tradition. However, the migration of portrait painters across the ocean that met the demand for portraits earlier in the century had at least temporarily ceased by 1769. The tidewater country was a wide open field for a portrait painter.

Peale had quite a clear understanding of his own gifts and of what he wished to do. He was a realist; he knew that it was his nature to observe and to paint what he saw. People were to be his subject matter. In a letter to his friend Bordley written after his return, he said of his situation in America, "I do not regret the loss of the Antiques, or the works of Raphael and Correggio, since I am obliged daily to portray the finest forms, a practise that made Titian excellent in colouring."[13] In another letter of 1772 he declared his determination to be independent of the practice of drawing upon the imagery of antique sculpture and the Italian Old Masters to compose their canvases, as he had seen West and Reynolds do.

Perhaps I have a good eye, that is all . . . A good painter of either Portrait or History, must be well acquainted with the Grecian and Roman statues, to be

Fig. f. Arthur Devis. A GENTLEMAN AND HIS DAUGHTER. c. 1745–47. Oil on canvas. Yale Center for British Art, New Haven, Connecticut. Paul Mellon Collection

Fig. g. Francis Hayman. MARGARET TYERS AND HER
HUSBAND. c. 1750–52. Oil on canvas. Yale Center
for British Art, New Haven, Connecticut. Paul
Mellon Collection

able to draw them at pleasure by memory, and account for every beauty, must
know the original cause of beauty in all he sees... These are more than I shall
ever have time or opportunity to know, but as I have variety of Characters to
paint, I must as Rembrandt did, make these my Antiques, and improve myself as
well as I can while I am providing for my support.[14]

Appeals to the example of Titian and Rembrandt show that the most important thing
Peale had learned in London was to know himself and to make conscious choices. He
had to create a new style to please his colonial public.

On his return, he found that the Barrister had been correct in saying that Marylanders did not wish miniatures. They would perhaps order a miniature for a lady to wear on
her wrist or pin upon her bosom. But the Maryland gentry were building high-
ceilinged, spacious houses, like the Hammond-Harwood house and the Chase-Lloyd
house in Annapolis. They wished portraits of themselves and their families, of lifesize,
even at full length, to hang in these houses. Although Peale had painted a full-length of
Pitt while in London, the problem presented by the wishes of his Maryland friends and
patrons was new and difficult for a man who had thought to be a miniature painter. His
mind went back to portraits in the exhibitions of London.

The pattern he selected to develop for Maryland was not the grandiose Italianate
examples of Reynolds or West, or the landscapes of Wilson: it was the conversation-
piece portrait. He had seen the small-scale conversation pieces of Arthur Devis (Fig. f)
and those of Francis Hayman (Fig. g) and Johann Zoffany on a larger, middling scale.
These showed the English gentry in their own living rooms or on the green lawns

opposite:

5. JOHN BEALE BORDLEY. 1770

John Beale Bordley was Peale's greatest friend and patron. Bordley had attended Peale's father's school and had developed a strong affection for the family. As a young lawyer, Bordley had helped the newly widowed Mrs. Peale and her family move to Annapolis, arranged to have her eldest son apprenticed to a saddler, and, a decade later, when Peale began to show promise as a painter, collected a fund to send him to London to study with Benjamin West.

During the stormy years before the Revolution, Bordley was a judge and member of the Governor's Council, but his gentle, kindly nature made him unhappy in colonial politics. In 1770, the year this portrait was painted, he and his brother-in-law, William Paca, came into possession of Wye Island in the Chesapeake. Bordley withdrew from politics to the life of a country gentleman, and turned his plantation into a self-sustaining progressive farm.

This portrait was commissioned by Edmund Jenings, Bordley's half brother. It combines the warm friendship and high regard the artist felt for Bordley and a warning to Great Britain from her colonies. The portrait was to be sent to Jenings in London, where it would serve as an American counterpart to Peale's earlier allegory of freedom, the portrait of William Pitt (see No. 3). Bordley is pictured as a defender of American liberties, standing firm against the expansion of Parliamentary power—an idea conveyed by the Latin words on the open book, "We observe the laws of England to be changed," and by the poisonous jimson weed growing at the base of the statue of English law. As Peale wrote Jenings, this native American weed "acts in the most violent manner and causes Death."

The history of the portrait is a mystery. Presumably shipped to London in 1771, it disappeared, to be rediscovered in America in the twentieth century, blackened with dirt, artist and subject unknown, until cleaning revealed Peale's signature and the date 1770. The jimson weed, which Peale had mentioned to Jenings in his letter of April 20, 1771, clearly identifies the subject as Bordley. (*The Barra Foundation, Inc.*)

outside their houses; their domestic English settings appealed to Peale's sense of fact. He set out to create portraiture in a size that would incorporate also something of the setting of life in Maryland. Arthur Devis, a rediscovery of our day, was a particularly congenial model for Peale. Born and trained at Preston, in Lancashire, Devis worked among a country gentry not unlike the gentry of Maryland in habit of life. When he moved to London in 1761 he continued to find clients of the same sort. He exhibited with the Free Society in 1762, 1763, 1767–70, 1775, and 1780 and was its president in 1768, when Peale was in London. Such conversation pieces presented no images of Italian grandeur: they were tranquil scenes of English life. People were portrayed in quiet enjoyment of their own homes and in their own familiar countryside.

Peale took the English conversation piece, enlarged it to lifesize, as his Maryland patrons desired, and made it speak of his own people and of the landscapes of the eastern and western shores. The result was a series of paintings of striking originality. Nothing like this had been done in American colonial painting. As the English sculptor-critic Michael Ayrton observed, "Receptivity and ability uniquely to transform for new purposes, visual information received from the past, may well serve as a definition of greatness in the visual arts."[15]

One of his best friends in Maryland, and a man of great intelligence, was the agriculturist John Beale Bordley (No. 5). Bordley's great interest was the improvement of agriculture. After he came into possession of a plantation on Wye Island in the Chesapeake, he gave up his quite onerous provincial responsibilities to turn his property into a self-sufficient farm village, where he pioneered in growing wheat instead of tobacco, and in raising sheep. In 1783, he removed to Philadelphia, where he founded the Philadelphia Society for Improving Agriculture, the first such society in the United

6. MORDECAI GIST. 1774

Peale's early Maryland portraits show great delicacy in drawing and tone and usually reflect the prosperity and accomplishments of their subjects. The elegantly dressed Mordecai Gist was a young Baltimorean who achieved great success as a merchant and sea captain before the Revolution. In this strong characterization, Gist is shown with the tools of his maritime trade—dividers, a copy of Euclid's *Geometry*, and a nautical chart. A brig under sail, seen through the window, shows the practical use to which these items were put. (*The Fine Arts Museums of San Francisco*)

opposite:

7. WILLIAM PACA. 1772

William Paca, brother-in-law of John Beale Bordley (see No. 5), was a prominent figure in Maryland politics. On February 19, 1827, just a few days before Peale's death, the artist wrote to Paca's son, John: "I knew your father when he was finishing his studies in the Laws. . . . He was a handsome man, more than 6 feet high, of portly appearance . . . graceful in his movements and complaisant to everyone; in short, his manners were of the first polish. In the early period, when the people's eyes first became opened to their rights, . . . [he] made the first stand for the independence of the People." (*Maryland Historical Society*)

States and still in existence. By example and by his writings he was instrumental in improving the art of husbandry in America. When Peale undertook Bordley's portrait, it was this aspect that the artist was anxious to show. He also wanted to illustrate the fact that, in the widening gap between the colonies and Britain, Bordley had been the only member of the Governor's Council who was on the side of America.

Peale shows him standing by a tree of the primeval forest. In the background, a pack horse is being loaded with wool. Bordley stands in an attitude of argument. An arm rests upon a book on which is written "Notamus Legos Anglicae mutari" (We observe

the laws of England to be changed). He points in demonstration to a statue of British liberty, at the base of whose pedestal grows a poisonous weed, the native American jimson weed, which every Marylander would know.

In scale and meaning, the Bordley is a new kind of portrait in America. Peale went on from this to paint an impressive gallery of the Whig leaders of the Chesapeake country. These portraits, precise in drawing, as delicate in color as a miniature, idyllic, yet penetrated by Peale's sense of fact, strike a unique note in American painting.

opposite:

8. WILLIAM STONE. 1774–75

A native of Bermuda, William Stone came to Baltimore on a maritime venture. After marrying into a prominent Maryland family, he made that city his home. In this ambitious portrait, Stone appears with his navigating instruments at hand; he holds a brass-mounted spyglass and a sextant lies at his feet. He points toward his Bermuda sloop, the *Charming Polly*, under sail in the bay. Stone was the owner of another sloop, the *Hornet*, which was later chartered to the Continental navy. It has been misidentified in the past as the vessel in the background. (*Maryland Historical Society*)

9. MRS. THOMAS HARWOOD. c. 1771

Margaret Strachan, whom Peale referred to as "Miss Peggy," was the daughter of William Strachan of "London Town," Ann Arundel County, Maryland. In 1772, she married Thomas Harwood, who was first treasurer of the western shore under the Council of Safety from 1776 until his death in 1804. His portrait, painted by Peale in 1775, is in the Henry Francis du Pont Winterthur Museum. Hers, it seems probable, was painted shortly before her marriage.

Charles Coleman Sellers thought Mrs. Harwood's portrait "the most vivid and charming of Peale's portraits of women, a personification of feminine grace and dignity." It is a fine example of the precise drawing and delicate muted color of the artist's Maryland style after his return from London. (*The Metropolitan Museum of Art*)

10. EDWARD LLOYD FAMILY. 1771

Peale made this picture of the Whig leader Edward Lloyd and his family a portrayal of a favorite theme—domestic harmony—as well as a symbol of the splendid life of the colonial gentry of Maryland. Edward Lloyd, the fourth of that name, was a friend and patron of Peale's; he had a house in Annapolis not far from Peale's painting room. Here, however, Lloyd is shown at "Wye House," his plantation in Talbot County, Maryland, where he lived in great luxury amidst vast wheat fields and a deer park, with a library that was reputed to be the finest in colonial Maryland. In this affectionate family portrait, we see Lloyd with his wife, Elizabeth Tayloe, of "Mount Airy," Richmond County, Virginia, whom he had married just four years earlier, and their first child, Anne. (*The Henry Francis du Pont Winterthur Museum*)

opposite:

11. WASHINGTON AS COLONEL OF THE VIRGINIA REGIMENT. 1772

Charles Willson Peale visited Mount Vernon in May of 1772 to paint this, our only likeness of George Washington before the Revolution. It commemorates Washington's service in the war against the French and their Indian allies. Washington wears the uniform of the Virginia regiment; in his pocket is a paper headed "Order of March," and at his side, the same sword he was to wear when he resigned his commission as commander in chief in 1783 and when he was inaugurated as president in 1789. On May 21, while the portrait was in progress, Washington wrote to the Reverend Jonathan Boucher of Annapolis, who had recommended the artist: "I am now contrary to all expectation under the hands of Mr. Peale; but in so grave—so sullen a mood—and now and then under the influence of Morpheus when some critical strokes are making, that I fancy the skill of this gentleman's pencil will be hard put to it, in describing to the world what manner of man I am."

This visit began a lifelong friendship between artist and soldier. Peale's seven life portraits of Washington give us a remarkable record of the growth of Washington's personality, from this unfamiliar young face at age forty, whose chief characteristic is reserve and stubborn will, to the face, resigned but still determined, of the old president, age sixty-seven. (*Washington and Lee University*)

William Paca (No. 7) stands at the bottom of his garden on the Severn River beside a monument to Cicero. William Stone (No. 8) stands before a sweep of the bay, holding a spyglass with a sextant at his feet. He points toward his sloop, *Charming Polly*, making down the bay with flags flying.

Peale painted Edward Lloyd, a great Whig leader of the eastern shore, without political overtones. He shows Lloyd at ease with wife and child in the garden of his home on the eastern shore (No. 10). Col. George Washington, painted at Mount Vernon, would stand before the dark, forest-covered mountains where he had won his reputation as a soldier fighting against the French and their Indian allies (No. 11). Peale's portraits of these leaders presented not only the subject's appearance, personality, and character, but setting, place, and personal interests in a way both new and distinctive in America.

PHILADELPHIA

To reach his sitters, Peale traveled from plantation to plantation, down the bay as far as Williamsburg and Norfolk. To the north, however, was the place of promise: the largest city in the colonies, Philadelphia.

At this point his London friend Edmund Jenings, a transplanted Marylander, intervened with his friends and relatives in America to help Peale establish himself: he ordered portraits of those of his friends who might help and become interested. Most important in its consequences was a portrait of John Dickinson of Philadelphia (No. 12), a lawyer whose "Letters from a Pennsylvania Farmer" had won an audience on both sides of the ocean. When Peale went to Philadelphia in 1769, Dickinson introduced him to his relatives, the Cadwaladers. Their interest and support were to be of great help and no doubt led to his deciding to move to Philadelphia instead of New York, a possibility he had also considered. As early as September 7, 1770, he wrote to John Cadwalader, "I

opposite:

12. JOHN DICKINSON. 1770

When Peale painted this portrait of John Dickinson in the summer of 1770, the Pennsylvania lawyer was already a well-known figure. His "Letters from a Pennsylvania Farmer"—an eloquent and reasoned defense of American rights—had begun to appear in colonial newspapers at the end of 1767. Dickinson was soon hailed as the "Benefactor of Mankind," and the "American Pitt." Peale wrote in the 1795 catalogue of his museum's collection that Dickinson's letters "may be said to have sown the seeds of the Revolution. They were written with great animation and read with uncommon attention."

Dickinson's portrait proved to be very important to Peale's career. Edmund Jenings had commissioned it—along with those of John Beale Bordley (No. 5) and Charles Carroll of Carrollton—to be sent to him in London. Jenings knew that these commissions would introduce Peale to people who could be helpful to him and would no doubt lead to other assignments, thereby assuring Peale of patronage when he returned to America in 1769. And indeed, Dickinson brought Peale to the attention of his cousin John Cadwalader (see No. 14), a wealthy Philadelphia merchant-planter. The support of these two men gave Peale valuable prestige as a portrait painter and encouraged him to move from Annapolis to Philadelphia.

Peale painted Dickinson with the falls of the Schuylkill River in the distance, in response to Jenings's request for American views in the backgrounds of his friends' portraits. (*Historical Society of Pennsylvania*)

13. MRS. JOHN DICKINSON AND HER DAUGHTER SALLY. 1773

Mary Norris married John Dickinson in 1770. Her portrait was to have been painted that year, as her husband's was (No. 12), but it was postponed until after the safe arrival of the baby, Sally, shown here in her mother's arms.

The birth of this child had a profound, almost religious significance for the parents. The child sits atop a stone pedestal, on the side of which is a relief showing a figure in the costume of antiquity offering a sacrifice—probably a symbol of thanksgiving—upon an altar.

Mrs. Dickinson was the daughter of Isaac Norris, the younger, for many years Speaker of the Pennsylvania Assembly and a powerful provincial leader. In the background is a distant view of Philadelphia with its two distinctive church spires, Christ Church and the First Presbyterian Church, as seen from "Fairhill," the Norris country house north of the city. (*Historical Society of Pennsylvania*)

14. JOHN CADWALADER FAMILY. 1772

Peale owed much of John Cadwalader's generous patronage to John Dickinson, Cadwalader's kinsman by blood and marriage. Commissions from the two men encouraged Peale to settle permanently in Philadelphia. Peale wrote to John Beale Bordley on July 29, 1772, "I am once more making a Tryal how far the Arts will be favoured in the City, I have now on hand . . . one composition of Mr. John Cadwalader Lady and Child . . . which is greatly admired . . . I have some prospect of the Quakers incouragement for I find that none of the Painters heretofore have pleased in Likeness—whether I can a little time will show." By November he was able to write that his painting business was flourishing and that "my reputation is greatly increased by a Number of New Yorkers . . . who have given me the character of being the best painter of America—that I paint more certain and handsomer likenesses than Copley."

Peale had great admiration for Cadwalader and here painted one of his best conversation pieces. With warmth and immediacy, he shows the young father, just in from the garden, offering a peach to the baby. The proud mother, Elizabeth Lloyd, sister of Edward Lloyd of Maryland (No. 10), holds their first child, Anne. (*Capt. John Cadwalader, U.S.N.R. [Ret.]*)

15. John Philip de Haas. 1772

In this portrait of John Philip de Haas,
Peale shows us an eighteenth-century
gentleman, nonchalantly at his ease, in a
setting suggestive of wealth and culture.
    De Haas, born in Holland, came to
America with his father in 1739 and
settled in Lebanon, Pennsylvania. He
served in the French and Indian Wars,
attaining the rank of major in 1764. The
oil painting in the background of this
portrait is thought to depict a scene from
the battle of Fort Pitt. At the time he
sat for Peale, De Haas was engaged in
the iron business and served as justice of
the peace for Lebanon County. (*National
Gallery of Art*)

am not certain that I shall not see Philadelphia this Winter for I have a great desire to
settle there and at leisure Times be a Visitor to Maryland, to do the Business I have here."

But first there were his debts in Annapolis. He took six years to pay off these debts.
Finally, in 1775, he was able to write to Edmund Jenings (August 29), "Except my
Debts of Gratitude I owe nothing on this side of the Atlantic." That autumn he went to
Philadelphia to prepare the way for his family to move there in the spring of 1776. He
made the move in time to hear the Declaration of Independence read from a platform
outside the Statehouse and to enlist in the militia unit of his neighborhood. In spite of
being a newcomer he was elected an officer by his fellow militiamen.

The war went badly for the colonials that autumn. Washington's army was driven
from New York City by a larger, better trained, and better equipped British force. As
the colonials retreated across New Jersey to shelter on the farther side of the Delaware,
the Pennsylvania militia were called out to defend their state. Led by Brig. Gen. John
Cadwalader, the Pennsylvanians marched toward Trenton. Though Peale's regiment
was not in the fighting at Trenton, a few days later they found themselves unexpectedly
in the front line at Princeton. In the first collision Gen. Hugh Mercer's advance unit of
Continentals was broken by a British bayonet charge; they were in full retreat just as
Peale's regiment came on the scene. Washington himself galloped up, reformed the
Pennsylvanians' battle line, and took his position with them. Other veteran units took

positions on either side. They "stood the fire without regarding Balls which whistled their thousand different notes around our heads, and what is very astonishing did little or no harm."[16] In a few minutes the enemy gave way and the battle was over. Peale marched with his unit to Morristown, where they stayed a few weeks, then marched home. Princeton was Peale's only battle. Yet the few minutes when the Pennsylvania militia stood their ground, with a veteran Pennsylvania battery on one side and veteran New England troops on the other, left an indelible impression on the young lieutenant (Fig. h).

During the British occupation of Philadelphia Peale was on patrol duty north of the city. He was at Valley Forge; but the Pennsylvania militia were mustered out of service, and Peale was a civilian during most of the next few years. In April, 1783, after the peace, he wrote a brief account of himself to Benjamin West: "You will naturally conclude that the arts must languish in a Country in trouble with Wars, yet when I could disengage myself from military life, I have not wanted employment. But I have done more in miniature than in any other manner, because these are more portable and therefore could be kept out of the way of a plundering enemy."[17] Always attracted to small, delicate work calling for precision and skill, Peale enjoyed painting miniatures, as at other times he repaired watches and clocks and mounted birds and insects for his museum. Wartime conditions rendered miniatures popular for a brief period only, perhaps fortunately, for Peale never developed in miniature the same kind of strong masculine portrayal that he achieved in his lifesize portraits.

16. GEORGE WASHINGTON. 1776

When Washington was sent in 1776 by the Continental
Congress to take command of an inexperienced American army in war against the greatest military power in
the world, his wife asked Peale to paint a miniature of
her husband for her. Since the general had already left
Philadelphia, Peale used as a model the three-quarter-
length portrait which he had just completed for John
Hancock, now in the Brooklyn Museum. This miniature, like Nos. 17-22, is reproduced actual size.
(*The Mount Vernon Ladies' Association of the Union*)

17. MARTHA WASHINGTON. 1776

Contemporaries described Martha Washington as an
active, cheerful person and a hostess of "perfect good
breeding." She was not fortunate in her portraits, but
this miniature, painted in May of 1776, perhaps comes
closest of all her likenesses to depicting the "sociable,
pretty kind of woman" a contemporary described in
1778. Peale is known to have painted two other miniatures, two three-quarter-length portraits and one half-
length of Mrs. Washington. (*The Mount Vernon Ladies'
Association of the Union*)

18. SILAS DEANE. 1776

A wealthy businessman and lawyer, Silas Deane represented Connecticut at both Continental Congresses.
This miniature was painted in 1776, before he was sent
to France as a secret agent of the Congress—the first
American to represent the colonies abroad. With Franklin and Arthur Lee, he negotiated substantial aid for the
colonies and enlisted in the American army trained
European officers, including Lafayette, De Kalb, and
Von Steuben. (*The Connecticut Historical Society*)

19. GEORGE WASHINGTON. 1779

This miniature was undoubtedly based on one of the
replicas Peale painted of his full-length *George Washington* (No. 26), now at the Pennsylvania Academy of
the Fine Arts. The hair ribbon seen here is not in the
original portrait but it does appear in the 1779 replica
made for Joseph Wilson, a Philadelphia merchant (now
at Princeton University). (*Private collection*)

20. COLONEL GEORGE BAYLOR. 1778

While Washington's troops were wintering at Valley
Forge, Peale was busy painting miniatures of his fellow
soldiers. George Baylor, commander of Virginia's Third
Continental Dragoons, sat for his portrait in April of
1778 just before the opening of the spring campaign.
Soon after, his command was wiped out in a surprise
attack, and Baylor was seriously wounded.
(*The Society of the Cincinnati*)

21. HENRY KNOX. 1778

"The father of the American Army Artillery," Henry
Knox, a former bookseller, became Washington's close
friend and trusted general. His skillful leadership at
key points, including the Germantown and Brandywine campaigns, the battles of Trenton, Monmouth,
and Yorktown, resulted in his being elected by Congress in 1785 as the United States's first Secretary of
War, a post he retained after the formation of Washington's cabinet in 1789. Knox sat for this miniature
during the winter of 1778 at Valley Forge. (*Private
collection*)

22. GEORGE WALTON. C. 1781

An energetic, fiery leader of the Whigs in Georgia,
George Walton served in the Continental Congress and
was a signer of the Declaration of Independence. He
commanded a Georgia regiment at the siege of Savan-
nah in 1778, was twice governor of his state, chief
justice of Georgia, and a United States Senator.

This miniature was probably painted shortly before
Walton left the Continental Congress in 1781. Three
years later Peale had still not received the eight guineas
he was owed for the miniature. He wrote Walton that
his son Raphaelle would be coming to Georgia to gather
specimens for the museum and that he would like to
collect the money still due. "Having a large family to
support," Peale wrote, "at this time it may be doing me
a greater favor than if you had paid me much sooner."
(*Yale University Art Gallery*)

23. Colonel Walter Stewart. 1781

Col. Walter Stewart commanded the Thirteenth and Third Pennsylvania Regiments of the line during the revolutionary war. He retired in January, 1783, with the brevet rank of brigadier general, and became a prominent merchant in Philadelphia. In this portrait he stands in military pose, wearing the sword of honor voted him by Congress when he brought the welcome news from Ticonderoga that the enemy had abandoned the great fort at Crown Point. Peale shows Stewart not in battle but with his regiment encamped for the night, muskets laid on long rails to support them from the damp, soldiers foraging for firewood or cooking their evening meal. When writing Stewart for payment, Peale expressed his desire "to have your approbation of the encampment." (*Private collection*)

24. MRS. WALTER STEWART. 1782

When Peale painted Deborah McClenahan
Stewart in 1782, the year following her
marriage to Walter Stewart (No. 23), he
created one of his most splendid woman's
portraits. The young bride stands in an
interior, leaning on a pier table where Peale
has arranged an informal still life of fruit,
books, sheet music, and guitar. These objects, and the quill which she holds in her
hand, poised as if to write, suggest her
interests and achievements. On each wrist
she wears a miniature, set in a bracelet of
pearls. The miniature on the right is of her
husband (unlocated). (*Private collection*)

25. THOMAS ROBINSON. c. 1784

This portrait was painted for Thomas Robinson, a wealthy Philadelphian, as a record of
his revolutionary war service. Robinson had
been lieutenant colonel of the Fourth Pennsylvania Regiment of the Continental Regiment. His commander, General ("Mad Anthony") Wayne, commended him for his
conduct at Ticonderoga, and George Washington also had a high opinion of Robinson
as an officer. Peale depicted him in military
uniform wearing the badge of the Order of
the Cincinnati. On the table beside him lie
his "Orderly Book" and military papers
inscribed "Return of the 21st Pennsylvania
Reg't." (*Independence National Historical
Park Collection*)

opposite:

26. WASHINGTON AT THE BATTLE OF PRINCETON. 1779

The Supreme Executive Council of Pennsylvania commissioned this portrait of George Washington for their council chamber in January, 1779, to commemorate the American victories of Trenton and Princeton. Peale painted it between January 20 and February 1, 1779, while Washington was in Philadelphia to confer with Congress. Washington is shown at the height of his physical vigor and military service. The general was a big man: six feet two or three inches tall and weighing about 220 pounds in his prime. His oval head was small in relation to the length of his body. His shoulders were narrow, arms and legs long, hands and feet very large. Jefferson described his carriage as "easy, erect and noble."

Peale had a soldier's respect for uniforms and the insignia of rank. If a replica of a painting was ordered, he would be careful to update the insignia according to the most recently issued orders, a practice that has enabled historians to assign fairly accurate dates to the copies. Washington here wears the blue uniform with buff facings of the general staff. The blue sash had been the insignia of the commander in chief since 1775. Washington's epaulets are without ornament, for it was not until June 18, 1780, that the colored ribbon was replaced by stars on the epaulets—three for the commander in chief, two for a major general, and one for a brigadier. The blue flag with a circle of thirteen stars was the battle flag carried by the army throughout the war until the flag of thirteen stars and stripes was adopted in 1784.

Peale painted many replicas of this picture, including one now at the Metropolitan Museum of Art. (*The Pennsylvania Academy of the Fine Arts*)

27. WASHINGTON, COMMANDER IN CHIEF OF THE FEDERAL ARMY. 1780

Peale's 1779 portrait of Washington (No. 26) proved instantly popular, and there were many requests for replicas. One Cuban diplomat ordered five. No doubt this convinced Peale to produce a mezzotint, and publication of the print was announced in the *Pennsylvania Packet* on August 26, 1780. As with his earlier Pitt mezzotint (see No. 3), Peale was not only the originator of the image but also acted as engraver, printer, and printseller.

The Washington mezzotint is masterful both in its technique and its great psychological force. It is unexcelled among the early graphic images of the general. (*The Metropolitan Museum of Art*)

PORTRAITS FOR THE CONTINENTAL CONGRESS

Washington came to Philadelphia in December, 1778, to consult with Congress. The war was going well. New England, New Jersey, and Pennsylvania were freed from British forces. In a mood of optimism the Supreme Executive Council of Pennsylvania on January 18, 1779, resolved to ask Peale to paint the general's portrait to hang in the council chamber "not only as a mark of the great respect that they bear to his Excellency, but that the contemplation of it may excite others to tread the same glorious and disinterested steps which lead to public happiness and private honors."

This gave an old tradition a new meaning. It had been customary in British colonial capitals to hang a portrait of the king in the capitol as a symbol of the larger loyalty that held the empire together. In 1779, the North American provinces differed greatly in

28. CONRAD-ALEXANDRE GÉRARD. 1779

Peale's portrait of French diplomat Conrad Gérard represents the hopes of the struggling republic as it looked to France for support in its war for independence. Gérard arrived in this country in November of 1778, bringing the first diplomatic recognition to the new nation. On September 3, 1779, the Continental Congress commissioned Peale to paint this portrait to be "placed in the council chamber of the United States." Always eager to use his art in the service of liberty, Peale made this portrait a political allegory. The bound fasces, symbol of authority, rests on a cornucopia, symbol of fruitfulness; the lyre overlays the cannon, the whole representing the harmony of nations that share the goals of peace and prosperity. At the right, France places a protective arm around young America, a quiver of arrows at her shoulder, while the two are entwined with a garland of flowers.

On September 18, 1779, after he had finished the portrait, Peale wrote to Gérard: "My anxiety to do well made me trouble you with several long sittings, and I have done my best to give satisfaction to the Honored Gentlemen of Congress at whose request you have granted me the honor and opportunity of transmitting to posterity my name as an artist." Congress, however, never claimed the portrait, probably because of the uncertainty of the times. It became the first in Peale's gallery of revolutionary war leaders. (*Independence National Historical Park Collection*)

government, customs, and habits of life; they were divided by disputes, jealousies, old quarrels, even by coinage. The United States of America did not yet exist. A new unity had slowly to be created. Everything was lacking: a government, a name, a flag, a song, a sense of Americans as one nation rather than thirteen. General Washington, who taught his officers to call themselves Americans rather than Virginians or Massachusetts men or Pennsylvanians, created in the army perhaps our first *national* institution. He became a symbol of the new nation.

Peale supplied the first images of him to satisfy an emerging national spirit. He had once painted Marylanders in settings symbolical of their lives: he was now to paint the tall Virginia general in a way symbolizing the victor in a war for American independence (No. 26). It is very different from the likenesses which Stuart was later to paint of the president as an old, venerable figure: the *Pater Patriae*. This is Washington at the height of his strength and military success, the man who had galloped up at Princeton to form the Pennsylvania militia into a battle line and taken position on horseback at their front. He leans against a cannon in that cross-legged attitude Peale had seen in British portraits as a symbol of elegant ease (see Fig. d). Captured Hessian and British battle flags lie at his feet. In the background a file of red-coated prisoners march past Nassau Hall.

Washington was a tall man, standing a head above the average soldier in his army. The uniform (preserved in the National Museum of American History, Washington, D.C.) in which he said farewell to his officers shows that he stood six feet two inches tall; but he was slender, of equal breadth from shoulder to hip, rather like Lincoln in physique. His great-nephew, George Washington Parke Custis, said his strength was in his "long, large, and sinewy limbs." It is that figure which Peale shows us. The oval head seems small in relation to the long body and long arms and legs; and the pose, which to Peale meant graceful relaxation, is not pleasing to our eyes. It is, nonetheless, the only likeness of the man at the height of his military career.

This portrait was immensely popular, and copies were made in the family workshop. One was ordered by Conrad-Alexandre Gérard, the French ambassador, as a present to the king of France. Another was taken to Spain by William Carmichael, the American chargé d'affaires. A third, ordered by William Laurens, who sailing to Holland on a diplomatic mission, was captured at sea by a British cruiser; the picture was taken to England as spoils of war. The Spanish minister, Don Juan de Mirailles, ordered one which was sent to his house in Havana, Cuba. Peale, writing to Barrister Carroll, speaks of "sundry others I have for private gentlemen—among these—Joseph Wilson, a Philadelphia merchant; Col. Frisby Tilghman of Maryland, one of Washington's military aides; Dr. Shields of Philadelphia; Gen. Nelson of Virginia; Elias Boudinot; the Washington family." These were full lengths; other replicas were made in half length.

In the fall of 1779 the Continental Congress asked Peale to paint Gérard, the French official who had brought the first diplomatic recognition to the struggling republic. Peale painted him before a window giving on the old Statehouse; behind him a marble group of France and America with arms about each other and a garland of flowers twined over their shoulders (No. 28).

PEALE'S GALLERY OF GREAT MEN

Gérard's picture was left in Peale's studio, possibly because of the uncertainty of the times, and there it became the first of a portrait gallery of leaders of the war, which, by an act of inspired artistic journalism, he now began to paint. By 1783 he could write to Edmund Jenings, "I have painted thirty or forty portraits of Principal Characters. The collection has cost me much time and labour and I mean to keep adding as many of those who are distinguished by their Actions or Office as opportunity will serve."[18]

The Gallery of Great Men, as it was to be called, thus came into existence only by historical circumstance and the interests of the time. Peale had already begun to form a gallery of paintings for his studio, while still in London. It was a common practice for artists to hang a selection of their work in an anteroom. If, like Reynolds or West, the artist was also a collector, the anteroom became a kind of museum, as may be seen in the painting by John Passmore the Younger entitled *Benjamin West's Picture Gallery* (c. 1828; Wadsworth Atheneum, Hartford), where the walls are shown hung with West's own work, from which a purchaser might pick one of which he would receive a replica.

29. FREDERIC WILLIAM AUGUSTUS, BARON VON STEUBEN. 1780

Baron von Steuben, a junior officer in the Prussian general staff during the Seven Years' War, was engaged in 1777 in Paris by the American commissioners, Franklin and Deane, to train the American army. Von Steuben knew no English when he presented himself to Washington at Valley Forge, but he quickly won favor by turning the "ragged Continentals" into an efficient fighting force. He was made inspector general with the rank of major general.

Peale painted Von Steuben wearing a rosette of rank on his chest; around his neck hangs what is probably the insignia of a Knight of the Margrave of Baden's Order of Fidelity. The artist wrote to the sitter on July 27, 1780, that the portrait "is highly approved of, or I am most egregiously flattered—yet when I can have the pleasure of seeing you here I hope to improve it." Von Steuben apparently did not claim the portrait until 1781, and Peale was able to duplicate it for his gallery of "distinguished characters." (*The Pennsylvania Academy of the Fine Arts*)

30. GENERAL OTHO HOLLAND WILLIAMS. 1782

By 1781 the idea of expanding his studio gallery into a monument to heroes of the revolutionary war had taken hold of Peale's imagination. In his autobiography he wrote that he planned to "make such a collection of Portraits to fill his Gallery as might be valuable in a future day. . . . The formation of this Gallery of Portraits," he went on, "gave him the opportunity of a more extended acquaintance with the military characters of those times."

Gen. Otho Holland Williams, one of the most dashing of the Maryland officers during the war for independence, was soon added to Peale's collection. After Williams led a decisive bayonet charge at the battle of Eutaw Springs, Congress voted him a sword of honor and the rank of brigadier general. This portrait was probably occasioned by that honor. (*Independence National Historical Park Collection*)

31. (BARON) JOHANN DE KALB. 1781–82

The son of a Bavarian peasant, Johann de Kalb rose by natural ability and the assumption of a fictitious title (a necessity for an officer in the eighteenth century) to the rank of brigadier in the French army, serving with distinction through the War of the Austrian Succession and the Seven Years' War. He introduced Lafayette to the American commissioners in France and sailed to America on the same ship with him in 1777.

Peale painted De Kalb in June, 1780, as he passed through Philadelphia, having been detached from Washington's army to serve under Gates in the southern army. Two months later, at the battle of Camden, De Kalb led his troops in desperate charges and hand-to-hand fighting until enemy bayonets brought him down, mortally wounded.

The fact that Peale possessed the only portrait of this national hero may have been a determining factor in the artist's decision to found a gallery of portraits of soldiers and statesmen. This portrait, a replica of one done for De Kalb in 1780, was painted specifically for Peale's museum collection. (*Independence National Historical Park Collection*)

32. GENERAL WILLIAM SMALLWOOD.
c. 1781–82

The character of William Smallwood may be read in his portrait, for despite Peale's attempt to render him as a congenial man, one still senses much of the general's hot-headed and choleric personality in this picture.

Smallwood's strength lay in administration and as a drillmaster. After De Kalb's death at Camden in 1780, he was named major general—in which rank Peale depicts him here—and placed under the command of Von Steuben with orders to join the southern army. The querulous Smallwood, however, resenting the idea of serving under a foreigner, objected; and instead he was dispatched to Maryland to raise troops and assemble supplies. In 1785, he was elected to Congress and in the same year governor of Maryland (1785–88). (*Independence National Historical Park Collection*)

33. COLONEL JOHN EAGER HOWARD. 1782

The name of this gallant and chivalrous officer, one of the best infantry commanders in the Continental army, still rings out in the song of his proud native state, "Maryland, My Maryland." John Howard became a national hero after leading a decisive charge at the battle of Cowpens, for which he was awarded the thanks of Congress and the silver medal he wears here. Peale probably painted the portrait when Howard came to Philadelphia to receive his honor.
(*Independence National Historical Park Collection*)

34. COLONEL WILLIAM (AUGUSTINE) WASHINGTON. c. 1782

In 1781, Congress voted William Washington —a distant relative of the general—a medal for leading a cavalry charge at a critical moment during the battle of Cowpens, where with eighty troopers he routed a numerically superior force. It was undoubtedly this exploit which won Washington a place in Peale's gallery. The artist gives us an attractive character study of an easygoing cavalryman, still wearing the coarse white linen fighting dress of the dragoons—a steady, unambitious person. Peale, who was usually careful in depicting the insignia of rank, endows Washington with a single epaulet, indicating the rank of captain. It has been suggested by Charles Coleman Sellers that this curious error occurred because one epaulet was all that was necessary to hold the sword belt to his shoulder—and Washington never troubled to add the second epaulet to which he was entitled. (*Independence National Historical Park Collection*)

35. GENERAL WILLIAM MOULTRIE. 1782

South Carolina-born William Moultrie became a national hero in 1776 with his courageous defense of the palmetto and sand fort guarding Charleston harbor. With four hundred men and thirty-two guns he repelled the attack of a British fleet of eight gunships, over one hundred guns, and four thousand troops. The fort in the background is probably based on James Peale's 1782 painting, *Sir Peter Parker's Attack Against Fort Moultrie* (Colonial Williamsburg). Over the fort flies the flag that was reportedly shot away during the battle but bravely replaced. On the left is a palmetto, the South Carolina state tree.

Moultrie was appointed a brigadier general shortly after this victory. He was captured by the British in 1780 after the fall of Charleston and imprisoned for nearly two years. Upon his release he was made major general, and in this portrait he wears two stars reflecting that promotion. Peale's original of this painting is unlocated, but this version and another, possibly by Rembrandt Peale, at the Gibbes Art Gallery in Charleston, illustrate the standard practice within the Peale family of replication and copying. (*National Portrait Gallery, Smithsonian Institution*)

63

While in London Peale had copied paintings in West's collection: *Elisha Restoring to Life the Shunammite's Son*, by West himself (No. 39); a *Landscape with a Group of Cows in Romantic Woody Scenery* by George Barrett and Sawrey Gilpin; a *Storm at Sea*, a *Moonlight at Sea*, and a *Ship on Fire* by the marine painter Francis Swaine; and an unidentified Italian painting of *Mercury and Argus*. In Maryland he added to this gallery works of his own. When in 1771 David Douglass's American Company played in the Annapolis Theatre, Peale painted its talented young star, *Nancy Hallam as Fidele in Cymbeline* (No. 37). When Peale and his wife, Rachel, lost a baby in 1772, he painted a portrait of the dead child, then added the weeping mother, and called the picture *Rachel Weeping* (No. 38). Naturally enough, his wife could not bear to see the picture, which was covered by a green curtain to be drawn aside for visitors. In 1773, he added the largest and most ambitious of his conversation groups, *The Peale Family* (No. 146), which, although it was displayed in the gallery, was not finished until 1808.

The Gallery of Great Men was an extension of the practice of the day, transformed by Peale into something quite different. It was always his instinct to change the old one-to-one-relation of the artist to his patron into the artist speaking to his fellow citizens. In the end, Peale's studio and gallery grew into a public museum; a new kind of institution was created. It bore at first the stamp of Peale's personality but was destined for a long life in American society.

Painting these portraits must also have contributed to a change in Peale's work. Most

37. Nancy Hallam as Fidele in Cymbeline. 1771

When the American Company, directed by David Douglass, played in Annapolis in the autumn of 1770, its young star, Miss Hallam, was a sensation. A poem in the *Maryland Gazette* of September 6 called on the "self-tutor'd Peale" to perpetuate by his brush "the nameless Grace that ev'ry Heart can charm." Peale responded to the poet's invocation, painting Hallam as she appeared in the scene from Shakespeare's *Cymbeline* in which Imogen, alone in the forest disguised as the boy Fidele, emerges from a cave into the presence of Bellarius and her royal brothers, whose identity she does not know. The Reverend Jonathan Boucher praised the painting in the *Gazette* on November 7, 1771: "In thee, Oh Peale, both excellencies join;/Venetian colors and the Greek design." The painting dramatized a moment when, as Boucher poeticized, "Tears fill each eye and passion heaves each breast."

It has been suggested that Peale, who is known to have painted stage sets for the Douglass company, may have painted the scenery for *Cymbeline* and that the cave and landscape scene shown in the portrait were his production. This theatrical portrait was a showpiece of Peale's Museum for many years. (*Colonial Williamsburg Foundation*)

38. RACHEL WEEPING. 1772 and probably 1776

Painted as a record of a personal tragedy all too familiar in eighteenth-century life, this picture depicts Peale's first wife, Rachel Brewer Peale, weeping over the body of their infant daughter, Margaret, who died during a smallpox epidemic that swept Annapolis in 1772. Peale originally painted the child alone, chin bound, arms tied down with white satin ribbons, ready for the grave. Several years later he enlarged the canvas to include his wife and a table of medicines to symbolize their futile attempt to save the baby's life. This stark, highly personal mourning picture was an unusual departure from the traditional portrayal of death. John Adams wrote that the picture of Peale's wife, "all bathed in tears, . . . struck me prodigiously." Rachel naturally could not bear to look at the picture, and it hung in Peale's painting room covered by a green curtain which was drawn aside for a visitor's viewing. At one time a legend on the curtain warned, "Before you draw this curtain Consider whether you will affect a Mother or Father who has lost a child." (*Philadelphia Museum of Art*)

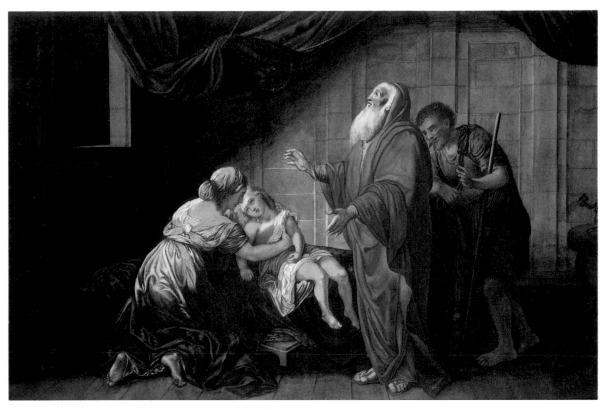

39. ELISHA RESTORING TO LIFE THE SHUNAMMITE'S SON. 1767

One of Peale's first tasks on arriving at Benjamin West's London studio was to copy in small size a
Biblical composition of West's *Elisha Restoring to Life the Shunammite's Son*. He took the painting
with him when he returned to Maryland, and it later became a feature in his exhibition gallery.
(*Private collection*)

of these likenesses were done quickly, in one or two sittings, as he was able to get time
from a busy soldier or politician. There was no time for the accessories of life he had
added to his earlier work. Here he concentrated on the clear delineation of character,
enough indication of uniform to show a man's rank and branch of service, recorded
soberly and simply. In France a neoclassic style of similar sobriety and simplicity was
created in the eighties by Jacques-Louis David to replace the rococo. For Peale there was
no rhetoric of ancient heroism, no nude figures inspired by antique sculpture, only a
sober coloring, precise drawing, and a striving for strong, direct characterization.

HATRED OF A TRAITOR

Both idealism and instinct were involved in Peale's reaction to the news of Benedict
Arnold's treason. The parade was an important means of propaganda to stir popular
emotion before the appearance of the daily newspaper and other modern forms of
communication. Such parades and pageants played roles in both the American and
French revolutions.

The news of Benedict Arnold's treason (September, 1780) caused a tumult of emotion in Philadelphia. Arnold was well known there. He had married a Philadelphia girl, Peggy Shippen, while serving as military governor of the city after its evacuation by the British. A leg wound received at the battle of Saratoga was slow to heal, and Arnold, with his leg propped up on a chair, had been a familiar sight to everyone in the city. Peale made use of it in the effigy he now improvised to express "the people's hatred of a traitor." He constructed a float upon a cart, with space under its floor for a boy to work the machinery (see No. 138). An effigy of Arnold sat upon the stage, his leg propped up before him; in front of him on a lighted transparency was a description of his treason. The effigy's head had two faces which revolved as the cart moved: one hand raised and lowered a mask; the other held a commission from the Devil. Behind the effigy stood the Devil himself in a long black robe, shaking a moneybag in one hand, a pitchfork in the other. As darkness gathered on September 30, 1780, the float moved slowly up and down the streets of the city behind fifes and drums playing the rogue's march. It was preceded by the cavalry of the city troop; behind came a company of militia, marching with lighted candles in the muzzles of their muskets, and behind these trooped a lot of boys carrying candles. Hour after hour the effigy moved through the dark streets until it came to High Street and the river, where it was set on fire and consumed.

THE AMERICAN NEOCLASSIC PORTRAIT

In early portraits, such as *John Dickinson* and *Mrs. John Dickinson and Her Daughter Sally* (Nos. 12, 13), faces are painted with the delicacy of a miniature; expressions are quiet and pensive; the figures are set against a background of shadow. By 1787, when Peale painted the great Whig lawyer *Thomas McKean and His Son, Thomas, Jr.* (see No. 155), the muted mood of the seventies had given way to more positive statements. A strong outline defines the forms; the light is even and clear; the drawing is exact; color, in broad areas, is almost enameled. The mood of the sitters is decisive.

Peale had arrived by his own intuitive development at the characteristics of what in European painting is called neoclassic portraiture. That is, he took the classical view, selecting the permanent, the enduring, and making a clear pictorial statement, being rational and objective in his approach. The romantics afterward emphasized the emotional; they sought transient moods of passion or of reverie; they made the portrait a study of the soul either under tension or withdrawn into itself in reverie.

So far as it was possible for a portrait painter to select his subjects, Peale chose to paint those whom he liked and admired; and in doing so he concentrated on the dominant note of character. The strong, objective statement of character without pictorial elaboration makes these portraits, done while the struggle for independence was as yet undecided and the republic unformed, a remarkable array. These are the faces of the competent, outgoing, able people who founded a nation. There are times when the austere simplicity of Peale's images surprises and disconcerts those accustomed to later, more flattering and idealized images of these same people.

One example is the "Constitutional Convention" portrait of George Washington

40. MRS. JACOB RUSH. 1786

When Peale visited Philadelphia in 1772, he met a young miniature painter named Mary ("Polly") Wrench. Handsome and accomplished—she was also a talented musician who sang and accompanied herself on the guitar—Polly supported her mother and younger brother by her painting, which Peale thought good for a young hand. Polly preferred to paint women, as she found it embarrassing to stare into the face of a gentleman.

Fourteen years later, Polly was the wife of Judge Jacob Rush (brother of the physician) and had given up portrait painting. Yet Peale portrayed her as an artist, with an air at once elegant, refined, and pensive. Before her are spread some of her ivories, her guitar, and sheet music entitled "The Blush of Aurora, a Favorite of the Muses." (*Private collection*)

41. CHARLES PETTIT. 1792

Charles Pettit was an attorney, a shrewd businessman, and a well-known financial authority. During the Revolution, as assistant quartermaster general of the Continental army, he was responsible for many reforms in the recording of accounts and cash. After the war, he was active in Philadelphia commercial circles. From 1785 to 1787, he served in Congress, and in 1788 was influential in the ratification of the federal Constitution. During the 1790s, Pettit was involved in the direction of the Insurance Company of North America, serving as president from 1796 to 1798 and from 1799 to his death in 1806. He was also a trustee of the University of Pennsylvania and a member of the American Philosophical Society.

Peale's clear, vigorous drawing, strong grasp of character, and muted color make this portrait one of the most pleasing examples of his neoclassic style. The composition is simple and unified; each detail counts—the writing table, the calfbound book, the easy relaxation of the pose. (*Worcester Art Museum*)

opposite:

42. GEORGE WASHINGTON. 1787

In the spring of 1787, Washington joined a group of political leaders assembling at Philadelphia for the purpose of revising the Articles of Confederation. Like the others, Washington was deeply concerned by the weakness and disunity of the colonies and feared the government was near collapse. "Are we to have the goodly fabric we were nine years raising, pulled over our heads?" he asked his friend Benjamin Lincoln.

When Washington arrived at Philadelphia, he was fifty-five years old. Peale, then in financial distress, thought a new mezzotint likeness of Washington might help him out of his difficulties, and wrote to Washington asking him to sit for a new portrait, from which he would make a print.

This portrait of the presiding officer of the Constitutional Convention shows the oval face, the deep eye sockets and heavy bone structure of brow and nose, the small eyes and mouth that appear in all of Peale's *Washingtons*. More important, it reveals "the noble, modest and gentlemanly urbanity and . . . graciousness" described by such contemporaries as the Marquis de Barbé-Marbois, secretary to the French minister, the Chevalier de la Luzerne. "He carries himself freely and with a sort of military grace," wrote Barbé-Marbois. "He is masculine looking, without his features being less gentle on that account." That is the man we see here. (*The Pennsylvania Academy of the Fine Arts*)

43. MRS. JAMES LATIMER. 1788

The wise old woman who looks out at us with a suggestion of good humor and amusement—so different from the grim certainties in her husband's face (No. 44)—is one of the most subtle character studies among Peale's portraits of women. She was born Sarah Geddes in Lancaster County, Pennsylvania, April 27, 1727, and married James Latimer on September 19, 1749. (*The Pennsylvania Academy of the Fine Arts*)

44. James Latimer. 1788

This formidable old veteran was born in the north of Ireland. At age sixteen, he accompanied his family to Chester County, Pennsylvania, where he became a prosperous merchant. After his marriage in 1749, he moved to Newport, Delaware. Here he owned several flour mills and participated in the West Indian trade. In 1756, he marched against the French and Indians as a captain; in 1776, as a lieutenant colonel of militia, he fought the British, and after the war served as a judge. Latimer attained national prominence when in 1787 he presided over the convention which made Delaware the first state to ratify the new federal Constitution. Peale's portrait of the crusty Latimer is an excellent example of his firmly drawn, incisively characterized neoclassic style. (*The Pennsylvania Academy of the Fine Arts*)

Fig. i. Professional card. 1790

Found in the papers of John Nicholson, this card was probably received at the time Peale painted Mrs. Nicholson and her son John Nicholson, Jr. (No. 158). (*Pennsylvania State Archives, Harrisburg*)

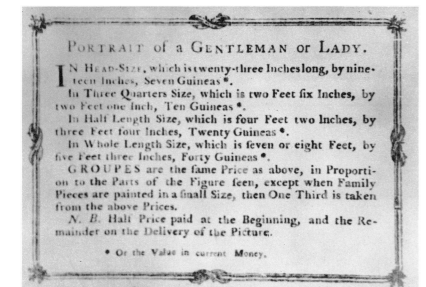

PORTRAIT of a GENTLEMAN or LADY.

IN Head-Size, which is twenty-three Inches long, by nineteen Inches, Seven Guineas *.

In Three Quarters Size, which is two Feet six Inches, by two Feet one Inch, Ten Guineas *.

In Half Length Size, which is four Feet two Inches, by three Feet four Inches, Twenty Guineas *.

In Whole Length Size, which is seven or eight Feet, by five Feet three Inches, Forty Guineas *.

GROUPES are the same Price as above, in Proportion to the Parts of the Figure seen, except when Family Pieces are painted in a small Size, then One Third is taken from the above Prices.

N. B. Half Price paid at the Beginning, and the Remainder on the Delivery of the Picture.

* Or the Value in current Money.

45. CAPTAIN JAMES JOSIAH. 1787

James Josiah, competent and confident, looks like the outstanding sea captain he was during the great period of Philadelphia's overseas commerce. He is shown in the cabin of his *St. Croix Packet*; a pair of dividers rests on a partially unrolled chart of the Asian waters to which he was to sail later that year. A compass is suspended from the cabin's ceiling. Josiah commanded a privateer in the war for independence, took part in the opening of the China trade, and captained one of the finest of the London packets. (*Allan Sussel*)

(No. 42), painted while he presided over the meetings in 1787 that resulted in "a more perfect union," which shows us the dignity and plain good sense, the modesty and firmness of character, that contemporaries saw and described. The foreigners who came to America, accustomed to the hauteur of European aristocrats, were invariably surprised by the mildness and simplicity they found in the face of this famous Washington whom they had crossed an ocean to see. Peale depicts that steady, brave man; a man of unflinching sense of duty; prudent, careful, reserved, not the demigod that later Americans wished to think him.

Peale's neoclassicism delineates a robust, clearly lighted world, revealing a wide range of character from the affable *Robert Goldsborough Family* (No. 157) to the unbending *James Latimer* (No. 44).

POSTWAR DEPRESSION YEARS

In 1783, forced to move from a rented house, Peale bought a house at Third and Lombard streets, to which he added a long, skylighted gallery to house his collection of portraits. His new quarters were to prove a success, but paying for them was a strain. A postwar depression had followed the peace. American merchants, excluded from their old trade within the British empire, eventually broke the monopoly of the East India Company and opened new sources of trade in India and China, in South America and the Pacific Northwest Coast. Meanwhile, times were hard. Payments for portraits were slow and fitful. The situation led Peale into various experiments to support his family. Reading of Philippe de Loutherbourg's success in London with a miniature theater of sound and light, Peale devised one of his own, setting it up at the end of his gallery. The experiment introduced the term "moving picture" into the language but hardly paid for itself.

Remembering the profits won by artists in London from engravings after their portraits, he next (in 1787) tried to transplant the engraved portrait to Philadelphia. With difficulty he obtained and prepared copperplates, and then executed mezzotints after a series of his portraits—Franklin, Lafayette, Washington, a popular preacher named Pilmore—and etched a street scene (Nos. 46–49).

On February 2, 1787, Peale wrote to Dr. David Ramsay, physician and historian of the war. The letter, written in that frank, outgoing tone of self-revelation that is part of Peale's charm, gives us a picture of the difficulty of printmaking in America in 1787:

> Of late I have begun one other great work, the Mezzotinto prints from my collection of portraits of illustrious Personages. This undertaking will cost me much Labour as I am obliged to take the plates from the rough and doing the whole business myself, even the impressing. I have just finished one of Doctr Franklin which I am giving out as a specimen of the size & manner I intend this series of prints. . . . My first intention was to have taken subscriptions for a Doz prints which I have selected out of the whole Collection of Heads, but on second

46. BENJAMIN FRANKLIN. 1787

Peale's exertions in establishing his museum had taken a heavy toll on his finances, and by the end of 1786 he was in a desperate state. "The charge of a large family and but little business in the portrait line at this time makes me very poor," he wrote to a Mrs. Smith on January 5, 1787.

In hopes of capitalizing on what seemed to be an increasing public interest in likenesses of leaders of the Revolution, Peale decided to make a series of mezzotints from the painted portraits in his museum. Franklin was the first subject; the likeness is based on Peale's 1785 portrait (see No. 140). (*The Metropolitan Museum of Art*)

47. THE MARQUIS DE LAFAYETTE. 1787

When a young French nobleman, not yet twenty years old, appeared in the colonies in the spring of 1777, offering to serve as a volunteer without pay in the colonies' war for independence, many congressmen at first distrusted him, as they did all foreign adventurers. His willingness to forego compensation, however, convinced Congress to give him the rank of major general, but without active command. Joining Washington's staff, he immediately endeared himself to the commander in chief. After Lafayette was wounded in the first battle for the defense of Philadelphia at the Brandywine, his youth, charm, and idealism became more widely appreciated, and his popularity grew. Peale painted his portrait in 1780. The original on which this mezzotint was based is with the Washington family pictures at Washington and Lee University. With high, receding forehead and smooth, youthful face, Lafayette was a difficult subject and the portrait is not one of Peale's successes.

Peale made this mezzotint in the spring of 1787 from the replica of the portrait in his museum; he sent three impressions together with the print of Franklin to Lafayette's wife in France on April 20, 1787. (*The Metropolitan Museum of Art*)

48. GEORGE WASHINGTON. 1787

Washington was to be the third subject for Peale's series of mezzotints and with "utmost reluctance," the artist asked the newly elected president of the Constitutional Convention for another sitting. "It gives me pain to make the request, but [for the] great desire I have to make a good mezzotinto print that your numerous friends may be gratified with a faithful likeness (several of whom I find is not satisfied with any of the portraits they have seen)."

Washington agreed to sit again (see No. 42), and the print was advertised in the September 26 issue of the *Pennsylvania Gazette.* "The likeness is esteemed the best that has been executed in print," the advertisement boasted. The cost for a framed engraving was two dollars.

Peale sent the Franklin, Lafayette, and this print to the general at Mount Vernon in October, asking Washington at the same time to visit his studio, when next in Philadelphia, to see "a pair of panthers, male and female, of full growth, most terrific animals." During the general's lifetime, the three prints hung in the music room at Mount Vernon. (*The Metropolitan Museum of Art*)

thought I have judged it best to propose only one at a time which I expect I shall be able to deliver in 6 weeks after I begin the work. . . . By this business of Prints I hope I shall get something in return for my great Expense of time and labour in making my Collection of Portraits.

In London a whole industry of printmaking and printselling—copperplate makers, engravers, print publishers, printsellers—existed to make and sell prints. In Philadelphia Peale had to do everything for himself. Sales were disappointing. In the autumn he tried an etching at a lower price but fared no better (No. 50). Peale was neither a businessman nor a salesman and after a year of struggle, he gave up the experiment. Prints of these engravings are extremely rare today.

Spurred by financial need, Peale was led into a variety of other experiments and inventions; and this is perhaps the place to speak of Peale the inventor and ingenious "improver," activities which will be described in detail by Brooke Hindle and Lillian Miller. His mechanical devices fall into categories that illustrate how Franklin's interests (other than electricity) were the needs and improvements of Peale's world. Peale's son Rembrandt thought that the time spent on his mechanical devices and inventions prevented his father from reaching his full potential as an artist. However, each time he returned to painting from one of these forays into invention (some of which lasted for years) his work seems to start with a new vigor.

49. THE REVEREND JOSEPH PILMORE. 1787

Joseph Pilmore, born in Yorkshire and educated in John Wesley's school at Kingswood, England, came to America to establish Methodism in Philadelphia. He was a powerful and successful itinerant missionary. After the war ended, he returned to England to be ordained a minister of the Anglican church. Back in Philadelphia, he became a popular preacher and was prominent among the members of the Anglican communion whose worship was close to Methodism. St. Paul's Church on Third Street, built to hold the crowds attracted by his preaching, was in its day the largest interior in the colonies. This mezzotint sold more widely than any other of Peale's mezzotints. (*The Metropolitan Museum of Art*)

50. The Accident in Lombard Street. 1787

Peale found the mezzotint process so laborious and time-consuming that he had no time to devote to sales. The prints did not sell well so he turned to the somewhat quicker technique of etching. On November 5, 1787, he advertised in the *Pennsylvania Packet* "A Perspective View of Lombard Street, being the first of an intended Series of Views taken of the principal Streets in Philadelphia. —Price one-quarter of a dollar." But the etching too did not sell and impressions are rare. The scene, an incident of Peale family life, contains these verses in the margin: "The pye from Bake-house she had brought/ But let it fall for want of thought/ And laughing Sweeps collect around/ The pye that's scatter'd on the ground." It may be the earliest genre street scene in American art as well as the first pure etching by an American artist. (*The Henry Francis du Pont Winterthur Museum*)

THE NATURAL HISTORY MUSEUM

L'histoire naturelle est la plus belle des Sciences—c'est elle qui nous montre tous les jours dans les Oeuvres de la Creation la toute puissance du Createur

(C. S. Rafinesque, in the accession book of Peale's Museum)

In a letter of 1788 to Benjamin West, Peale told him that for two or three years he had studied and labored to create an exhibition of moving pictures. This, he said, had injured his health and straitened his circumstances. He had now turned to a new and no less arduous undertaking: "That is the preserving Birds, Beasts, etc., to form a Museum, and by constant application I have made a considerable progress in collecting, considering the difficulties I have laboured under, having all to learn and no opportunity of getting assistance." [19]

The museum was to be the answer to Peale's financial distress and to his instinct to speak to a broad public. A museum, now taken as a normal part of civic life, was then quite novel. The British Museum had opened its doors in 1759. Peale must have heard talk of it in London, but there is no evidence that he had seen it. Access to it was limited. Waiting for tickets of admission sometimes lasted months and a visit, when allowed, was brief and hurried.

Only a most unusual mind would have taken such a leap into the unknown as to project a museum in Philadelphia in the 1780s.[20] It arose from a request by Dr. Christian Friedrich Michaelis, the son of a professor at the University of Göttingen and physician of a Hessian regiment in the British service. The elder Michaelis asked his son to bring back examples of the huge bones found here and there in our forest continent. These huge bones that had aroused the curiosity of the learned world were supposed to be those of a living creature. Dr. Michaelis was unable to acquire any and asked Peale to make drawings of some found at Big Bone Lick, Kentucky, belonging to Dr. John Morgan of Philadelphia. The bones were brought to Peale's gallery for his convenience in making the drawings and there roused such curiosity that he was inspired to collect other curiosities. Beginning with things that he could exhibit just as found, he progressed

51. Golden Pheasants

Many leading Americans of Peale's day played significant roles in the development of his museum. George Washington not only headed the annual subscription list, but contributed these two golden pheasants, a gift to him from Lafayette. The earliest of Peale's mountings, they are shown here in a restoration of the original exhibit, with Peale's Museum labels at their feet. Peale wrote to Washington on February 27, 1787, acknowledging receipt of one of the pheasants: "Your obliging favor of the Body of the Golden Pheasant I have received in good condition altho by a stage two Days after the receipt of your Letter, the delay was vexatious yet I was richly paid in being able to preserve so much beauty. . . . When you have the misfortune of loosing the others if the weather should be warm be pleased to order the Bowels to be taken out and some pepper put into the Body. But no salt which would injure the feathers." (*Museum of Comparative Zoology, Harvard University*)

52. William Birch. BACK
OF THE STATE HOUSE,
PHILADELPHIA. 1799

Peale's Museum was housed
in the hall of the American
Philosophical Society from
1794 until 1810. In 1802,
the collection expanded to
the upper floors of the Statehouse, and from 1810 to
1827 the entire museum
was concentrated there. In
this print, one of a group
of visiting Indians gestures
toward Philosophical Hall,
seen in the center back-
ground with a sign reading
"MUSEUM" over its door.
(*The Library Company
of Philadelphia*)

to collecting and preserving birds, animals, insects—"a work so difficult," he said
ruefully afterward, "that had he known what he was about to undertake, he would
perhaps have rather put his hand into the fire. But such is the bewitching study of
Nature, that it expands the mind to embrace object after object, and the desire is still fed
in an endless maze and contemplation of the wondrous works of Creation."[21]

"... the bewitching study of Nature..."

That study carried him into a new career. Friends donated specimens; Peale and his
sons became ardent collectors of animals, birds, and insects; he discovered the use of
arsenic as a preservative; the museum grew and grew. The seaborne commerce of
Philadelphia made contributions. Sea captains brought back a variety of creatures from
their voyages—antelope, serpents, monkeys, apes—from places as distant as Tasmania.
Washington presented a pair of Chinese pheasants, sent him through Lafayette by the
king of France (No. 51). Peale kept living animals first in an open-air zoo and when they
died, stuffed and mounted the skins. The collection soon outgrew Peale's gallery. He
was allowed to rent space in the building newly erected by the American Philosophical
Society just behind Independence Hall (No. 52). When the Statehouse was left vacant
by the removal of the federal government to Washington and the state government to
Lancaster in the interior of the state, Peale was granted use of its empty second floor and
tower room. There the museum was to remain during his lifetime, becoming our first
(although unofficial) national museum. Expeditions sent to the far ends of the continent
—Lewis and Clark, Pike, Long—deposited specimens there. The founders of American

53. THE LONG ROOM. 1822

With his museum, Peale set out "to bring into one view a world in miniature." The best visual document of the contents and arrangement of the museum is this watercolor of the Long Room, which extended across the entire Chestnut Street side on the second floor of the Statehouse. Cases of birds flank the left wall; portraits of great men are hung above. At the right are cases displaying insects, minerals, and fossils; on the cases rest busts of George Washington, scientist Benjamin Rush, and Dr. Philip Syng Physick. On the right wall are four of Peale's landscapes made near his Germantown farm.

This drawing was begun by Peale, who used his "painter's quadrant." The detail was completed by Titian Ramsay Peale II in the summer of 1822 as a preliminary study for *The Artist in His Museum* (No. 75). In a letter to his son Rubens of August 4, 1822, Peale reports: "I drew the lines with my Machine, I set Titian at work to fill it up with his water Colours." (*The Detroit Institute of Arts*)

54. THE EXHUMATION OF THE MASTODON. 1806–8

The high point of Peale's museum career was the excavation from a glacial bog near Newburgh, New York, in 1801 of two nearly complete skeletons of a mastodon. One of these was mounted in the museum with the aid of Dr. Caspar Wistar, the country's leading anatomist; the few missing portions were either restored in *papier maché* or carved in wood by the sculptor William Rush. The other skeleton was taken to England by Rembrandt and Rubens Peale in an unsuccessful attempt to raise money through its exhibition. When the French scientist Cuvier published the mastodon as representative of an extinct species, it was a dramatic demonstration of the fact that over geological time species could become extinct, an issue that was still being debated at that time. Peale, through his own perseverance, had found scientific information that had not been known before.

Peale began this picture in 1806 to record the event, but kept adding to the canvas until 1808. The completed work contains about seventy-five figures, including family members and friends whom Peale wished to associate with the momentous discovery. Some twenty of these are identifiable portraits, but not all of them represent people present at the time. At the left of the tent, standing with folded arms, Peale portrayed his fellow naturalist, Alexander Wilson, author of *American Ornithology*. Climbing a ladder in the foreground is John Masten, owner of the farm on which the excavation took place. Peale himself stands with arm extended, holding a large drawing of the bones. Next to him, from left to right, are Mrs. Hannah Peale in Quaker cap, possibly Mrs. Rembrandt Peale, and members of the Peale family: Rembrandt, Sybilla, Elizabeth, Rubens (with glasses), and Raphaelle. James Peale may be seen between the two poles. In the group to the right of Wilson, we see Peale's deceased second wife, Elizabeth DePeyster Peale, scolding her youngest son Titian Ramsay II; her sister and brother-in-law, Major and Mrs. John Stagg, stand slightly behind her. Coleman and Sophonisba Sellers are shown under a green umbrella, while the two younger Peale boys—Linnaeus and Franklin—push a log in the pit with a long pole.

The painting dramatizes a critical moment in the excavation when a violent thunderstorm threatened to flood the pit and bring the search to an end. (*The Peale Museum*)

natural history—Alexander Wilson, Benjamin Smith Barton, Dr. John D. Godman —gathered about it.

In 1805 Peale published a guide, *A Walk with a Friend Through the Philadelphia Museum*, from which we learn that some ninety species of mammals, labeled in Latin, French, and English, were shown in the Room of Mammals. The Long Room (No. 53) on the Chestnut Street side was devoted to birds, some seven hundred specimens, arranged according to the Linnaean system, in glass-fronted cases, the backs of which were painted landscapes illustrating their different habitats. Between the windows on the north wall were cases holding some four thousand species of insects. An ingenious pair of revolving microscopes allowed close examination of small specimens. The mineral collection was also displayed on the north wall. Above the cases hung, row on row, the portraits of illustrious men. In a third room was a marine collection.

A portion of the museum remained in Philosophical Hall. The mounted skeleton of the mastodon was there and a room of what we would now call ethnology, containing North and South Sea artifacts amplified by lifesize figures in wax of American Indian chiefs and South Sea natives.

The outstanding scientific discovery of the museum was the mastodon. Excavated by Peale in 1801, it was "far the first fossil skeleton ever mounted in America . . . and it was probably the second in the world."[22] One must bear in mind that our ideas of geological time and of extinct species did not then exist. The huge bones, teeth, tusks, and other fragments of very large creatures found in various parts of the world, most frequently in North America, had puzzled and teased the minds of scientists since the 1730s. In 1798, Thomas Jefferson, as president of the American Philosophical Society, appointed a committee to collect information relative to American antiquities, both natural and archaeological. Jefferson was its chairman; the others were Dr. Caspar Wistar, the country's leading anatomist; Charles Willson Peale; Dr. Adam Seybert, mineralogist and chemist; George Turner; Gen. James Wilkinson, the commanding general of the army; and Maj. Jonathan Williams, its chief engineer officer and Franklin's grand-nephew.

In 1801, Peale led an expedition, partly financed by the Philosophical Society, which recovered two nearly complete skeletons and portions of others from glacial bogs near Newburgh, New York. One of these skeletons was mounted in the society's hall. Missing bones were carved in wood by the sculptor William Rush. Missing portions of the head were restored in *papier maché*, a red line indicating the restored parts. A second skeleton was taken to London by Peale's son Rembrandt for exhibition. The climax came when Baron Georges-Léopold Cuvier, the great French naturalist, reviewing Peale's discovery and other previous finds in 1806, named the incognitum a new species, the mastodon, and wrote, *"il n'y a pas le moindre preuve, le moindre témoignage propre à faire croire qu'il y en ait encore ni en Amerique, ni ailleurs, aucun individu vivant."*[23] The first extinct species accepted by science! Peale had helped add to man's understanding of geologic time, whose realization was one of the great intellectual events of the nineteenth century (No. 54).

Peale's Museum was far ahead in another way. Its creator, a child of the Enlightenment and of the first New World republic, thought of his museum as an instrument for rational pleasure and the instruction of the public. For long after his time, the museums appearing in Europe reflected the more socially stratified structure of that society. The European museum was directed toward artists, savants, and amateurs of science and art, not toward the populace. When the British Museum opened in 1759, "applicants had first to present themselves at the porter's lodge, then fill in their name, condition and address in the porter's register, then pass the scrutiny of the librarians, then wait until their ticket had been formally issued . . . It was a process that took several weeks and two or three visits."[24] The Louvre opened in 1793. "The public was admitted on three days in every ten: the rest were reserved for artists and for those admitted by special pass."[25] In the open society of America, Peale's Museum not only was accessible to everyone but offered lectures, concerts, and a sales desk where printed guides were given out and souvenirs (in the form of one's own silhouette) were available for purchase. Peale summed up his ideal of rational pleasure and self-instruction in the placard over the entrance of the south door of the Statehouse:

> The book of Nature open—
> —Explore the wond'rous work.
> A solemn Institute of laws eternal
> Whose unaltered page no time can change,
> No copier can corrupt.[26]

In popular education Peale's Museum was a hundred years ahead of its time.[27]

THE COLUMBIANUM

Peale's energies were more and more absorbed by collecting and mounting specimens; studying the best works of science in order to identify and label his specimens; installing and arranging; announcing, with a flair for publicity, accessions and improvements. In 1794, he announced in the press that he would retire from portrait painting in favor of his sons Rembrandt and Raphaelle. Nevertheless, in that same year, Peale launched a new project, the founding of an academy of art in Philadelphia. Peale believed that American artists needed both public exhibition of their works and a professional art school, such as the Royal Academy provided in London. Many such academies had been founded in European capitals since the sixteenth century but up until 1794 no American city had had a sufficient number of artists to form such an organization. Now, because the French Revolution and a long period of war had brought hard times for artists in England and on the Continent, a number of painters, sculptors, and engravers had migrated to the New World. By 1794, Peale thought the artists' time had come and took the lead in organizing the Columbianum, or American Academy of Fine Arts.

The Columbianum was formed on December 29, 1794. It was short-lived, however, a victim of the political passions of the times. The group split over a resolution asking President Washington to be honorary patron of the Columbianum, as King George was of the Royal Academy in London. This seems innocent enough in our eyes, and a reasonable move to give the academy a national character. But at this moment the fear of

55. THE STAIRCASE GROUP: RAPHAELLE AND TITIAN RAMSAY PEALE I. 1795

This painting was done as a show-piece for the first exhibition of the "Columbianum, or American Academy of Painting, Sculpture, Architecture and Engraving," which opened in the Statehouse in Philadelphia in 1795—the first contemporary group exhibition in America.

Peale intended the lifesize painting of his sons climbing a winding stairway as a "deception," deliberately meant to fool the viewer into believing the subjects were real. Even his method of installing the painting added to the deception. Instead of being hung on the wall, the painting was set into a doorway with an actual step built out into the room at the base of the painted steps. The illusion was so successful that according to Rembrandt Peale, when George Washington visited the museum (where the painting had been moved) in 1797, he "bowed politely to the painted figures which he afterwards acknowledged he thought were living persons." (*Philadelphia Museum of Art*)

"monarchy" haunted the leftward-thinking sympathizers of revolutionary France. An angry dispute followed. Peale's faction stayed united long enough to open the Columbianum's one and only exhibition on April 30, 1795, in the Senate chamber of the Statehouse.

Peale exhibited five portraits of his friends. In addition, thinking he should contribute something more than the usual portrait, he painted a lifesize *trompe l'oeil* picture of his two sons, Titian (above) and Raphaelle, going up a stairway (No. 55). They are a "deception," in a natural pose wholly unlike an ordinary portrait; the canvas was set in a door frame which seemed to lead into a winding stairway, and which was continued by actual stairs projecting outward and down to the floor. It is a notable example of the sense of fact that was Peale's gift and reveals a new breadth and force that can be attributed to a technique he had recently adopted. He had begun to paint with long brushes of twice the normal length. In his autobiography he says, speaking of 1795, "He made his Pencil sticks of more than twice the usual length of such tools . . . having of late accustomed himself to paint portraits with very long brushes." Thirty years earlier Gainsborough had done the same to achieve a simpler and broader style, and the technique was just as effective for Peale.

PEALE'S LANDSCAPES

The museum's popular success made Peale well-to-do. In 1810, his son Rubens, his principal assistant, was placed in charge of the museum. Peale bought a farm of over one hundred acres in the rolling countryside near Germantown and retired to enjoy the country life that his friend Thomas Jefferson considered the best of human existence. On the property was a stone house, a stone barn and springhouse, numerous wooden outbuildings, and a stream with two small falls. He called it "Belfield." Here he spent his time farming, embellishing the grounds of Belfield with walks and pavilions, and making inventions.

Finally, about 1815, he turned again to painting, his eyes as he said, "now opened to see his folly of making various machines, which cost labor and money and no real profit." This was the period, c. 1815–17, of his landscapes in oil, and of a new series of portraits.

The naturalism of Peale's vision had always made him ill at ease with the eighteenth-century tradition of decorative Italianate landscape. Years earlier, one of his most generous patrons in America, John Cadwalader, had asked him in 1769 to paint landscapes for his new house on Second Street, Philadelphia, presumably to be mounted in panels over the mantels.[28] Peale was familiar with the English style of overmantel landscape. He had certainly seen the grand Italian views of Richard Wilson (see Fig. c); Francesco Zuccarelli's pastoral scenes with peasants dancing in the foreground; the picturesque views of ruins and castles; hunting parties in the grounds of a distant country house. All were equally remote from Peale's naturalistic mind and subject matter. The American landscape offered nothing that suggested such picturesque elements, although the Chesapeake and Delaware bays offered beautiful effects of light, cloud, and sky over expanses of water and low horizons. The backgrounds of his early portraits show that Peale painted these effects delightfully, but nevertheless, decorative overmantel landscapes baffled him. To him an overmantel meant an idyll or an Italianate landscape. William Williams had painted such pictures in Philadelphia (an example is in the Newark Museum), and Peale owned an engraving of such a landscape by Claude Lorrain; Peale's friend Bordley, an amateur artist, had painted a *Temple of Apollo* (Fig. j) after it. Peale knew the mode. He even went to Bordley's place on Wye Island, hoping to find a subject for Cadwalader's pictures but nothing came of it. He delayed so long that Cadwalader eventually ordered landscapes from London, whereupon Peale wrote in relief: "I hope you will pardon my neglect of the Landscapes for really too much diffidence prevented my attempts after nature had lost her green mantle. The pieces you get from London I hope will be very clever. I could not promise myself anything of that way . . . worthy of the Place you intended."[29] Cadwalader, though disappointed, continued to be Peale's chief patron in Philadelphia.[30]

Peale's feeling for landscape was expressed earlier in his career in a letter to Edmund Jenings about the education of Bordley's sons at Eton: "I wish their master may teach them to sketch from Nature, I mean Landscape; it may be very useful, will certainly be a great amusement. One rude line from Nature is worth an hundred from copies, enlarges the Ideas, and makes one see and feel with such venerations as are worthy of the author."[31]

To solve his own difficulty of painting landscapes as a faithful transcript of nature, he built a machine which he called "a painter's quadrant."[32] Judging by drawings that appear to have been done by its aid (No. 56) and by the landscapes which he contributed to James Trenchard's *Columbian Magazine*, it must have been some form of *camera obscura*, a chamber in which the real image of an object is received through a small opening or lens and focused on a facing surface.

Fig. j. John Beale Bordley after Claude Lorrain. TEMPLE OF APOLLO. 1776. Oil on canvas. Philadelphia Museum of Art. Given by Mrs. Walter C. Janney in memory of her late husband, a former Trustee of the Museum

56. EUTAW (?). c. 1788

In his autobiography, Peale mentions going with Gen. Otho Holland Williams (No. 30) to paint a portrait of his father-in-law, William Smith, at his country seat of "Eutaw" (No. 156), named for the battle in which General Williams had led a famous charge. On Sunday, October 12, Peale wrote in his diary, "went with Genl. Williams to his country seat four miles distant, where I made three drawings with the machine [Peale's 'painter's quadrant'] and returned in the evening." It seems probable that this drawing is the product of that excursion.

Peale's working method is shown in this sketch. A few quick lines in pencil, confirmed in ink, represent accurately but artlessly a level landscape looking across a small stream to various farm buildings among trees. Pencil notations on the drawing may have served as a guide for more finished work in the studio. (*American Philosophical Society*)

When Trenchard, a fellow soldier in the Revolution, started the *Columbian Magazine* in 1786, he had asked Peale for illustrations. Peale responded with a series of views of the countryside around Philadelphia and views of the town (Nos. 57–62), which Trenchard engraved. In the small scale of a magazine page, Peale's directness and innocence of eye are engaging and effective.

It was not lack of sentiment for nature that made landscape a small part of his artistic output. When he sailed up the Hudson River in 1801 to dig for the mastodon, he was greatly stirred by the mountain scenery. "The grand scenes . . . so enraptured me that I would, if I could, have made drawings with both hands at the same instant," he said; and he filled a sketchbook with studies of the river's banks (No. 63). These direct transcripts of what he saw, jotted over with notes about historic events or people associated

57. A N.W. VIEW OF THE STATE HOUSE IN PHILADELPHIA TAKEN 1778. 1787

In 1786, when James Trenchard, a Philadelphia engraver, started the *Columbian Magazine, a Monthly Miscellany*, he enlisted the aid of his friend Charles Willson Peale in providing illustrations. "A N.W. View of the State House" appeared in the July, 1787, issue, the first in a series of views of Philadelphia and its environs which Peale developed for the magazine. The Statehouse, already revered as the site of the Continental Congress and the signing of the Declaration of Independence, was that summer the setting for the Constitutional Convention. The modest size and manner of the engraving disguise the strong emotion that lies behind it; the text that accompanied the plate described the Statehouse as "a building which will, perhaps, become more interesting in the history of the world, than any of the celebrated fabrics of Greece or Rome."

Peale's drawing, probably made with the aid of his "painter's quadrant," had been done nine years earlier and incorporated in his full-length portrait of Conrad-Alexandre Gérard (No. 28). (*Private collection*)

58. PERSPECTIVE VIEW OF THE COUNTRY BETWEEN WILMINGTON AND THE DELAWARE. 1787

While this landscape, which appeared in the April, 1787, issue of the *Columbian*, does not show an artist's or an engraver's name, it is thought to be far beyond the scope of Trenchard or any other engraver then working in America. Only Peale could have composed a landscape so subtle and convincing. (*Robert G. Stewart*)

59. AN EAST VIEW OF GRAY'S FERRY, ON THE RIVER SCHUYLKILL. 1787

The road leading south from Philadelphia crossed the Schuylkill River at Gray's Ferry, where a floating bridge was constructed during occupation of the city by the British army. Peale's rendering of this familiar landmark is one of his freshest and most effective landscape views. It was engraved by Trenchard for the frontispiece of the August, 1787, issue of the *Columbian Magazine*. (*The Library Company of Philadelphia*)

60. A SOUTH EAST VIEW OF CHRIST'S CHURCH. 1787

This unsigned plate is clearly a product of the joint effort of Peale and Trenchard, Peale working with his "painter's quadrant." The engraving appeared in the *Columbian Magazine* of December, 1787. It is not keyed into the text but accompanies the final installment of an article on "Considerations of Religion . . . By A. Z." (*The Library Company of Philadelphia*)

61. An East View of Gray's Ferry, near Philadelphia, with the Triumphal Arches, & Erected for the Reception of General Washington. 1789

Washington's journey from Mount Vernon to New York City for his inauguration as first president of the United States was a series of festive receptions. Crossing Gray's Ferry bridge on April 20, he found it arched over with laurel and colors. In such patriotic pageantry Peale was, as always, active. It is said that he had arranged for his fifteen-year-old daughter Angelica to lower a civic crown of laurel upon the head of the president-elect when he passed under the western arch. Washington, however, quietly pushed the wreath aside and gave Angelica a kiss, "much to her embarrassment at the time—but remembered afterward with pride and pleasure," as her brother Titian noted. This engraving appeared in the May, 1789, issue of the *Columbian*. (*Bowdoin College Library*)

62. View of Several Public Buildings, in Philadelphia. 1790

Published in the *Columbian Magazine* of January, 1790, as an unsigned plate, this engraving is closely related to Peale's other work for the magazine. The buildings, identified in an accompanying key, are from left to right: the Protestant Episcopal Academy, not entirely finished; the county courthouse; the Statehouse; the hall of the American Philosophical Society; a front view of the hall of the Library Company of Philadelphia; and Carpenters' Hall. (*The Library Company of Philadelphia*)

View of West point from the side of the mountain

63. VIEW OF WEST POINT FROM THE SIDE OF THE MOUNTAIN, in sketchbook entitled "Highlands of the Hudson." 1801

Peale embarked at New York City on the sloop *Priscilla*, of Albany, on June 18, 1801, for West Point; from there he planned to travel by land to Newburgh and the site where gigantic bones were reported to have been found. The bold and picturesque mountain scenery of the Hudson excited him greatly. He wrote to his friend, the surveyor Andrew Ellicott: "The grand scenes presented in our passage through the highlands so enraptured me that I would, if I could, have made drawings with both hands at the same Instant, and the rapidity of our sailing with a fair wind and tide rendered more rapid by the confinement of mountains, permitted me only to make hasty sketches, these for the number of 17 views of the most striking and interesting by the events of the late war. I retouched them on my return and I hope to finish more correctly in my next trip."

Peale finished the drawings in watercolor and kept them as souvenirs of the memorable journey that resulted in the discovery of the mastodon. He gave the sketches to his son Titian Ramsay II after the latter's return from Long's expedition to the Rocky Mountains. A later owner had them bound in leather. (*American Philosophical Society*)

with each place, have the same factual interest and innocence of eye as the images done for Trenchard. The freshness of his vision is more striking if compared to the generalized, conventional landscape painted in America by such European-trained artists as Beck, Corne, Groombridge, and Winstanley, whom the convulsions of the Napoleonic wars had brought to these shores in the last decade of the eighteenth century.

Now years later, painting at his Germantown farm for his own pleasure, he turned

64. BELFIELD. 1815–16

In 1810, at the age of sixty-nine, Peale retired to a farm he called "Belfield," just outside of
Philadelphia. Here he engaged in a vigorous round of farming activities, all of which he considered
"healthy amusements." He also painted over fifteen views of his farm and its environs. Perhaps
referring to this painting, he wrote his daughter Angelica on November 22, 1815: "I have . . .
painted . . . a tolerable large landscape . . . a View of the Garden and most of the Buildings, as seen
from what we call my seat in the Walk to the Mill." (*Private collection*)

opposite top:

65. MILL BANK. 1818

The landscapes painted at "Belfield" were primarily a diversion for Peale. In a letter to his
daughter Angelica in September, 1817, he writes, "To fill up my time I take delight in the study
of Landscapes and if I continue my diligence I may in the issue produce something clever. But as
my work is altogether for amusement, I may not be so industrious as I ought to be in order to
excell in the art." "Mill Bank" was the home of Nathan Sellers, father of Peale's son-in-law,
Coleman Sellers, and the first of the inventive engineer-manufacturer type in the Sellers family;
for a hundred years his descendants were distinguished in Pennsylvania iron mining and machine
design. (*Private collection*)

opposite bottom:

66. SELLERS HALL. c. 1818

Peale painted this view of the original homestead of the Sellers family and "Mill Bank" (No. 65) for
Coleman Sellers. They are among the most luminous and pleasing of his landscapes. (*Private collection*)

to landscapes in oil. In 1815, there was no landscape tradition in the United States except the topographic view, which Peale had practiced earlier in his drawings for Trenchard's *Columbian Magazine*. Peale picked up this thread once more, drawing familiar scenes about "Belfield" with his painter's quadrant (Nos. 64–66), but adding something of the charming luminosity one sees in the backgrounds of his portraits. The results are documentary, and one misses the sense of changing light that gives life to landscape; yet it may have been the experience of painting out-of-doors, under the sky, that led to the last phase of his development as an artist.

THE LAST PORTRAITS

The old man was nearing eighty when he returned to painting portraits. He went to Washington in 1818 to add a likeness of President Monroe to his gallery, and portraits of other new leaders of the republic (Nos. 67, 68). His further aim was to secure a place for his son Titian Ramsay Peale on the expedition into the unknown West, to be commanded by Maj. Stephen H. Long (No. 129). The Long Expedition stirred the imagination of

67. JOHN QUINCY ADAMS. 1818

In 1818, Peale went to Washington, where he hoped, among other things, to enlist federal support for his museum. While there he also intended to add portraits of President Monroe and other political leaders of the day to his gallery collection. Men like Secretary of State Adams and Senators Henry Clay and John C. Calhoun came to sit for their portraits in the capital. In his diary, John Quincy Adams wrote that the seventy-seven-year-old Peale "has made a Caricature of my Portrait." Yet Peale's painting reflects much of the intellectual pride and rigidity of the man whose wisdom and integrity he came to respect. (*Historical Society of Pennsylvania*)

68. HENRY CLAY. 1818

When Peale painted this portrait in the autumn of 1818, Henry Clay was Speaker of the House and on his way to becoming a figure of national prominence. Clay's reputation and position entitled him, in Peale's mind, to a place in his Gallery of Great Men.

In Peale's portrait, Clay's face retains the softness of youth. He is the young orator who had come to Washington in 1806 as a vigorous representative of the West, and through insouciant charm and extraordinary eloquence quickly rose to party leadership. The great tragic struggles that were to carve his face into the gaunt and furrowed countenance so familiar to us today lay ahead—the efforts to prevent the union from being destroyed by sectional antagonisms, to defend the commercial and manufacturing interests of the country, and to become president of the United States. Peale's Clay is still a young and cheerful man, the leader who had won the affection of Americans. The portrait is one of Peale's most interesting records of character. (*Historical Society of Pennsylvania*)

the country. Peale painted its five scientists for the museum: Maj. Stephen H. Long, its leader; William Baldwin, botanist, who died worn out by the hardships of the expedition; A.E. Jessup, geologist; Thomas Say, geologist (No. 90); and Titian Ramsay Peale, naturalist (No. 130). He had previously painted for the museum Charles-Alexandre Lesueur, the French naturalist, who had come to Philadelphia in 1816 (see No. 76).

In portraits of these scientists and in those of himself and his family (Nos. 69–73), the artist's deepened insight into human character is conveyed in the richest and most subtle style of his long career. In his old age he had become aware that visual experience is created by light. He planned his pictures in terms of light. Something also entered into his style from the encaustic medium which Rembrandt Peale had learned in Paris, and that his father had adopted. Peale painted his brother James (No. 74), a man of gentle and retiring nature, who had been content to live quietly all his life in the shadow of his more aggressive brother Charles. James is shown as a miniature painter, examining by the light of an Argand lamp a miniature painted by his daughter Rosalba. Peale had always drawn expressively: in this portrait the slow movement of the heavy, old figure is admirably suggested. But at eighty Peale, experimenting to the last, was working with light. He let the direct light of the lamp fall upon the lower portion of the head, the upper part receiving only the soft glow through the lampshade, making the whole canvas a study in subtle gradations of light.

The portrait was done for the museum. After all his efforts to obtain support for the museum from the legislature of Pennsylvania and from the federal government, he was obliged at last to obtain incorporation (but no money) from the city councils of Philadelphia (1821). Peale appointed a board of trustees and a staff of scientific lecturers. The trustees, in grateful recognition of the artist's role, asked him to paint a self-portrait for the museum.

The commission meant a great deal to Peale. The artistic problem he set for himself was to place the figure in a dark foreground against a light background, the source of light coming from behind with only a secondary reflected light upon the head. He made first a study of his own head in half-light (Frontispiece). At this point Peale's use of light places him in the advancing forefront of his art. And there he stands, raising the curtain to reveal the wonders of nature and of art to the people of the young republic for which he had fought as a soldier and labored as a man.

In *The Artist in His Museum* (No. 75) Peale depicted himself as he wished to be

69, 70. SOPHONISBA AND COLEMAN SELLERS. 1805

The wedding of Peale's daughter Sophonisba and Coleman Sellers, son of Nathan, was to be a formal affair in the late fall of 1805. But, with the blessings of both fathers, who disliked social parades, the two eloped. Announcing the news to his wife the morning after the wedding, Coleman's father pretended to read aloud from the newspaper: "Marriage Notice. At the home of Squire Moore, Montgomery County, Coleman Sellers, son of Nathan Sellers the tinker, to Sophonisba Angusciola Peale, daughter of Charles Willson Peale the showman."

These cabinet-size watercolors were almost certainly done at the time of their marriage. (*Private collection*)

71. COLEMAN SELLERS.
c. 1811

Coleman Sellers was a mechanical engineer by trade and had the same inventive spirit as his father-in-law. Together they worked on projects varying from the development of a mail pouch to the construction of a magnet which would lift three hundred pounds. Coleman took an active interest in the museum, and on its incorporation in 1821 was named one of its five trustees. (*Private collection*)

remembered, in the midst of his life's work. Behind the curtain is the Long Room of his museum. His palette and brushes rest on the table; his taxidermy tools, the jaw and bones of the mastodon, and a wild turkey (a specimen collected on the Missouri River by his son Titian) are at his feet. Half-seen behind the curtain is the mastodon. The long rows of cases contain the world of nature; above are the portraits, row on row, of illustrious men. The spectators in the museum represent the self-education in the Great Book of Nature which was Peale's ideal for the institution.

Charles Willson Peale was born on April 15, 1741. He died at Philadelphia, February 22, 1827, eighty-six years later, and was buried in St. Peter's churchyard, a stone's throw from where he had lived at the corner of Third and Lombard streets. He was an artist of a strong, simple, severe neoclassic style; a pioneer in American natural history and in the development of the public museum; and a man of great skill, ingenuity, and benevolence.

72. Mrs. Charles Willson Peale (Hannah Moore). 1816

Peale married his third wife, Hannah Moore, a Quaker, in 1805. In a letter written to his son Raphaelle on September 7, a month after the wedding, Peale described her as "A Person of suitable years to me [she was fifty-one, he was sixty-four] a *friend* and uncommonly cheerful for her time of life, although as plain as any amongst friends."

When painting this portrait, the third he did of Hannah, Peale at first experimented with a new method—using a large magnifying glass—that had been suggested by his son Rembrandt. "Although the effect was pleasing," he wrote to Rembrandt on February 20, "yet through so great a medium of glass I lost sight of the minute markings, so essential to a well-finished portrait, and therefore I laid the apparatus aside, and finished the picture in the common mode, and I believe it is the best portrait that I have ever executed." Heavy crackling in the portrait indicates that Peale was experimenting with pigments as well as the "new method." (*Museum of Fine Arts, Boston*)

73. SELF-PORTRAIT. 1822

A gift for his daughter Sophonisba Sellers, this portrait was exhibited at the Pennsylvania Academy in 1822 with a note, "Painted in the 81st year of his age without spectacles." The old artist might well have taken pride not only in his eyesight but in the sober power of this artistic statement, worthy of a Dutch seventeenth-century artist. Intelligence, a capacity for piercing observation, and strong will are the traits that emerge most strongly from this self-portrait. (*Private collection*)

74. JAMES PEALE BY LAMPLIGHT. 1822

In a letter to his son Rembrandt of December 19, 1822, Peale described this portrait of his brother James: "He is looking at a miniature picture by an argand lamp. The brightest light is on the end of his nose downward, the forehead has only the light through the shade of the lamp, a miniature palette and pencil on the table, this to show that he is a painter. On the shade of the lamp I shall put that he served in the Battle of Long Island, White Plains, Trenton, Brandywine, Germantown and at Monmouth. You know it is common to ornament the shades of lamps with the English coat of arms. I think this is noting that my brother has deserved well of his country."

The inscription on the lampshade proved artistically inexpedient, and the portrait became a tribute not to a military career but to a brother's affection for a gentle old man and to the poetry of light. (*The Detroit Institute of Arts*)

opposite:

75. THE ARTIST IN HIS MUSEUM. 1822

This monumental portrait is Peale's autobiography. Asked by the museum trustees to paint a lifesize full-length portrait of himself, he wrote to his son Rembrandt on July 23, 1822: "I think it important that I should not only make it a lasting ornament to my art as a painter, but also that the design should be expressive that I bring forth into public view the beauties of nature and art, the rise and progress of the Museum." Drawing aside a curtain, Peale invites us into his museum. We see the Long Room with its cases of birds lining the left wall and the portraits of illustrious men above them. In the left foreground, by his taxidermist's tools, is a fine specimen of wild turkey brought back by Titian from the Long Expedition. At the right, a table holds his palette and brushes. On the floor beside the table are a mastodon jaw and tibia; the mounted skeleton stands half-seen behind. In the perspective of the gallery, Peale illustrated his idea of the educational meaning of the museum. One figure, with folded arms, gazing at the birds, stands meditating on what he sees; a father is instructing his son, who holds an open book; a Quaker woman throws up her hands in astonishment as she catches sight of the mastodon.

Peale, whose artistic skills had always lain in his drawing, surprises us that at age eighty-one he should make the canvas an experiment in subtleties of light. Indeed, the difficulties presented by the lighting were such that he took the unusual step of making a preparatory sketch (see the Frontispiece). He stands, a dark figure in a black suit, against the lighted distance, a secondary light reflected on his head by means of a mirror, making his figure one of strong darks and half-lights. The canvas was especially admired by artists, who appreciated its novelty, the difficulty of handling the lighting problem, and the success of its solution. (*The Pennsylvania Academy of the Fine Arts*)

Charles Willson Peale's

SCIENCE

AND

TECHNOLOGY

—

BROOKE HINDLE

II

CHARLES WILLSON PEALE is most remembered as a painter, and this indeed was the field of his most enduring achievement. He thought of himself, however, as having a second career and lavished most of the last half of his life on his museum and on natural history. He had several other careers as well, not only soldier, politician, and farmer, but, conspicuously, inventor and developer of varied mechanical devices. Peale's ability to create and innovate in such apparently unrelated areas as art, science, and technology baffles the modern mind, conscious of the intricate specialization required to contribute to any one of those fields today. It can be understood only by seeking to enter Peale's world.

In fact, Peale's diverse activities and accomplishments were neither unrelated nor unparalleled. They are related in that each depended primarily upon his unusual and highly developed capacity for visual thinking—for manipulating images in his mind. They are paralleled by artist-scientists and artist-inventors of his own and earlier days. Of these, the first to come to mind is always Leonardo da Vinci, who contributed at the highest level in each of the three fields. Other, if lesser, Renaissance figures are also relatively easy to name, for example, Francesco di Giorgio Martini and Albrecht Dürer.

Somehow it has been easier to recognize Renaissance men who succeeded in two or more fields than to notice Americans of Peale's era who boasted such diversity. They were, however, not at all unusual. Peale himself was well acquainted with several, the most obvious being Robert Fulton who, before turning to the design of canals, submarines, and, finally, steamboats, had studied painting under Benjamin West as Peale had, though a generation later. Peale was familiar too with the architect-artist-inventors Benjamin Henry Latrobe and William Thornton. Each is best known for his architecture —itself a fusion of art and engineering—but each also painted, sketched, and made maps; one did geological surveys and the other wrote music. Like Latrobe and Thornton, Thomas Jefferson (No. 142) lacked Peale's and Fulton's artisan-art beginning but boasted a similar range of interest in architecture, mechanisms, and natural history. As a friend of Peale, he provided sustaining support.

Most comparable in the quality of his art and in the importance of his other achievements was Samuel F. B. Morse, who also studied under West some thirty-five years after Peale. Peale may have known him; his son Rembrandt certainly did. While in New York City, Rembrandt served as president of the expiring American Academy of Fine Arts in competition with Morse's new and rising National Academy of Design. Morse was a leading portraitist and, indeed, the first art professor in the country (at New York University) before he turned to work on the telegraph. In that invention, he put new scientific knowledge to practical and profitable use by applying the same capacity in visual thinking Peale enjoyed.[1]

The consistent, broad, and remarkably adaptable strength of visual thinking must be recognized. Everyone has the capacity to think visually; we now know that it is one of only two modes of human thought, the other being the mode cultivated in the three R's and in the schools generally: verbal, linear, arithmetic, and analytical. By contrast, visual thinking interprets simultaneous, complex images. It is the basis for the recognition of people and places and for orienting ourselves in space. It has to be relied upon more than verbal, linear thought for painting, sculpture, and all two- or three-dimensional design. The cultivation of visual thinking was the basis of nearly all pre-industrial technology, which is where Peale began—in the trade of saddlery.[2]

Charles Willson Peale was a product of the artisan culture of his day. He learned his trade as generations of craftsmen had, through a traditional apprenticeship. In America, apprenticeships were loosely administered; the powerful guild systems which controlled them in Europe had not been transferred here. On the other hand, apprenticeship indentures and obligations of both master and apprentice were supervised through the court system. Although he strained against the power of his master, Peale completed an apprenticeship of nearly eight years before setting up his own saddlery and harness-making shop.

His training as an artisan conditioned him for the rest of his life and explains the strengths and weaknesses he displayed in his varied occupations. It was, overwhelmingly, a non-verbal learning process in which he learned by doing, by watching the master perform his manipulations, and by measuring his own product against good pieces of finished work. He acquired sufficient knowledge to make acceptable saddles and harnesses —but more importantly for his future work, he cultivated a manner of learning and a mode of thinking.

When saddlery proved insufficiently remunerative, he moved through a succession of other trades with an ease that astonishes us today—and that would have been impossible in the more rigidly controlled environment of England. Having gotten the rudiments of metalworking in his own trade, he soon began silversmithing on the side, producing bridles, shoe buckles, and finger rings. Then, by repairing a set of watches, "he acquired knowledge of such machines" and decided to advertise for clock- and watch-repair work.[3] After all, this was a trade that could be learned by doing, well-made clocks providing perfect models for emulation and well-running clocks a perfect test of success. Finally, a sort of hobby, painting, caught him in the same year he opened his saddlery shop, in 1762, and came increasingly to absorb his efforts. He gradually moved toward serious portrait painting, which demanded ever better models and better masters.

Peale's ability to teach himself one trade after another was far from unique, although only the most talented craftsmen could hope to succeed in such shifts. Another who demonstrated great mobility was the steamboat pioneer of the 1780s, John Fitch, whom Peale knew. Fitch was apprenticed as a clockmaker in Connecticut, but when he finished his training, he set himself up, instead, as a brass founder. On the side, he undertook the manufacture of potash. He then moved to New Jersey, where he bought a set of tools, always the essential requirement for any practice, and set up as a silversmith. He succeeded well in this endeavor but when the war for independence intruded he became a gunsmith, contracting to repair and rebuild muskets, and then served as a soldier. He did a copperplate engraving of a map without instruction, and he built his first steam engine without ever having seen one. Like Peale, he moved from one trade to another without apparent hesitancy.[4]

In Peale's world, painting had a recognized position in the spectrum of trades and crafts. It was a superior position and one that brought its practitioners into intimate contact with the social and political leaders of the day. It also had the potential for bringing them a good income—and even wealth and position, as Benjamin West's great success dramatically emphasized. But the fine and the mechanical or useful arts were understood, and Peale specifically understood them, to be part of the same continuum. The learning process was identical: learning by doing, observing the master's style and technique, and, especially, copying and seeking to excel the best models. At the center was the same translation of mental images into material form through the application of manual dexterity and skill.[5]

Peale's first art instructor, John Hesselius, made clear how exactly similar the learning of painting could be to learning a mechanical trade. As Peale later recalled, "Mr. Hesselius painted the half of a face for him, leaving the other half to be finished by Peale, who also saw Mr. Hesselius paint two Portraits" (see Fig. a). This opportunity, he understood, "infinitely lightened the difficulties in a new art."[6]

By the time Peale sailed for England in 1766, painting had become his career, and it remained so until sometime after his announcement in 1784 that he would devote his energies to a natural history museum. Yet, he never gave up art but returned to painting at irregular intervals and used it effectively in his museum work. In conjunction with, or in addition to, these major occupations, he engaged in many handicrafts and mechanical efforts that were new to him. He approached everything he did with the conviction he must have learned in his early trades that perseverance would conquer all difficulties. As he put it, "an industrious habit" was the key to success.[7]

When he and his sons complained that he may have failed of maximum fulfillment by the neglect of art, his great career, they reflected a common attitude which favored specialization. Specialization is not new to our day but ancient, and such old maxims as "Shoemaker stick to your last," recommended the concentration of effort in a single area. Although drifting from one trade to another was common in America, it was disparaged as ending in failure rather than success. Indeed, Peale's conclusion from his own early experience was "that the carrying on so many different trades at the same time only embarrassed his circumstances the more."[8]

On the other hand, the vocational mobility characteristic of Peale's world had the potential to produce new combinations, new adaptations, and truly new developments. American success in laying unique foundations for industrialization, a success which occurred during Peale's lifetime, rested in part on this advantage. Peale's own contributions to technology and to science owe much to his ability to transcend narrow occupational boundaries and to think out large, new pictures.

Peale was at heart an artisan with a developed capacity for manipulating mental images whether for making saddles, painting portraits, mounting specimens, or designing exhibits. He had applied this mental and manipulative talent during the Revolution to experiments with telescopic sights for rifles, and after his later retirement to "Belfield" he applied it to improving a variety of farm mechanisms. A natural history museum called for continuing application of this capability from the most mundane matters of designing cases and providing utilities to Peale's highest aim in science: to classifying all the varieties and species, genera and orders of nature, that came within his purview.

But even given Peale's applicable talents, why would he suddenly decide to take that large step from art to the establishment and management of a museum? First of all, the step did not seem as large then as it does today. The artist-naturalist combination was a familiar one, required by the continuing needs of natural history. Peale already knew William Bartram (No. 144), botanist and superior painter of plants, and he also knew of such predecessors as Mark Catesby, who had illustrated and written the *Natural History of Carolina, Florida, and the Bahama Islands* in 1754. He came to know many others: Alexander Wilson, the artist-ornithologist; Charles-Alexandre Lesueur, the French-born artist-naturalist (No. 76); and, of course, his own artist-naturalist sons, especially the two Titian Ramsay Peales.

Another and perhaps more directly pertinent impetus to the founding of the museum was the opportunity he sensed to benefit himself materially and in reputation, at the same time that he performed an important service to society. Art was, even for Peale, an unreliable career; a portraitist tended to work out his market, and there was little continuing demand for other sorts of painting. His ever growing family required a growing income—which a successful museum might provide. He had experienced the intensity of interest in natural "curiosities" and he knew of the importance scientists attached to the study of nature. Admissions revenues alone might carry a flourishing museum. In addition, it was not unreasonable to think that an enlightened government, as governments in other countries had, might support such a museum.

Beyond the chance to apply his special talents productively and profitably, Peale without question saw that he had a rare opportunity to carry through a great project. From that moment in 1784 when visitors grew excited about the mastodon bones he was sketching, he was in a position to do for natural history what none of the professors, scientists, or collectors in the country were able to do. He could collect, preserve, classify, and present in a realistic and orderly fashion the actual specimens of nature. He could provide a resource and encouragement for scholars; at the same time, he could construct understandable, direct experiences for a wide public. He could build a broad educational institution. He surely did not see this entire vista at the start but with his ability to take complex patterns into view, he saw some of it.

Peale began with a little museum of his own, an art museum comprised mostly of his

When the French artist-
naturalist Charles-Alexandre
Lesueur came to the United
States in 1816 to serve as
assistant to William Maclure, a
geologist and philanthropist of
American science, his reputation
was already well established.
As a member of a French exploring expedition to Australia, he
and his compatriot Francois
Péron are credited with discov-
ering over 2,500 new species.

Lesueur lived in Philadelphia
for nine years and during that
time was active in the American
Philosophical Society and the
Academy of Natural Sciences
and was particularly close
to the Peales. He contributed
illustrations both to John D.
Godman's *American Natural
History* (see No. 91) and to
Thomas Say's *American Entomology* (see No. 90). Peale
admired him greatly, and in
1818 added this portrait—one
of his strongest—to the
museum collection. Lesueur was
the first to study the marine life
of the Great Lakes, an interest
reflected by Peale's inclusion of
an eel specimen in the portrait.
(*Academy of Natural Sciences
of Philadelphia*)

own paintings. His gallery became larger than the studio collection maintained by most painters, expanded by his paintings of Revolutionary leaders and "ingenious men in different branches of science."[9] In 1782, he added a long skylighted gallery to his house to show them off. By then, he had already begun to think about some of the problems of museum planning and management.

He often retold the story of how he was stimulated to expand his collections into the first true museum of natural history in the country. First, his brother-in-law, Nathaniel Ramsay, became so excited by the mastodon bones Peale had in his studio to sketch that Ramsay declared, "he would have gone 20 miles to see such a collection."[10] From scientists Peale got mixed reactions to the idea of starting a museum of natural history. David Rittenhouse (No. 77) responded negatively that there might be "considerable amusement" in launching a museum but Peale "might rest assured that it would be a very unprofitable labor."[11] Probably Peale did not perceive that behind that answer lurked, first, a feeling that an experienced painter was not likely to become a respectable scientist and, second, that in his own pursuit of science Rittenhouse had never found much financial reward.

77. DAVID RITTENHOUSE. 1791

The three major statesmen of science in Peale's era—Rittenhouse, Franklin, and Jefferson—were all well known to Peale. He painted his first portrait of Rittenhouse in 1772, at an early stage of their friendship but after Rittenhouse had already attained recognition as America's leading astronomer. During the Revolution, the two were associated in experimenting with telescopic sights for rifles and also as leaders of the radical "Furious Whigs."

    This 1791 portrait was painted by Peale at the direction of the American Philosophical Society, shortly after Rittenhouse succeeded Franklin as president of that premier scientific organization. After Peale came to live in Philosophical Hall in 1794, he became one of the most faithful members in attending society meetings, over most of which Rittenhouse presided. In that organization, both men had developed further their friendship with Thomas Jefferson, who paid Rittenhouse his greatest compliment. He called him one of nature's masterworks: "the world has but one Rittenhouse, and . . . it never had one before." (*American Philosophical Society*)

Fortunately, others, notably Robert Patterson, professor of mathematics at the University of Pennsylvania, saw more possibilities of success. Patterson even contributed the museum's first specimen, a paddlefish. Both Patterson and Rittenhouse along with other members of the American Philosophical Society conveyed to Peale the sense that the scientific value of such an institution might be great—if it were properly directed. When Benjamin Franklin (No. 140), president of the society, returned from his resoundingly successful mission to France in 1785, he added his interest to that of the others—plus the carcass of an Angora cat. The formation of the museum was formally announced on July 7, 1786, and two weeks later Peale was elected a member of the philosophical society. Thereafter, Peale enjoyed the society's encouragement, heeded its continuing demand that science be served, and tried to respond to its sometimes inadequate understanding of the real problems in this improbable dream.

In building his museum, Peale had to learn the required museum trades by doing. How, for example, did one preserve and mount animal specimens? Along with the cat, Franklin lent Peale a pamphlet obtained from the French naturalist Louis M. J. Daubenton which Peale copied into his letter book, "Directions for Preserving Birds & C." The trial did not work well, and the cat had to be discarded, but Peale persevered. He seems to have experimented first with turpentine, then moved to arsenic solutions and, for larger animals, to bichloride of mercury. When he had trouble obtaining glass eyes, he turned to black sealing wax for the smaller specimens. For the larger mammals, he molded glass in the form of small cups and painted the inside surfaces to resemble the appearance of eyes. This was just the sort of thing that Peale, the artist and risen mechanic, could do so well. He continued to find better procedures, no doubt consulting other books along the way. By the time he gained a fuller knowledge of European techniques, he was convinced that his were superior; time has confirmed their effectiveness.[12]

His taxidermy proved effective very early in preserving and mounting birds; this is strikingly evident in the Chinese golden pheasants that still survive (No. 51). These had been given to George Washington by Lafayette from the Royal Aviary in Paris. At Peale's request, Washington sent them on at their death, and they became an attraction of his museum. They also marked Peale's rising enthusiasm for birds.

This enthusiasm owed something to the ease with which birds could be preserved for museum display, their plumage, beaks, and claws retaining a lifelike appearance without the problems certain other animals presented. Also, because they were relatively small, they could be accommodated in larger numbers than quadrupeds, mounted in more realistic settings, and exhibited in more instructive patterns of classification (Nos. 78–80). The museum ultimately boasted a collection of over 1,600, and Peale mounted many of them in the famous Long Room in identically sized cases along one wall. Here he innovated in a way that he, as a talented artist, was peculiarly able to do. Instead of leaving the case white or monochrome, he painted in a scene showing foliage and terrain appropriate to its habitat, set the bird on a branch or a rock, and arranged it in a pose sometimes taken from life.

After preservation and mounting, classification was the major problem Peale confronted. Specimens are the "real things" of natural history. They were direct and unimpeachable scientific sources which were magnified in their importance because the

78. The White-Headed or Bald Eagle

Peale was fascinated by birds, and he soon learned to preserve and mount them very effectively in animated but natural attitudes. He painted watercolor backgrounds of the habitats for each species, the first time that anyone had displayed museum specimens in natural surroundings. This bald eagle—which Peale preferred to call the "White-Headed Eagle" as more accurate—is one of the few mounts surviving from Peale's Museum. It had been a museum pet, living for years in a cage high above the zoo Peale kept as part of his museum. Peale included the eagle in his self-portrait, *The Artist in His Museum* (No. 75), where it can be seen in its glass habitat on the top tier of shelves at the left. In his autobiography he reports: "This Eagle had been so long domesticated, that Peale could without fear stroke him with his hand, nay it knew him so well that when [Peale] was walking in the State House Garden, it would utter cries expressive of its pleasure on seeing him. He had in Gold Letters on his cage *Feed me daily 100 years*; however, it did not live in captivity only 15 years, however that was long enough to cost Peale at least 300$ for its food." (*Museum of Comparative Zoology, Harvard University*)

opposite:

79. Alexander Lawson after Alexander Wilson. White-Headed Eagle. 1811

Alexander Wilson's drawing of the White-Headed Eagle for his publication *American Ornithology* was almost certainly based on the mounted bald eagle from Peale's Museum (No. 78). Wilson, a Scottish poet and artist-naturalist, was inspired by the Peales to make the study of birds his life work. His *American Ornithology*, published in nine volumes from 1808 to 1813 and continued in three volumes by Charles-Lucien Bonaparte, is a classic of both science and literature and did much to establish scientific nomenclature among other naturalists. It was based on the Peale collection of birds, which, by this time, comprised the best arranged and most complete department in the museum. Wilson's work provides an excellent documentary record of the museum's exhibits, since he based his drawings on museum mounts and cited the museum catalogue numbers so that his readers would not only have a description and drawing, but a type specimen.

    This hand-colored print was engraved by a fellow Scotsman, Alexander Lawson, who had, along with the Peales, encouraged Wilson to undertake his monumental study. (*Academy of Natural Sciences of Philadelphia*)

scientists of Peale's day gave their first attention to taxonomy or classification. Indeed, the largest early American contribution to Western science had been in natural history precisely because America's animals and plants had to be collected so they could be classified along with already known forms of life.[13]

Although the eighteenth century was the great era of classification, the results were only partially satisfactory. Peale found that the best available help was where he least needed it; the generally accepted Linnaean method of classification was especially successful in botany. Although Peale expressed his interest in "the examination of the distinguishing characters of animals, vegetables, minerals," he left the vegetable kingdom largely alone.[14] Why?

The answer is deceptively simple. The prior problems of preserving and mounting could not be satisfactorily solved for botanical specimens. Flowers and fresh plants are conspicuously difficult to preserve and to present in a lifelike manner. Peale received one set of wax flowers but never used this technique himself—although he later did excellent human wax figures. At their best, wax and even glass flowers are only replicas; they are not "real" specimens. Better than a museum for plants was the botanical garden and in 1787, members of the American Philosophical Society were seeking to establish a scientifically administered garden of this sort. Peale's neglect of this kingdom of nature

White-headed Eagle.

80. American Wild Turkey

Peale's friend Benjamin Franklin would have preferred the turkey rather than the eagle as our national bird. "Eagles," he wrote, "have been found in all countries, but the Turkey was peculiar to ours. He is, besides, . . . a bird of courage, and would not hesitate to attack a grenadier of the British guards, who should presume to invade his farm-yard with a red coat on." The turkey must have held a particular significance for Peale, too, for it is prominently featured in the foreground of his self-portrait, *The Artist in His Museum* (No. 75). There, it is shown as an unmounted specimen, lying beside the taxidermy instruments which the artist used to transform its limp body into a lifelike mounted bird.

This mounted specimen from Peale's Museum may well be the turkey that Titian Ramsay Peale II brought back from Major Long's western expedition of 1819–20. Titian used the specimen as a model for the drawing of turkeys which he made for Charles-Lucien Bonaparte's continuation of Wilson's *American Ornithology*. (*Museum of Comparative Zoology, Harvard University*)

foreshadowed the practice of natural history museums to the present time. Even when they have competent botanists on their staffs, they seldom open their herbaria to museum visitors.

In seeking to classify quadrupeds, insects, and other members of the animal kingdom, Peale obtained occasional help from philosophical society members. For example, Patterson went with him to the University of Pennsylvania library, where together they looked through the great *Histoire Naturelle*, by then at its thirty-eighth volume, by the Comte de Buffon, the leading French naturalist. He was one of a small handful of scientists whose classification, especially of animals, had to be followed. Peale responded immediately and frequently thereafter referred to Buffon, sometimes resisted him, and on occasion corrected him with a degree of relish. He called the errors he detected in Buffon, "surprising" and "very extraordinary." At Buffon's acceptance of the idea that life in America had degenerated and was smaller than in Europe, Peale bristled, remarking that Buffon must have "either a great *Antipathy to America* or to *Truth*."[15]

What was needed, however, was to find someone with a competent knowledge of classification systems who would work his way through the arrangement of Peale's collections. This person fell to him quite by accident. In the wake of the French Revolution, a displaced French nobleman and naturalist, Ambroise-Marie-François-Joseph Palisot de Beauvois, arrived in Philadelphia in 1793. Peale seized the opportunity Beauvois's presence offered by engaging him to write a scientific catalogue of his collections. The publication of such a catalogue had long been demanded by philosophical society members as a debt owing to science but it was quite beyond Peale's ability. He had neither the specific knowledge required nor the time needed to gain that knowledge.

Peale envisaged, and Beauvois set to work on, a catalogue of museum holdings that would run between three and five hundred pages, but would be issued in a series of installments. Beginning with quadrupeds, the first fifty-six-page segment was published without date, but probably in 1795, as a *Catalogue raisonné du museum de Mr. C. W. Peale.*[16] Only Beauvois's name was listed as the compiler and his French text ended abruptly in the middle of the thirty-seventh entry. Peale's contributions were specifically identified: life-habit comments on the hyena and the jackal which he had observed from specimens sent, live, for his museum. Great care was observed in naming and cataloging the animals, and Beauvois added life-habit notes on several he had observed in Africa, Latin

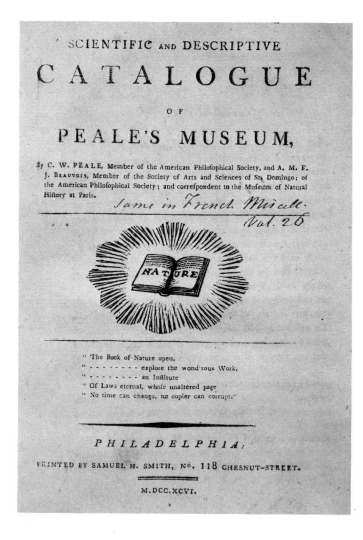

81. *A Scientific and Descriptive Catalogue of Peale's Museum.* 1796

Peale hoped that a formal catalogue of the museum's collection would establish its scientific character. The work, written largely by the French naturalist Palisot de Beauvois, was to appear in parts, with the whole eventually becoming an octavo volume of from three to five hundred pages. However, because of lack of funds, only this fifty-six-page catalogue was produced. (*American Philosophical Society*)

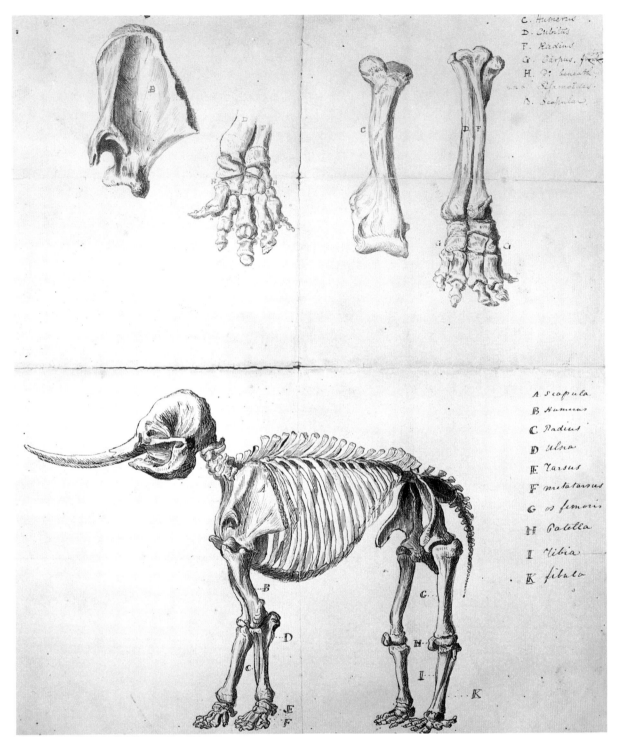

C. *Humerus*
D. *Cubitus*
F. *Radius*
G. *Carpus*
H. *D: beneath*
Sesmoides
B. *Scapula*

A *Scapula*
B *Humerus*
C *Radius*
D *Ulna*
E *Tarsus*
F *metatarsus*
G *os femoris*
H *Patella*
I *Tibia*
K *fibula*

82. Rembrandt Peale. WORKING SKETCH OF THE MASTODON. 1801

The recovery of buried mastodon bones, and the mounting and displaying of a complete
skeleton represented Peale's greatest single contribution to science. Putting the bones
back into their natural form posed many problems, and Rembrandt Peale's drawing was
intended as a guide in this work. (*American Philosophical Society*)

America, and France. The primary authorities cited were Buffon, Linnaeus, and the *Encyclopédie Méthodique*.

A translator had to be hired to render the text into English, and an English edition was issued in 1796 as *A Scientific and Descriptive Catalogue of Peale's Museum* (No. 81).[17] The chief difference between this and the French edition was that Peale and Beauvois were now listed as joint authors, although Peale had written only a tiny part of it. He did add another life-habit note, on the opossum, which was among the sixteen additional animals included in the English edition. More important, perhaps, than what Peale actually wrote, was the fact that the conception and the collection were wholly his and the two men had worked closely together as Beauvois proceeded through the writing.

Beauvois went home in 1798 after another turn of the French merry-go-round, and, without him, no further installments of the catalogue were ever issued. In the museum, Peale continued to classify and mount specimens until he had over 200 quadrupeds, 1,600 birds, 3 stands of insects (perhaps 4,000), and 11 cases of minerals. He talked and wrote of continuing the catalogue, recognizing its scientific value and its advantage in attracting visitors. Unfortunately, he could not find either the required funding or a competent classifier, and in 1802, he predicted correctly that it was "not likely ever to be finished printing."[18]

The catalogue mentioned one enthusiasm kindled with the birth of the museum that still burned; this was the riddle of the mammoth—introduced in the catalogue because of several teeth exhibited in the museum. The authors classified the mammoth next to their elephant, of which the museum showed a tooth and a tail. The catalogue pointed to unanswered questions: whether the bones were of a different kind of animal from the elephant and whether those found in Siberia were from the same kind of animal as the American bones. Note was taken of recent finds of bones—mostly teeth—in New Jersey, Pennsylvania, Ohio, Maryland, Virginia, and South Carolina.[19]

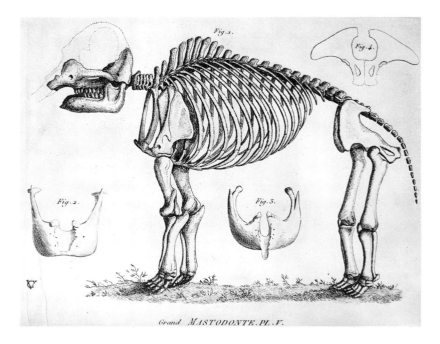

Grand *MASTODONTE. PL. V.*

83. Peale's mastodon, from Cuvier's *Recherches sur les Ossemens Fossiles des Quadrupedes.* 1812

When Georges Cuvier, a leading French scientist of the day, wrote and illustrated an article on Peale's mastodon, it represented scientific acknowledgment of the importance of Peale's finding. Cuvier's description of the mastodon as an extinct species dramatized the reality that species could indeed die out. (*American Philosophical Society*)

Peale's recurring pursuit of the mammoth brought him finally to what may be regarded as his greatest contribution of new knowledge to natural history. Discoveries of giant bones were often brought to his attention and they always awakened renewed enthusiasm. One of them he was asked to sketch: an enormous molar brought back from the upper Susquehanna by David Rittenhouse. The drawing was published in 1786 in the *Columbian Magazine*. In 1793, he followed a lead to Bladensburg, Maryland, in the vain hope of finding a complete skeleton.[20] Then, eight years later, he fell upon a notice in the 1801 *Medical Repository* of the bones of a very large animal found in New York State.[21] Peale feared that whatever was there would be dispersed and what he needed was a complete skeleton that could be mounted and displayed in his museum.

Almost like a shot, he was off. He stopped with his DePeyster in-laws in New York to marshall his forces. Then, well introduced, he moved on to John Masten's farm near Newburgh where, on the granary floor, he found most of the bones of "the great incognitum" that Masten had begun to pull out of a marl pit some three years before. Peale, after some clever negotiating, was able to buy the bones plus the right to dig for the remainder.

The dig was happily memorialized by Peale himself in his *Exhumation of the Mastodon* (No. 54). To finance the dig, he displayed some of the recovered bones to the philosophical society and obtained a loan of five hundred dollars, without interest. Before Jefferson's agreement to lend Navy pumps could arrive, Peale got other pumps in New York City and he collected wood, tents, tools, and laborers for the operation. To lower the water in the pit and permit digging for the deeper bones he set up a chain pump powered by a common treadmill worked by boys. He made no attempt to record the precise level or situation of the bones and although he urged caution upon the unpracticed workers, they did not dig out each bone carefully but lugged out the larger ones with a team of oxen. One resultant loss was that "fixing the ox chains, perhaps, to one of the tusks broke the upper part of the head to pieces."[22]

Peale next extended his search a few miles west to Joseph Barber's and Peter Millspaw's lands, where digs were made for bones missing from the first skeleton. The result was the uncovering of another nearly complete skeleton. Now, missing or broken elements in either skeleton could be replaced with carved wooden replicas, fashioned after sound bones found either in the other, or among a variety of bones randomly recovered at other sites. Peale took the skeletons back to Philadelphia, where he concentrated on mounting the first one while his sons, Rembrandt and Rubens, laid plans for taking the second on tour. They would lecture on it in England and, perhaps, they could sell it for a large sum in France.[23]

The overwhelming importance of these finds was that they were the skeletons of an animal that had never been seen or known in life. They challenged the "great chain of being" theory that all of life was connected by almost imperceptible gradients, one to another, and that all had existed from the initial creation and would continue to exist in this foreordained relationship. Now, the possibility of some species becoming extinct threatened this harmonious universe.

Thomas Jefferson (No. 142) was deeply involved in the question of extinct species. He himself had put together the incomplete bones of the "megalonyx," which he identified as a giant clawed animal similar to a tiger; it later turned out to be a sloth. The mastodon skeleton was even more exciting, and one of Jefferson's hopes was that the famous Lewis and Clark Expedition might resolve the question of whether this giant still roamed the western plains. At that time he and many others were uncertain about its extinction.

Peale's success in recovering two nearly complete skeletons, where finding one had long been merely a dream, had a great and expanding impact not only on paleontology but on the human imagination. Scientific interest in the find rose rapidly. In Philadelphia Caspar Wistar, an expert on comparative anatomy, was happy to advise as he studied the difference between these bones and those of the elephant. The leading scholar of the day, Georges Cuvier, was anxious to obtain casts, which Peale supplied.[24] French, German, and British scientists wrote and came to visit to learn more of this find.

84. Titian Ramsay Peale II. THE MAMMOTH SKELETON. 1821

Titian Ramsay Peale II was only a small child when his father exhumed the bones of the American mastodon. In 1821, twenty years after the exciting discovery, he made this drawing of the mastodon as it appeared in reconstruction in the Peale Museum. It was reproduced as an engraving in *American Natural History* (first published in 1826–28) by John D. Godman. (*American Philosophical Society*)

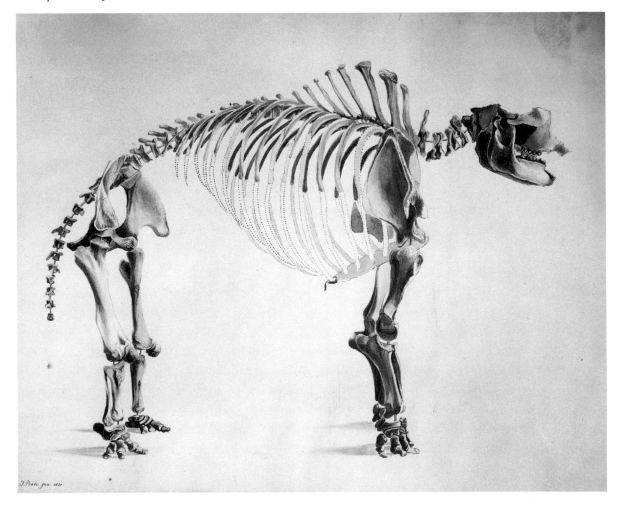

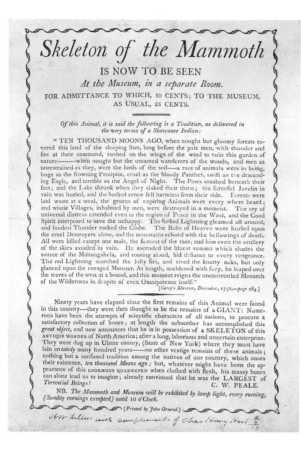

85. Broadside advertising the mastodon exhibition

The discovery and reconstruction of two complete skeletons of "the great American Incognitum" became overnight an event of international fame. Eager to retrieve his expenses in the expedition while the excitement was at its peak, Peale sent the museum factotum, Moses Williams, through the town on horseback, wearing an Indian costume, to distribute this broadside. (*American Philosophical Society*)

Peale had two objectives to fulfill, as he did in all of his museum work. First, he had to satisfy the scientific community and, second, he had to reach out to the broader public with both an educational mission and a financial need. From the beginning, he planned to recover the costs of obtaining and mounting the mastodon by an admission charge. This proved relatively easy at a charge of fifty cents. The mounted specimen stood 11 feet high, 17 feet 6 inches long, and 5 feet 8 inches wide. On December 24, 1801, it was placed on public display—and the crowds poured in (No. 85). Their readiness to pay twice what they had already paid for admission to the rest of the museum was an objective measure of the great appeal of the big skeleton. It long remained the prime drawing card of the museum, almost of the city; it was so big! Mammoth, still the name it went by, became a byword, a synonym for "enormous."

As for the second skeleton, Rembrandt and Rubens did take it to England, where they awakened less enthusiasm than they had hoped. While abroad, Rembrandt published a lengthy pamphlet on the skeleton in which the chief issue he raised was the renewed assertion that the teeth were those of a carnivorous beast. This, the authority of Georges Cuvier, the leading naturalist after the deaths of Linnaeus and Buffon, ultimately established as wrong; the mastodon was herbivorous. The pamphlet, however, was well done and effectively illustrated. The Peales were at least able to pay for their trip out of the proceeds from exhibiting the skeleton, and Rembrandt and Raphaelle then took the skeleton on a tour of the American South in 1804.[25]

More dramatically than most specimens, the mastodon offered a major response to the two, often conflicting, museum goals. First, it advanced science directly and immediately by providing new, reliable information on a species but dimly known from scattered bone finds. Peale's uncovering and mounting the skeleton probably represented his greatest single personal contribution to science. It raised stimulating questions with which scientists had to grapple. Second, in regard to the museum's mission to the public, it offered the greatest attraction Peale would ever find.

These wonderful results, all flowing from Peale's mastodon dig, resoundingly confirmed his faith in the "open book of nature." This view of nature was an outlook that flourished in the romantic wing of the Enlightenment, that philosophical setting of the American and French revolutions. Indeed it was distinctly related to the egalitarianism of both revolutions as well as to the resentments of the artisan community against the upper and learned classes. The "open book of nature" concept represented a reaction against sterile scholasticism but also against all academic pretensions to special knowledge. It held that the truth of science was not restricted to those who read Latin or understood fluxions but was accessible to all who would observe and study nature directly. It was especially applicable to natural history, where living things had to be the ultimate source and where mounted specimens were unarguably superior to verbal descriptions of even the greatest authority.[26]

As Peale put it, "the great book of nature may be opened and studied, leaf by leaf, and a knowledge gained of the character which the great Creator has stamped on each being."[27] The "open book of nature" became virtually the motto of his museum, his "world in miniature," which he saw as the "open book" dramatized. He used it as the museum logo on the catalogue and on museum tickets, where it appeared as a book, opened flat, with "Nature" written large across it (Nos. 81, 86).

The view of science projected in the "open book of nature" concept had received further confirmation in Peale's training as an artist. In art, one of the reigning dicta called for the artist to copy nature directly. Paintings by masters were to be observed and used as models—but ultimately the supreme model was nature itself. Portraits as

86. Ticket to the museum. 1788

Tickets to the museum were issued in varying forms, but none has the charm of the first —casual, and with a touch of humor, engraved by Peale himself. During the Constitutional Convention year, it was issued to delegates and visitors, among them many old friends of the artist. (*Elise Peale Patterson de Gelpi-Toro*)

well as landscapes had to be based upon the living original as the model. It was but a short step from this approach to mounting an animal in the setting and stance observed in life.

But, the "open book of nature" had only limited appeal to most scientists. Natural philosophers, such as Rittenhouse and Patterson, knew that their analyses of physical phenomena rested on long and arduous study of mathematics and Newtonian mechanics. They believed that an uninstructed observer could make only limited contributions to the already complex structure of science. European naturalists similarly believed that fundamental contributions to natural history had to rest on good knowledge of the taxonomic structure and even of the Latin descriptors in general use. They encouraged amateur naturalists to bring in new varieties and species, but felt that their role was inferior to that of the scientific classifier.

Consequently, while most scientists responded to Peale's work, recognizing his genuine contributions, they responded with restraint. Peale's correspondence suggests that he got answers to a minority of the letters he wrote. He complained to Beauvois that ideas he sent to the Académie des Sciences in Paris were not even acknowledged, giving "little encouragement to further communication." He bristled to Cuvier that he had not even known whether the bones he sent had reached him until he saw a published notice of them.[28]

87. Alexander Wilson. CLARK'S CROW AND LEWIS'S WOODPECKER. 1808

These working drawings were executed by Alexander Wilson in Peale's Museum from skins brought back by the Lewis and Clark Expedition. On President Jefferson's order, the explorers deposited many skins and skeletons collected on the expedition in the museum, since no one else was ready and able to preserve and mount them. Peale himself also made a drawing of the woodpecker (No. 124).

These drawings were turned over to Alexander Lawson, who engraved them for *American Ornithology*. They have been cut and trimmed, presumably for ease in copying the image onto the plate and for flexibility in arrangement. (*Academy of Natural Sciences of Philadelphia*)

1. *Louisiana Tanager.* 2. *Clarks Crow.* 3. *Lewis Woodpecker.*

88. Alexander Lawson after Alexander Wilson. 1. LOUISIANA TANAGER. 2. CLARK'S CROW.
3. LEWIS'S WOODPECKER. 1811

This plate, illustrating three bird specimens brought back by the Lewis and Clark Expedition,
was developed from the preliminary drawings (No. 87) executed in Peale's Museum by Wilson.
A comparison between the drawings and this finished plate indicates that the engraver did not
simply reproduce Wilson's sketches. Lawson softened the incisive contours of the birds, filled
in the feather patterns only suggested by the artist, and added a sense of three-dimensionality.
Like other illustrations in *American Ornithology*, this print was hand-colored; John H.
Hopkins and Alexander Rider are among the colorists known to have worked on the plates
in this particular volume. They may have used pigments ground by Peale. Wilson specifically
mentions "one of the richest yellows" as a product "from the laboratory of Messrs. Peale and
Son, of the Museum"; this could well be the brilliant yellow seen here on the wings and
neck of the Louisiana tanager. (*Academy of Natural Sciences of Philadelphia*)

On the face of things, Peale often had reason for bitterness. On the other hand, his view of science was only partially acceptable to the scientific community and instead of modifying his faith in the "open book of nature," he tilted against the hierarchy of science. He almost invited disappointment by assuming that he could simply strike up correspondences with Cuvier, with Sir Joseph Banks, president of the Royal Society, and with Franklin, the most honored scientist in the country. When several of the distinguished group he invited to become members of his museum board failed to respond, Peale wrote them, "I have taken the liberty of electing you."[29] He kept inviting Samuel Latham Mitchill, Columbia College professor and editor of the *Medical Repository*, to visit his museum and when he repeatedly failed to do so on his visits to the city, Peale chided him, "Can I suppose that you have not a love for natural history?"[30]

In the end, the most enduring contribution the museum made to the advancement of science was through the encouragement its specimens and activities gave to study. This was a result Peale expected and sought to stimulate, his earliest clear success being achieved in the work of Alexander Wilson. Wilson was an immigrant Scottish schoolmaster whom Peale first met in 1802 when he and his son Rubens were out shooting birds to mount in the museum. Wilson was interested in natural history but mostly in botany, at least while in touch with William Bartram, on whose land his school was located. When he visited the museum, however, Peale was able to communicate his own enthusiasm for birds, and the schoolmaster became an indefatigable bird collector. From this beginning, Wilson went on to publish nine carefully illustrated volumes on American birds, a more comprehensive work than any previously published.

Wilson worked with the museum collections, based some of his illustrations upon its mountings (Nos. 87, 88), and regularly added to its holdings. His first volume appeared in 1808 and the ninth just before his death in 1813. He was a studious classifier who insisted on classical names in preference to Peale's advocacy of vernacular or descriptive names—and he won the support of a significant segment of the science community. One of the most interesting investigations he made with Peale was their study of the flight of birds (No. 89). In order to determine the lift of varied wing forms, they used a crossbow to experiment with differently designed arrows—simulating the flight of birds.[31]

Peale's relationship to the professionalization of natural history was evidenced in the influence his museum had upon founders and early members of the Academy of Natural Sciences of Philadelphia, founded in 1812. The academy became the leading Philadelphia institution for the study of natural history, carrying forward several of Peale's aspirations. The founders were nearly all amateurs who made their living in other occupations: an apothecary, a practicing physician, a dentist, a distiller, and a couple of others, all dedicated to the avocation of natural history.[32] The academy, founded shortly after Peale's retirement to "Belfield," recognized the museum by electing Rubens Peale, then director of the museum, to membership in 1813.

Several systematic studies of American natural history appeared just before and just after Peale's death, all by members of the academy who had been heavily influenced by the museum. Thomas Say (No. 90) began in 1817 with the installments of his three-

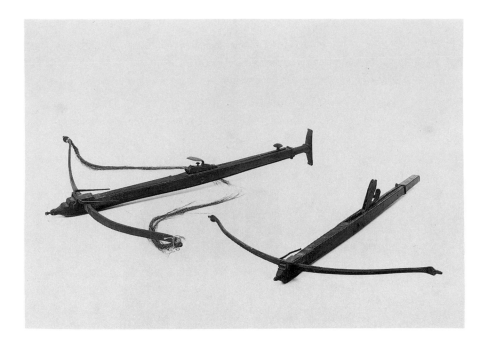

volume *American Entomology*, completed in 1828. This work bore the imprint of the museum and the impress of two generations of Peales. His six-volume *American Conchology* appeared in the 1830s. Richard Harlan's *Fauna Americana*, the first taxonomic study of American zoology, came out in 1825; Harlan also felt the museum influence. John D. Godman, who became Peale's grandson-in-law in 1821, published his three-volume *American Natural History* between 1826 and 1828 (see No. 91). In sum, these works represented the fulfillment of Peale's faith that the dedicated study of the "open book" would lead inexorably to new knowledge.

A more personal link between Peale and this new scholarship was his own son, Titian Ramsay II. Titian, his second son by that name, was born in 1799 and early flowered into the most competent naturalist in the family. His particular interest was insects, just as his namesake brother's had been, and he assembled a notable collection of butterflies, which he mounted with particular effectiveness (No. 92). The academy recognized his work by electing him a member in 1817, just as its journal was established and the wealthy naturalist, William Maclure, became president, turning the institution from the amateur into the professional realm.[33] The Long Expedition of 1818–21 into unexplored portions of the Louisiana territory drew its scientific contingent largely from the academy. Thomas Say went as zoologist, and Titian Peale as assistant naturalist.

Although Titian's work and that of many of the other scientific naturalists as well was related to the museum's expanding collections as a fundamental source, that was not the most visible role of the museum. The museum as Peale developed it, and even more under Rubens as director, was primarily an educational institution that offered reliable information in the form of natural history exhibits to a broad public. Peale was determined that the exhibits be well preserved, authentically mounted, and classified in accordance with the best scientific taxonomy. In this ideal, he succeeded remarkably

90. THOMAS SAY (before restoration). 1819

As Peale's interest turned more and more to the study of natural history, he began to add portraits of scientists to his gallery of distinguished men. Many of these were men he had worked with, or who had used the museum's collections. Thomas Say, known as the father of American ento-mology and conchology, was one of a group of students of natural history who grew up around Peale's Museum. Say is even said occasionally to have spent the night in the museum under the great mastodon skeleton.

This self-trained naturalist, an indefatigable and unsparing scholar, was a founder of the Academy of Natural Sciences of Philadelphia and its first curator. In 1819, he joined the Long Expedition into the Indian territories west of the Mississippi as zoologist; this portrait was painted shortly before his departure. His three-volume publication, *American Entomology*, included exquisite illustrations by Charles Lesueur (No. 76) and Titian Ramsay Peale II (No. 130) and bore the imprint of Peale's Philadelphia Museum. In 1822, he was appointed to the faculty of the museum as part of Peale's effort to broaden the museum's reach as an educational institution. (*Academy of Natural Sciences of Philadelphia*)

well, but in a way that reflected at the same time his own personality and values. Just as his art and his emotional fondness for birds were evident in the manner in which he presented them, so did the other categories of natural history respond to his impress.

To begin with, he had an anthropocentric approach to natural history. The collection of his own portraits which had been a nucleus of his initial museum continued to be featured and expanded, notably by portraits of scientists Rembrandt did in Europe. He wrote seriously of mounting a real human being, speculating that Franklin would have contributed his own body for the purpose. Short of that, he did include a variety of excellent wax likenesses in his collections. In terms of actual mounted specimens, monkeys most resembled humans and consequently Peale evinced a special interest in them. This spread as well to the other quadrupeds, among whom they were classified. Peale was also particularly interested in observing living animals and led his children into a similar interest, lectured about them—and mounted and labeled them with inescapable verve. Although because of their size only a limited number of quadrupeds could be accommodated, they became a great attraction (Nos. 93–95).[34]

Other forms of animal life were reasonably well represented in the museum: the birds, of course, reptiles, fish, and invertebrates—mostly insects. As with quadrupeds, he observed some of the snakes in life before mounting them in order to discover their life habits; some he exhibited live. He taught his children to handle rattlesnakes and designed a fine exhibit incorporating a lens focused upon the poison ducts in the fangs. Peale was anxious to offer a collection of fish that would instruct Europeans in American varieties and kept inviting contributions while he combed, especially, the New York fish markets for specimens. This last category remained only partially developed although his marine room, which contained shells, corals, and amphibia in addition to fish, was a successful concept (No. 96).[35]

He collected insects in large numbers, displaying some 4,000 by 1804. A special feature was his use of an adjustable, compound microscope and revolving lens to view the smaller specimens. This was typical of Peale's innovative approach, which was always concerned with the appeal and effectiveness each display had to the visitor. Yet, appeal was not permitted to supersede preservation; butterflies, which were intrinsically attractive, were protected from the light in specially designed cases.

Ethnology, or the study of the varieties of mankind, was bound to be fun for Peale, who was delighted to be able to include man within the animal kingdom. Visitors responded happily to his display of clothing and artifacts of various human cultures because they could relate personally to the different ways other peoples took care of familiar needs. Most of these items came to the museum by donation from individuals or from government expeditions. Peale announced his chief interest as "primitive" man, particularly soliciting Indian and African articles, although very few African items came to him. The North American Indian was, understandably, best represented (Nos. 97–100). China, of course, did not represent a primitive culture; the numerous items from that country reflected the growing American trade with the Far East (Nos. 101–103). Trade also accounted for Polynesian and Latin American artifacts (Nos. 104, 105). Peale was able to exhibit ornaments, instruments, weapons, an Indian canoe, and a Chinese plow and wheelbarrow. Most spectacular were his wax-faced manikins:

Drawn by C.A.Lesueur. Eng.ᵈ by G.B.Ellis.

91. George B. Ellis after Charles A. Lesueur. PRONGHORN ANTILOPE

The illustrations in John Godman's three-volume classic *American Natural History*
(1826–28) were largely based on Peale's museum mountings. The newly discovered
pronghorn antelope—or "forked horned antelope," as Peale with his taste for plain
descriptive names preferred to call it—was a subject of great interest to naturalists of that
day. In 1805, Lewis and Clark sent a specimen of this new species to Peale. Although
the skins were badly damaged, Peale was able to make a mounting of it, as he wrote to
Thomas Jefferson on April 5, 1806: "The skins of the several antilopes was so badly
managed in the Skinning, and also so much eaten by dermests, that it was with much
difficulty I could mount one of them, but being so interesting an Animal, I conceived it
was better to have one even in bad condition, than to let it be wanting in the Museum."

Godman, who married Peale's granddaughter Angelica, was appointed to a chair in
physiology at the museum in 1821, along with Thomas Say in zoology (No. 90), Richard
Harlan in comparative anatomy, and Gerard Troost in mineralogy (No. 120). The
number of productive naturalists associated with the museum indicates how influential
and effective Peale's Museum was. In the end, the most enduring contribution Peale
made to the advancement of science was the encouragement the museum's specimens and
activities gave to scholarship. (*American Philosophical Society*)

130

92. Moth and butterfly mounts, arranged by Titian Ramsay Peale II

Titian Ramsay Peale was an enthusiastic collector of insects, an interest he had in common with his deceased half brother and namesake, Titian I. Titian II prepared the text and illustrations for a book which he never completed, to be called "The Butterflies of North America," the manuscript of which is now at the American Museum of Natural History, New York. He was a great field collector and devised these ingenious mountings to house his collections. He placed the insects between two separated layers of glass, and then bound the whole within covers like a book so that the glass could be turned like a page. Notes on the contents were inscribed on the "endpapers." Because the butterflies and moths were protected from the light, they have retained an amazing brilliance. There are nearly one hundred of these boxes, some of which bear the mark of Peale's Museum and have handwritten notations by Titian II. A portion of his butterflies were collected during his father's lifetime, but many were found after 1830. Nevertheless, a goodly number of these boxes must have been available to interested scholars and scientists during the final years of the museum. (*Academy of Natural Sciences of Philadelphia*)

93. Titian Ramsay Peale II. Bat, Moose, and Monkey. 1821–22

Charles Willson Peale's Museum included not only mounted specimens but also living animals. He observed them closely to discover their life habits before he mounted them, and took a decidedly anthropocentric view of their characters. In his "Lectures on Natural History," given in 1799-1800, he observed: "If we study the manners of . . . animals in general, we shall find amongst them, most excellent models of *friendship*, *constancy*, *parental care*, and every *social virtue*"—the very same traits he loved to capture in portraiture. The bat, for instance, provided an illustration of domestic tenderness. His article "The Maternal Affection of the Bat" described an incident which had taken place in the spring of 1823. A boy who had found a young red bat left his house to bring it to the museum. On his way, he passed the place where he had captured the little bat. "The mother [bat] made her appearance, followed the boy for two squares, flying around him, and finally alighted on his breast, such was her anxiety to save her offspring. Both were brought to the Museum, the young one firmly adhering to its mother's teat." (*American Philosophical Society*)

THE FAMOUS GRISLY BEAR

hitherto unseen in the inhabited countries, and entirely unknown untill the celebrated A. MACKENZIE gave some account of that extraordinary animal, having met him in the neighbourhood of the Rocky Mountains, by 56. degrees N. L. in his ever memorable expedition to the Pacific Ocean, through the north-western continent of America.

THIS ANIMAL was born in the spring of the year 1802. not far from the sources of the river Missoury, about 4500. miles from Philadelphia, in a country inhabited by an indian nation called the Cattanahowes. He is the firſt of his specie that ever was seen, and seems to be a separate class of White Bear, which differs from those known to and described by the naturaliſts, as well in point of colour, as in point of inclinations. His hair is a kind of straw colour or light sorrel, neither hard nor stiff, but somewhat like wool. His inclinations are so ferocious, that he follows the tracks of men, and attacks them with undaunted fury. Mackenzie's own expressions respecting that extraordinary beaſt, are as follows: " We perceived "along the river, tracks of large bears, some of which were nine inches wide "and of a proportionate length. We saw one of their dens, or winter-quar- "ters, called wattee, which was ten feet deep, five feet high, and six feet "wide; but we had not yet seen one of those animals. The Indians en- "tertain great apprehenſion of this kind of bear, which is called the GRISLY "BEAR; and they never venture to attack it but in a party of at leaſt three "or four".

By the ſize of this one, who has hardly attained the third part of his bigneſs, by the length of his claws, when yet so young, one may form an idea of the powerful ſtrength of that dangerous animal, which may be conſidered as the moſt formidable wild beaſt of the continent of America.

During the short time he will remain in this place, the GRISLY BEAR may be seen at every hour of the day, at *the museum*

The price of entrance *is half a dollar. 25 cents & half price for children. N.B. I gave the french man liberty to exhibit the Bear two weeks in the Hall of the State-House.*

24013

94. Broadside describing *The Famous Grisly Bear*. 1804

In the summer of 1803 an "Indian trader from New Orleans" brought Peale a live grizzly bear to exhibit in his museum. It was the first time such an animal had been seen in Philadelphia, and its ferocity made it a notable attraction. When it broke loose from its cage in Philosophical Hall, however, Peale was forced to shoot it.

Peale sent this broadside to Thomas Jefferson on March 18, 1804, informing him in an accompanying letter that a hindquarter from the bear was "being sent by the mail stage." (*Library of Congress*)

a Chinese "Laborer and Gentleman," the Indian sachems Blue Jacket and Red Cloud, a Hawaiian, a Society Islander, and a few others, attired in donated clothing and accouterments.[36]

These exhibits did not rest upon the same level of scholarship that informed his animal exhibits, nor did they stimulate the same level of scientific writing; ethnology was simply not as active a field at that time. Peale's personal feelings pervaded his exhibits and his comments on them; he noted, for example, that visiting Indians had the same distaste for nude paintings as he had. He published one essay of his own, entitled "The Bow," on an African prince's bow that came to his museum. This was a human-interest news note—the tragic story of the captured black who had brought the bow to America, preserving it through a life of servitude in South Carolina.[37]

At the opposite end of the scale from man were minerals. Peale approached minerals with at least three differing interests: as objects for scientific study, as useful resources, and as attractions. He arranged them in glass cases, according to the classification of the English mineralogist Richard Kirwan, keying each specimen to a page reference in a book kept nearby where the visitor could find additional information. Minerals of economic value were featured: clays for porcelain, earths for pigments, sulfur, bitumens (that is, pitch or asphalt), native gold, silver, iron, and other ores (No. 106). Fossils, chiefly of shells and marine life, were displayed in the same section. Then there were curiosities—crowd-pleasers—such as Vesuvius lava, insects enclosed in amber, and a petrified bird's nest with eggs (No. 107).[38]

In all of his exhibitry, Peale sought to combine popular appeal and education with

95. Titian Ramsay Peale II. Missouri Bears

None of Charles Willson Peale's mounted mammals survive, but many naturalists, among them his son Titian Ramsay, used actual museum exhibits as models for book illustrations. This is a typical exhibit: the animals are arranged in a family group and are shown in natural poses, with an indication of their habitat. These bears were presented to the museum on January 28, 1808, by President Jefferson, who had received them from the explorer Zebulon Pike. Peale acknowledged the gift in a letter to Jefferson on January 29: "The Bears I received to day, in good health. . . . I shall take the precaution of Chaining them untill we can know their dispositions. If they can be kept together, it will furnish the opportunity trying whether they will breed in a domesticated State, a desirable object with me. Can we obtain their exact age? The register of the Museum should contain every interesting particular about them, as we hope to see them get their full groath + also to ascertain what they might weigh when they acquire their full size." As cubs, the two bears were docile and playful, but unfortunately, when mature, were too dangerous to be allowed to live. (*American Philosophical Society*)

T.R.Peale delin.

MISSOURI BEAR.
Ursus horribilis: Ord.

96. Shells collected by Titian Ramsay Peale II

Peale's Marine Room included a great variety of aquatic life. At the center was an enormous Chama shell which was "3 feet long and 185 lbs. weight" and which proved irresistible to tourists, who persisted in carving their names on it. The *Guide* described the arrangement and contents of the room: large fish—including a hammerhead shark and swordfish—and amphibious animals were displayed at opposite ends of the room; smaller "Fishes, Lizards, Tortoises, Snakes, Snakes with two heads c." were shown, living and preserved, in two large glass cases. On top of these Peale had arranged "artificial Rock-work supporting Marine productions, such as Corals, Sea Fans, Feathers, c." And, in cases between the windows, were "a Classical arrangement of Shells, Corals, Sponges, c." Charles Willson Peale himself collected many shells with Thomas Say (No. 90) but their whereabouts are not known. The shells illustrated here (*Drupa morum*) were collected by Titian Ramsay Peale and were displayed in the museum after 1836. (*Academy of Natural Sciences of Philadelphia*)

97. Ojibwa Man's Snowshoes

As Americans pressed into the interior of the continent, they began to send American Indian artifacts to the museum. In 1795, the Indian nations of the Northwest Territory and their British allies had been defeated by "Mad Anthony" Wayne at Fallen Timbers, and Wayne sent pipes smoked at the treaty fire as well as a buffalo-skin mantle. The Lewis and Clark Expedition of 1804 resulted in deposits of many treasures over a period of years.

Many of the superb pieces originally in Peale's Museum, including the Lewis and Clark collection, are now preserved at the Peabody Museum of Archaeology and Ethnology at Harvard University. (*Peabody Museum, Harvard University*)

98. Algonquin Beaver Bowl

George Turner, revolutionary war veteran and federal judge in the Northwest Territory, collected a variety of Indian objects while riding the circuit. In 1797, he gave a number of these to the museum and to the American Philosophical Society. Each received a similar bowl, now counted among the rarest examples of early American Indian art. This bowl bears Charles Willson Peale's inscription on its rounded side: "Indian Sculpture of a Beaver/presented by Judge Turner." The bowl at the American Philosophical Society is listed as Kaskaskian, from Southern Illinois. (*Peabody Museum, Harvard University*)

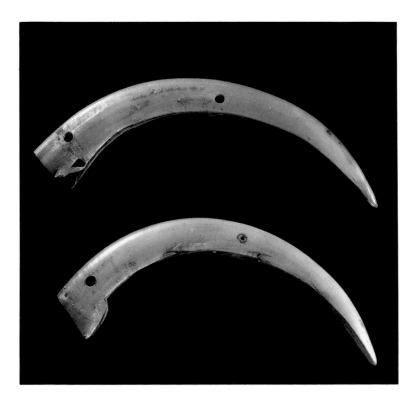

99. Grizzly Bear Ornaments

These two bear claws are each perforated and were probably part of a bear-claw necklace typically worn by the Plains Indians. (*Peabody Museum, Harvard University*)

scientific accuracy, and his success in this endeavor is the best measure of his contribution both to science and to museum development. It was because of the scientific base upon which he built his exhibits that he was able to attract and stimulate that coterie of productive scientific naturalists. His ability to reach and instruct a broad public, and to keep them coming back to his museum, rested upon a larger complex of concerns and actions, including many of importance to museum directors today. Indeed, in a remarkable way, Peale traversed much of the ground that museum directors ever since, especially natural history museum directors, have had to cover. This included a series of direct necessities: collection, preservation, paleontological digs, mounting, display, labeling, the use of wax manikins, and catalogues. Peale also paid rewarding attention to museum lighting, heating, advertising, guides, journals, and books. He experimented creatively with related lectures, audio-visual aids, music, and demonstrators. He was especially concerned with funding, believing from the beginning that his museum deserved to become a national institution, supported by the federal government.

In fact, he proved a master at putting the museum on a paying basis, although he

100. Choctaw Necklace

This brilliantly colored Indian adornment was presented to the museum on January 9, 1828. (*Peabody Museum, Harvard University*)

101. Model of a Chinese Lady's Foot and Leg with Silk Shoe

In 1792, Peale had declared his intention to the museum's Board of Visitors to include "the arms, dresses, tools and utensils of the aborigenes of divers countries." Although the ethnographic department of the museum was never developed as fully as other areas, the artifacts of alien cultures were very popular with the public. To help form his museum collections, Peale had solicited the "Assistance of the Curious," and sea captains proved a particularly fruitful source. In 1797, Richard Dale, who had been John Paul Jones's second-in-command at the famous battle between the *Bon Homme Richard* and the *Serapis*, responded with a "model of Chinese ladies foot," which he had brought back from his pioneering three-year voyage to Canton. The model, which illustrates the characteristically tiny and misshapen foot that results from the custom of foot binding, was one of many items received from China as trade between the United States and the Far East increased. (*Peabody Museum, Harvard University*)

102. Chinese Abacus or Counting Board

This "instrument on which the Chinese make their arithmetical calculations" was presented to the museum by George Meminger in February, 1791. (*Peabody Museum, Harvard University*)

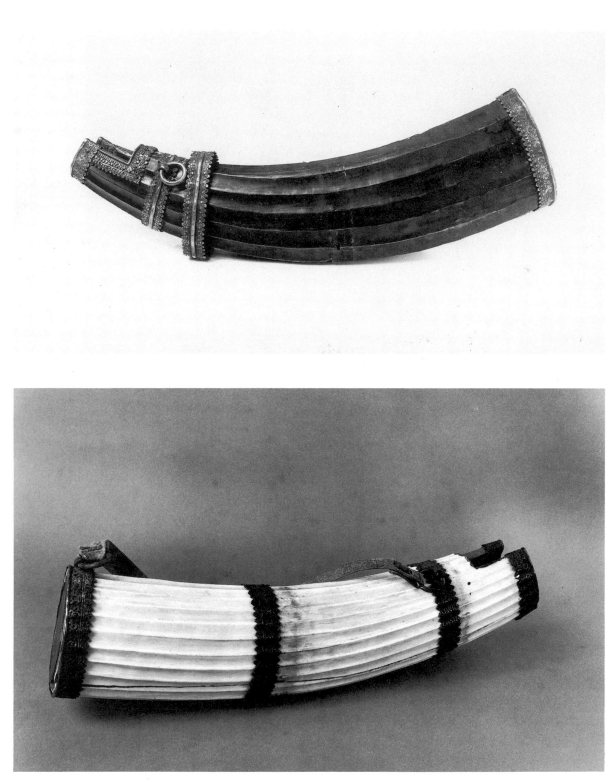

103. Horn Canteen and Ivory Canteen

These "Canteens made of Ivory and Buffaloe Horns" from India were part of a large gift from
George Harrison in 1804, which also included "embossed helmets" and a coat of fish-scale armor
"covered with crimson velvet richly studded with gold . . . the Dress of an Emperor or Commander-
in-Chief" of India or Persia. Harrison was a young diplomat of the Revolution and later navy
agent at Philadelphia, where he was in an excellent position to be helpful to Peale. He made many
gifts to the museum over a twenty-year period, beginning with South Sea artifacts in 1788, the
first in the museum collection. (*Peabody Museum, Harvard University*)

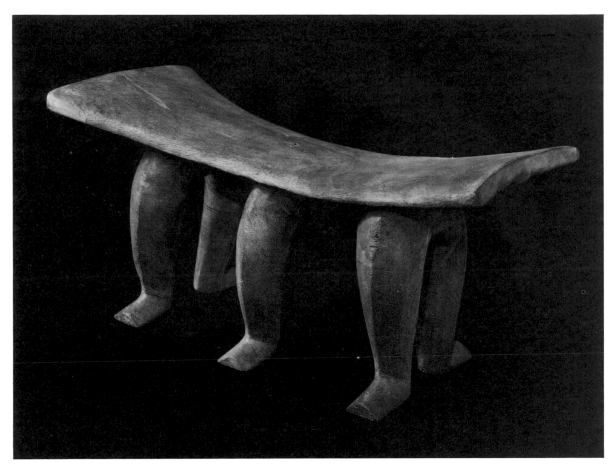

104. Fiji Headrest

The Fiji headrest was one of many gifts which the museum received from merchants eager to publicize their products or accomplishments. In this instance, two New Yorkers—Capt. Edmund Fanning and his associate, Mr. Coles—were calling attention to Fanning's discovery of "New York Island" in the South Seas and his succession of trading expeditions to that area. Among the objects Fanning and Coles presented to the museum on June 6, 1808, was a "wooden pillow from the Fegee Islands." That same day, Charles Willson Peale, in acknowledging the gift, responded to their offer to collect additional items for the museum by giving them detailed instructions that revealed his priorities in acquisition as well as his methods of preservation. He asked for "Utensils and weapons &c which serve to give us a knowledge of their customs, may be useful & well as curious—subjects of natural History, such a[s] snakes Lizards and Insects (except Butterflies) can be preserved in Rum & thuse easily brought here to be after-wards displayed; a Single bottle may contain a multitude of different subjects. But if any Quadrupedes were attempted to be brought (except they were of the Smallest kind which also might be put into Spirits) but if large, to take the Skin leaving in them the Bones of the Head and feet. Soft soap will preserve them much better than salt." (*Peabody Museum, Harvard University*)

never ceased complaining that the enterprise was not federally funded. Over time, he received limited varieties of federal, state, and city aid, but the museum from its beginning depended overwhelmingly on admission revenues. The twenty-five-cent admission charge with which he began was never altered, although the Mammoth Room charge was added for that specific attraction.

Certainly the American Philosophical Society intended to encourage Peale in 1794 when it rented all but two rooms in Philosophical Hall to him for housing both his museum and his family. This permitted him to move the museum from its initial

105. Hawaiian Crested Helmet

In 1790, Capt. Robert Gray, returning from a three-year voyage around the world, was triumphantly welcomed by the city of Boston. In a march up State Street to greet the governor, he was preceded by the "Crown Prince of Owyhee," who wore a brilliant feather cape and headdress. This helmet is thought to be the one presented to Washington by Gray and sent to the museum by the president in 1792—the first government deposit to the museum. (*Peabody Museum, Harvard University*)

106. Sulfur from the collection of Adam Seybert (1773–1825)

With an eye to bringing the nation's natural resources into view, the museum's "Visitors and Directors" in 1792 advised greater attention to mineralogy. In the next year, Peale completed a display in glass-covered drawers with labels which included a note on the potential usefulness of each specimen. With the appearance of the second edition of Richard Kirwan's *Elements of Mineralogy* (1794–96), the specimens were keyed to this text in order to facilitate study. When American minerals received full attention for the first time in Parker Cleaveland's *Elementary Treatise on Mineralogy and Geology* (1816), the museum collection was again enlarged and rearranged with this as its guide.

As in other departments of the museum, the emphasis was on American materials, particularly ores and clays, but with a comparative representation from other parts of the world, bringing together the first organized and effective public display of minerals and geological materials in the United States. When the contents of the museum were sold, the mineral collection was apparently dispersed and is now untraceable. This sample, selected on the basis of information in the museum accession book, is drawn from the collection of Peale's good friend, Adam Seybert of Philadelphia. (*Academy of Natural Sciences of Philadelphia*)

107. A Fossilized Bird's Nest from the collection of Adam Seybert (1773–1825)

Among the many mineral specimens listed in the museum accession book, Peale noted a number of fossils and "petrifications," including "a Petrific Incrustation of a Bird's Nest and Eggs," which would have resembled this specimen from the Seybert Collection. (*Academy of Natural Sciences of Philadelphia*)

establishment in an extension to his home at Third and Lombard streets (No. 111). With his good public-relations sense, Peale staged a parade to the new site with boy volunteers carrying some of the bigger and more popular items: the bison, tigers, and panthers. But the rental was only a little less than the going rate, and the largest advantage Peale was given was the quasi-public location, adjacent to the Statehouse, in a fine position to catch crowds (No. 62). This was support, but not direct financial support.

Continuing growth of his collections and the 1799 vote to move the state government to Lancaster led Peale to petition for space in the old Statehouse, and for "legislative patronage."[39] In 1802, he was rented, at a relatively high rate, the upper floor and tower and, except on election days, the Declaration chamber on the main floor. In 1810, he continued to use Philosophical Hall as well, displaying the mastodon there.

By 1810, the museum was flourishing. Although even Jefferson ultimately proved not supportive of Peale's desire to bring it under federal patronage, it continued to grow and attract crowds. Now at the age of sixty-nine, Peale decided to turn over the direction of the museum to his son Rubens and to retire to farmland he had purchased a bit beyond the city limits. Rubens counted upon being able to increase revenues still further in agreeing to pay his father four thousand dollars each year.

For a time the museum prospered as Rubens anticipated, and the elder Peale

To the CITIZENS

OF THE

United States of America.

MR. PEALE respectfully informs the Public, That having formed a design to establish a MUSEUM, for a collection, arrangement and preservation of the objects of natural history and things useful and curious, in June 1785, he began to collect subjects, and to preserve and arrange them in the Linnæan method. His labours herein have been great, and disappointments many—especially respecting proper methods of preserving dead animals from the ravage of moths and worms. In vain he hath fought, from men, information of the effectual methods used in foreign countries: and after experiencing the most promising ways recommended in such books as he had read, they proved ineffectual to prevent depredations by the vermin of America. But, in making various other experiments, he at length discovered a method of preservation, which he is persuaded will prove effectual: it has a very favourable appearance in practice, and far surpasses all others that have come to his knowledge. Nevertheless, it will be obliging in gentlemen to inform him of the best practices in Europe, or elsewhere.

The difficulties in preserving subjects being thus overcome and the Museum having advanced to be an object of attention to some individuals—who, it is hoped, may gain from it information, which, with pleasing and elevated ruminations, will bring them nearer to the Great-First-Cause—he is therefore the more earnestly bent on enlarging the collection with a greater variety of beasts, birds, fishes, insects, reptiles, vegetables, minerals, shells, fossils, medals, old coins, and of utensils, cloathing, arms, dyes and colours, or materials for colouring or for physic, from amongst the Indian, African, or other savage people; and all particulars, although but in model or delineation, promising to be useful in advancing knowledge and the arts; in a word, all that is likely to be beneficial, curious or entertaining to the citizens of the new world. But, alas! in compleating the design, a collection of all animated Nature, alone (in the infinite variety of which the wonderfully delights—so great—so vast) requiring an age to enlarge it to the full consideration of a national magnitude; and yet these and other subjects are to be unremittingly pursued, and far as possible obtained, by an individual of but slender circumstances.

All the national museums in the world (as far as he is informed) were from beginnings of individuals: the Public are therefore the more chearfully solicited to help forward this tender plant, while it is yet under the nurturing care and anxious attention of its present possessor, and until it shall have grown into maturity, and become a favorite establishment in the hands of the great Public of the American States. He hopes this may be the case: For—" with harmony small beginnings eff. & great things."

Much might be said of the importance that such a collection and arrangement would be of to society: but the present address means only to give a concise report of the rise and progress of this infant design, and excite exertion in the friends of science, favorable to it: A design that, whilst countenanced by the Public, may grow into a great national museum, or repository of valuable rarities, for more generally diffusing an increase of knowledge in the works of the Creator——God, alone wise!——At all events, Mr. PEALE intends to prosecute the design with such means as are in his power. Should it happily receive the smiles of the Public, the progress will be proportionably great; whereas, if it is to depend only upon his solitary efforts, the progress must be so slow, that the whole may fall through, not for want of men so superior abilities, but for a successor equally zealous in building up and enlarging the noble fabric, for the emolument of mankind—a fabric which, with due attention, must be continually improving to the end of time.

With sentiments of gratitude, Mr. PEALE thanks the friends to the Museum, who have beneficially added to his collection a number of precious curiosities, from many parts of the world:—from Africa, from India, from China, from the Islands of the great Pacific Ocean, and from different parts of America; some whereof are the more curious, as they have been but very recently discovered, even by the great voyagers of Europe.

He respectfully asks a continuance of their favors; and the assistance of all persons who may be possessed of things curious, that they can spare; whether they be of America, or any other part of the world: all will command his grateful acknowledgments; and such deposits will surely be pleasing to men of genius, lovers of science, as well as obliging to their

Thankful and humble Servant,

CHARLES WILSON PEALE.

Note. Mr. PEALE keeps a regular register of the subjects of his Museum, arranged systematically; together with the names of the promoters of this important institution. *Philadelphia, Feb. 1, 1790.*

Experience thus far has justified the above statement, and posterity will do justice to the labours of CWPeale

108. Broadside addressed *To the Citizens of the United States of America.* 1790

In this broadside of February 1, 1790, not four years after he had announced the formation of his museum, Peale issued his first call for a national museum. Expressing the hope that his institution would grow to maturity "in the hands of the Great Public of the American states," he attempted to ensure its permanence by bringing it under the aegis of the federal government. He repeatedly tried to persuade congressmen and government officials to take over his museum, but the country was not ready for such responsibility. Years later, in 1846, a national museum—the Smithsonian Institution—did come into being, the result of a bequest from an English scientist, James Smithson. By that time, however, the contents of Peale's Museum had been dispersed. (*Massachusetts Historical Society*)

luxuriated in his newfound landed status. Working very hard, he nevertheless behaved much like a gentleman farmer, sparing "no pains to make machines for very many uses" with virtually no feeling for what might be financially feasible.[40] (And losses had no tax-shelter advantage in that day!) Far from making a profit, he spent nearly the whole of what he received from Rubens just to keep going. On his side Rubens weakened the scientific thrust of the museum in efforts to gain greater profit—and in the end found that slipping away too. His father increasingly reentered the museum scene; in 1822, Rubens withdrew and Charles Willson resumed his position as "Manager."

He returned the museum to earlier patterns and to a degree of stability. By 1827, he had completed plans for moving the museum to a new building, the Philadelphia Arcade, on Chestnut Street between Sixth and Seventh—a move that his death in that year left to his successors.

Peale's Museum raised a standard. It was the first of its kind in America, and in certain respects pioneered in the world. Its prospering led to imitators and competitors of many sorts, some of them highlighting the unusual, bizarre, and even fraudulent in order to attract paying visitors. P. T. Barnum is undeservedly known as the worst of those who put profits before concern for truth or education (and he did finally buy the successor museum to Peale's in 1849). Closest to Peale's objectives were the museums established by his sons in Baltimore and New York, but each failed after a little success.

Peale's ability to manipulate mental images in designing and building or rebuilding aspects of the three-dimensional world was the primary reason for the unique

109. Museum Annual Subscription. 1794

Although Peale's hope for a national endowment for his museum was not to be fulfilled, President Washington headed the list of annual subscriptions, a fund-raising effort Peale undertook in 1794. Vice-President Adams and members of the Cabinet, Senate, and House also signed for tickets. By the end of January, 159 individuals had enrolled, at one dollar apiece. Subscribers' names were entered in a record book bound in red morocco, the title and preamble engrossed in Peale's hand. (*Historical Society of Pennsylvania*)

NATURE

Of grains are Mountains form'd

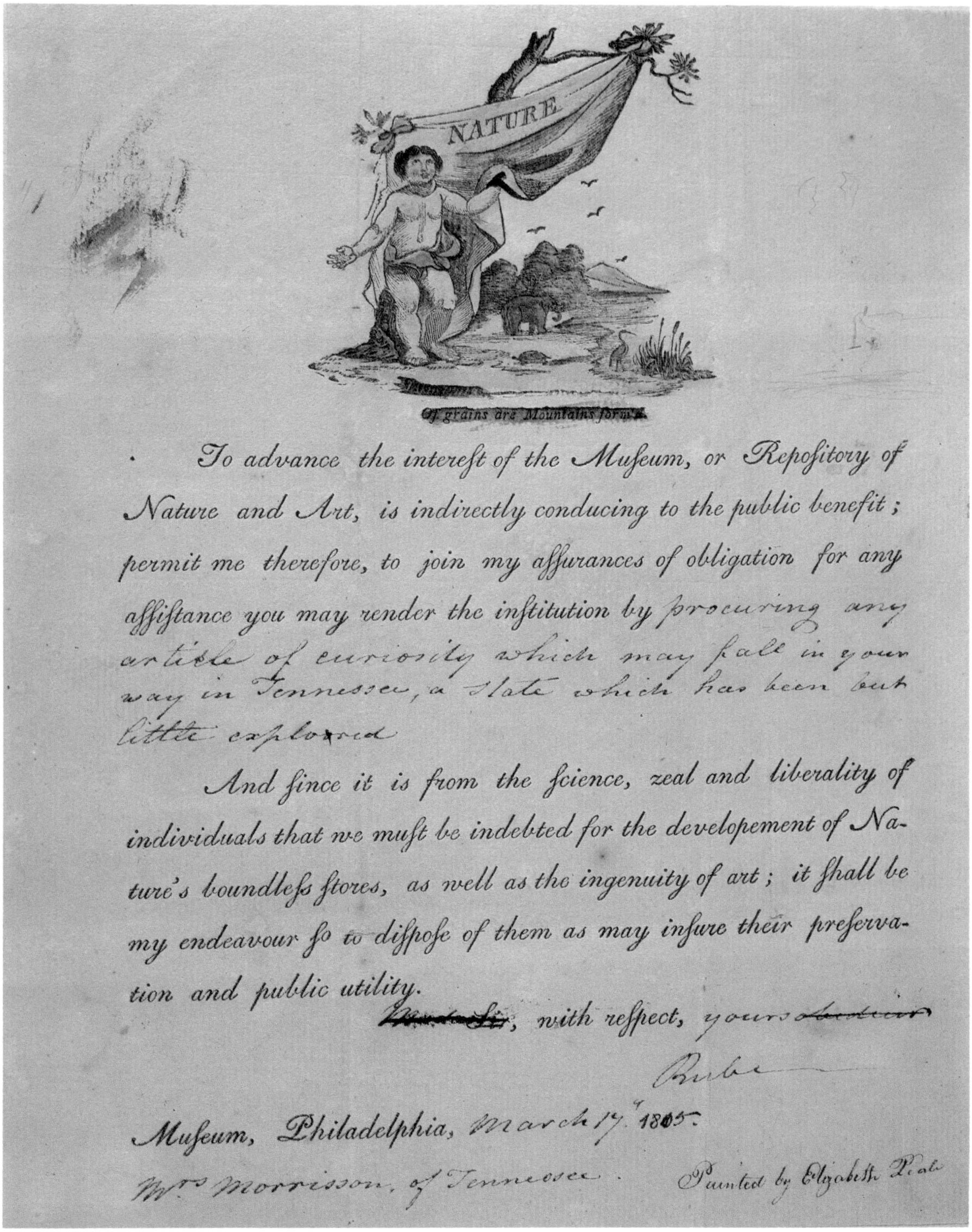

To advance the intereſt of the Muſeum, or Repoſitory of Nature and Art, is indirectly conducing to the public benefit; permit me therefore, to join my aſſurances of obligation for any aſſiſtance you may render the inſtitution by procuring any article of curiosity which may fall in your way in Tennessee, a State which has been but little explored

And ſince it is from the ſcience, zeal and liberality of individuals that we muſt be indebted for the developement of Nature's boundleſs ſtores, as well as the ingenuity of art; it ſhall be my endeavour ſo to diſpoſe of them as may inſure their preſervation and public utility.

~~Most ob. Sir~~, with reſpect, yours ~~obedient~~

Rube—

Muſeum, Philadelphia, March 17th 1805

Mrs Morrisson, of Tennessee.

Painted by Elizabeth Peale

110. Museum Gift Acknowledgment. c. 1805

From the first, Peale and his successors did all in their power to encourage gifts, accepting everything, culling out the useless, always listing donor with object. Unneeded gifts and second-best duplicates were used as exchanges for specimens from other collectors. Purchases were limited to objects which might attract enough additional visitors to cover their cost. Peale designed this card of acknowledgment in conjunction with the expansion of the museum into the Statehouse in 1802. This particular acknowledgment was colored by his daughter Elizabeth and signed by his son Rubens, who, in 1805, was in charge of the daily administration of the museum. (*American Philosophical Society*)

achievements of his museum, but this ability had its purest expression in his technology and mechanical inventiveness. His whole tour through life led him to believe that he could comprehend any museum problem. Nothing was beyond or beneath him. He sought expert advice and he trained and made use of assistants of many sorts, but he did not turn over basic problems to others. He attacked them himself. He especially delighted in attacking material or technological problems for which there was no existing or obvious solution. Time after time, he entered new fields of striving, eager to learn their basics "by doing" just as he had in undertaking new trades. His achievement is to be measured in his ever-active inventiveness rather than in specific inventions—although these forays did bring him two patents.

Like most mechanics and craftsmen, Peale engaged primarily in adapting and applying, innovating only when that was necessary. He was notably sensitive to new devices, to new ways of making and doing things, and to the inventors responsible. This sensitivity was underlined when Peale decided that an appropriate response to his American Philosophical Society election was to present a drawing and description of John Cram's "fan chair" (No. 167) at their next meeting.[41] This was a foot-actuated fan that drove flies away. Peale had Cram at work at the time, making a barrel organ for the museum, and he continued to use Cram's talents. Jefferson was sufficiently interested to acquire one of the chairs for himself.

Peale was especially sensitive to inventions that might be of direct utility in the museum and at the same time attract attention by their novelty. The Argand lamp, for example, had been brought back from France by Franklin, and Peale installed several in the museum. During Rubens's tenure as director, he decided to carry through a project his father had considered: lighting the museum by gas. Gas-lighting was still a novelty although it had been successfully used in London for nearly a decade when Rubens got a system going in the museum (No. 112). The first system had to be given up because of the offensive smell and the second because of fears of fire.[42]

111. Unidentified artist. CHARLES WILLSON PEALE'S HOME. c. 1790

An oil sketch by an unidentified hand shows the Peale home with its skylighted portrait gallery at Third and Lombard, site of the museum during the early years from 1784 to 1794. At right is the small addition for "moving pictures," later to become the museum's Marine Room. (*American Philosophical Society*)

112. Letter from Peale to his daughter Angelica, May 5, 1816, with drawing of museum gasworks

One purpose of Peale's Museum was to promote scientific advance, and Peale, therefore, was always interested in new inventions, especially if they would also attract people to the museum. Gaslight filled this double purpose perfectly: by lighting a large public building, Peale's Museum would demonstrate the potential of gas, thereby stepping into the forefront of scientific progress; and at the same time, gaslight would in itself be a wonderful evening entertainment. Indeed, the museum's evening "illuminations" attracted more visitors than by day, many drawn in merely by the novelty of such a scene after sundown. Museum income greatly increased, but fear of fire or explosion forced removal of the gasworks in 1820.

On May 5, 1816, Peale wrote to his daughter Angelica explaining the installation of gaslight. In high spirits, he was now sure that his museum was destined to "be the admiration of the world." (*American Philosophical Society*)

148

113. Models for Improvements in the Common Fireplace. 1796–97

In Peale's time, as towns and farms replaced the virgin forests of the new continent, fuel conservation became as important as it is today. In 1795, the American Philosophical Society offered a premium of sixty dollars "For the best construction of stoves or fireplaces." Charles Willson Peale and his son Raphaelle received the award for a plan showing how a sliding panel door and chimney damper could stop active burning but prolong heating from the hot coals and heated iron. Although the two Peales were awarded a patent, the fireplace was never produced commercially. (*American Philosophical Society*)

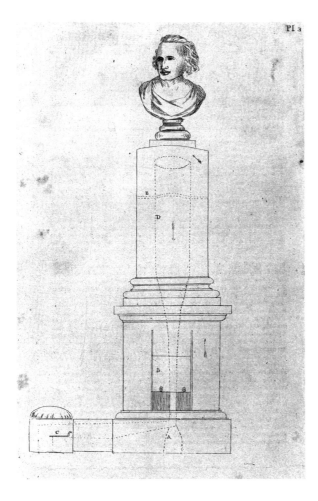

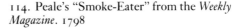

114. Peale's "Smoke-Eater" from the *Weekly Magazine*. 1798

Peale, always interested in inventions and devices that addressed the problems of daily life, built a stove for his museum in January, 1796, based on a new French device. It was designed to consume its own smoke, hence the name "Smoke-Eater." By forcing the smoke into a pipe and back through the heart of the fire, the combustible elements in the smoke were burnt before being drawn into the chimney, thus reducing smoke and soot. Peale gave it the form of a pillar capped by a bust probably of his own making. (*American Philosophical Society*)

Heating was equally unresolved, especially in large buildings. Peale was introduced to this inquiry by the ideas of his son, Raphaelle, and the two began by taking down a Rittenhouse fireplace (an improvement upon Franklin's) in their parlor. After trying several fireplace designs, the two won a philosophical society prize for a plan the chief feature of which was a closable, iron door at the front which could, in conjunction with the damper, stop active burning but prolong heating from the hot coals and heated iron (No. 113). Despite the award of a patent on top of the prize, the fireplace did not prove useful.[43]

In the museum, Peale installed instead a new French device, dubbed the "Smoke-Eater" (No. 114). This was a stove that ran the smoke back through the firebox, causing further combustion of unburned particles. It had a positive effect in reducing smoke, though it was not as good as Rumford's contemporary smoke shelf, which is still a feature of fireplace chimneys. The tall, columnar form of the "Smoke-Eater" surmounted by a bust made it highly visible, and Peale's published write-ups called it to the attention of potential visitors.[44]

In addition to utilities, Peale picked up on a variety of devices, some of which became celebrated attractions. After all, his first actual step toward broadening his picture gallery into a museum had begun with the 1785 application of the "Eidophusikon" invented in London. Peale called his version "Perspective Views with Changeable Effects; or, Nature Delineated, and in Motion." He offered several scenes in which turning on and off and moving multiple lights and moving several components within each scene gave motion and apparent motion to flat, painted surfaces—earning the nickname, "moving pictures."[45]

Much like his relationship with John Cram was Peale's association with John Isaac Hawkins and with his twin devices, the polygraph and the physiognotrace. Both were forms of the pantograph, which had been used for copying letters and designs since the seventeenth century. Hawkins had made other contributions to the museum, in music as well as mechanical devices, and when he returned to England in 1802 he left his American rights to the polygraph in Peale's hands; the physiognotrace he made available to the museum without royalty.

Both men expected much from the polygraph (No. 115), which could produce as many as five simultaneous copies of a handwritten letter—by giving exactly the same motion to duplicate pens. Peale hoped to be able to pay Hawkins his royalty and still realize handsome profits from the patented device but it proved too delicate and too expensive. It required constant fiddling and attention which only such enthusiasts as Thomas Jefferson and Benjamin Henry Latrobe were ready to put up with. Jefferson and Peale conducted a remarkably lengthy correspondence over many years in efforts to perfect the contraption.[46] It never worked easily, but it is responsible for much of the existing corpus of Jefferson and Latrobe letters.

The physiognotrace (No. 116), a pantograph designed to produce silhouettes, derived from a French invention of 1786. Hawkins's version was much simplified and more direct, having a brass finger that could be moved physically around the profile of the subject, actuating a point that sketched a reduced image of the profile.[47] It was used with vast success in the museum. Moses Williams, a former black slave who had been given to Peale, apparently as payment for a portrait in the Maryland days, operated the machine, first as an employee, and then as a concessionaire. He charged eight cents for four copies of a guest's silhouette, all cut from a single sketching; he soon had a booming business.

Peale explained carefully how he was led into designing his bridge—that too was conceived as an adjunct to the museum. It was first developed with the thought of bridging Walnut and Sixth streets to provide a connection between State House Square, upon which the museum stood, and Washington Square, upon which development seemed possible. As soon as he worked out an arch-bridge design, his vision expanded. Why not make it long enough to cross the Schuylkill, where a permanent bridge had so long been needed? His 390-foot bridge, incredibly, was to be constructed of layers of planks laid crosswise and held together only by nails and trunnels or wooden pegs (No. 118). It had no stringers and no source of rigidity save the wooden railings that ran along its upper surface. He built a small model that supported "12 Indians and all stout men"—although when one person crossed it alone, it deformed enough to cause concern.[48]

In this instance, Peale had not acquired enough "fingertip knowledge" from experience to conceive a successful bridge, and he was in no position to use the alternative approach of calculating stresses and strains. His patent bridge did not represent a satisfactory design, but fortunately no one tried to build it and its most permanent embodiment was in a tiny model placed in one of his bird cases.

Although the bridge did not serve future bridge builders, it did serve the museum. Peale obtained from his wartime friend, Thomas Paine, a model of his iron bridge and more than doubled the importance of either by displaying the scale models together in his Model Room. This, following the practice of the London Society of Arts and other European institutions, offered the visitor a "repository of machines." Here were displayed "implements of Husbandry, Models, Machinery, and improvements of tools," including a threshing machine, a clothes washer, and even Jefferson's plow—these devices did not work well yet could pique the imagination of the viewer.[49]

115. Polygraph sold to Thomas Jefferson by Charles Willson Peale

To the polygraph we owe the preservation in precise duplicate of most of Peale's correspondence, as well as that of Thomas Jefferson and the architect Benjamin Henry Latrobe. The device was invented by Peale's friend, the English composer John Isaac Hawkins, who gave the American rights to the museum. In principle, the polygraph was a version of the pantograph, which had been used for copying letters and designs since the seventeenth century. It was basically a writing desk over which two or more pens moved in unison. Peale and Hawkins had high hopes for profiting from sales of the machine, but although Peale and Jefferson together made many improvements in the device, it required constant attention, which only enthusiasts were willing to give it. (*University of Virginia, Charlottesville*)

116. Drawing and explanation of the physiognotrace. 1803

John Isaac Hawkins's invention of 1802 made it possible to trace one's own features in small size on paper, to be scissored out along the indented line. He gave Peale the right to use it in the museum, where it started a nationwide rage for silhouettes. Peale sent this description of the device to Thomas Jefferson, January 28, 1803. "A" is a sliding board adjustable to the height of the sitter, who rests his or her cheek against the projection "D." As the brass gnomon is guided around the profile, it is traced in reduced size on the paper fastened at top, "d." The silhouette would then be scissored by the skillful hand of Moses Williams, Peale's former slave, who became a well-to-do landowner as a result of the small fees he collected. Amies's Dove Mill banknote paper, twice folded, was used in making the four copies, to which the embossed stamp of the museum was added. Over 8,500 silhouettes were cut during the physiognotrace's first year of operation. (*Jefferson Papers, Library of Congress*)

117. Baron Alexander von Humboldt. 1804

In 1804, the German naturalist Baron von Humboldt visited Peale's Museum and paused to have his silhouette taken. Von Humboldt was delighted with the museum and its proprietor and enthusiastically endorsed Peale's plan to make the museum a national institution. (*Private collection*)

None of Peale's mechanical designs or adaptations brought him much personal profit but nearly all advanced the cause of the museum. Because he believed it himself, he was a master at convincing his visitors that they could, themselves, turn the pages of the "open book of nature." They might discover new knowledge of life and they might invent yet unperfected devices. If the objective of good education is to stimulate the imagination toward productive learning, Peale's Museum was an imaginative educational institution.

The educational success of the museum rested on his balance of popular appeal and scientific accuracy. He began with excellent taxidermy and the mounting of specimens in natural postures which, whenever possible, he established through observation in life. He used habitat settings with rocks, moss, and appropriate props, including painted backgrounds. Small insects were mounted to be viewed through a microscope. He provided succinct information on his labels. His attention to heating and lighting permitted him to open the museum in the evening and keep it bearable during the winter season.

Peale hoped to extend the reach of the museum's educational efforts through its publications. His catalogue coupled scientific classification with interesting observations on life habits of animals, but it was a research tool that helped very little in informing the public. Peale sought a broader audience through his museum press, which published an eight-page *Guide to the Philadelphia Museum* in 1805 (No. 119) and, in 1824, the first number of a periodical entitled, *The Philadelphia Museum, or Register of Natural History and the Arts*. This magazine presented reliable information in a popular vein but, like the catalogue, it did not awaken enough support to continue.

In promoting the museum to the public, Peale explored most of the media used today. In addition to publications, he offered organ concerts and other musical events. Scientific demonstrations and lectures were an early feature, especially on electricity and chemistry. During Rubens's tenure, magic lantern presentations were offered (Fig. k).

118. The Patent Wooden Bridge, from Peale's *Essay on Building Wooden Bridges*. 1797

From this idea for a bridge, conceived in the winter of 1796–97, Peale, as usual, expected great things. Easily erected of cheap materials, the bridge, he believed, would accelerate the westward advance of civilization. At the time, he hoped that his design would be selected by the city of Philadelphia and become the first permanent bridge over the Schuylkill River. Peale sent his design to the philosophical society, took out a patent, published a descriptive pamphlet, and built a model for exhibition in the museum. "The model," he recorded in his autobiography, "was placed in the passage in the Philosophical Hall, and the strength of it was so great that 12 Indians and all stout men stood on it and did it no injury." Fortunately, no one tried to build the bridge, for it would not have worked over such a large distance as the Schuylkill. Peale, who had mastered so many skills, was not equipped to cope with the engineering problems involved in building a 390-foot arch. (*American Philosophical Society*)

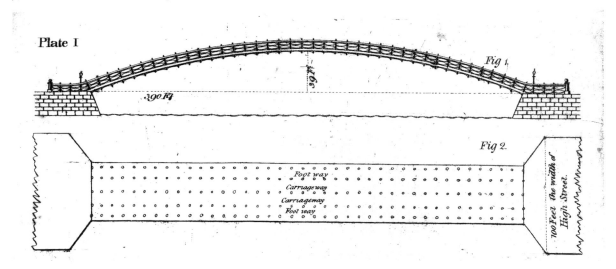

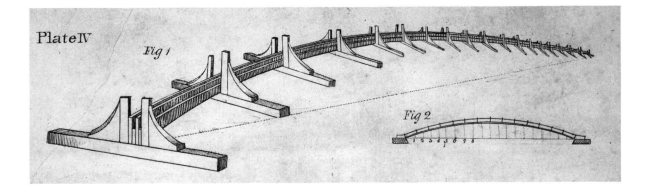

GUIDE

TO THE

PHILADELPHIA MUSEUM.

ADMITTANCE 25 CENTS.

THIS Museum is the property of Charles W. Peale, who began it in 1785, with some bones of the Mammoth and the Paddle-Fish, which were then added to his Picture Gallery: Shortly after, relinquishing his profession as a Portrait Painter, his exertions were directed and have been ever since devoted to the present establishment. His persevering industry has been so far crowned with success—and when the plans now preparing for execution shall be accomplished, the Institution, in point of arrangement, preservation and number, will rival in value and utility any of a similar nature.

IN 1802, the Legislature of Pennsylvania, influenced by an idea of its increasing utility, granted for the use of the Museum, the greater part of the Statehouse, where it is now displayed in a manner better becoming the importance of the Institution, and more worthy of the State which gave it birth.

From 1804 to 1826, every purchaser of a ticket to Peale's Museum was given a copy of this eight-page guide, listing the contents of each room. The guide accompanied the visitor through the Quadruped Room, down the Long Room, into the Marine Room, then across to Philosophical Hall and the Mammoth Room, Model Room, and Antique Room. (*American Philosophical Society*)

Peale's major effort to extend the educational impact of his exhibits was through the lecture series he offered in the fall and winter of 1799–1800 and 1800–1801. In each case he gave the introductory lecture at the University of Pennsylvania, celebrating the museum's relationships with the university and indicating the intended reach of the lectures. Calling the first series "Natural History" and the second "The Science of Nature," he published the introduction to each series but not the remaining lectures, all of which he presented in the museum. There he realized the true novelty of these courses: noting that, "It is not easy to convey in words a distinct idea of the form of an *Animal*," he lectured directly from the museum specimens displayed in front of him.[50] He thus was able to show off his source, adding its scientific classification and many of his own life stories. He made comparisons both of one species to another and of one scientist's conclusions with another's or with his own.

This pioneering approach did not awaken the public response for which Peale had hoped, but, rightly, he continued to believe in it. In 1823, he planned but did not carry through a third series. At some point, his lectures were deposited in the Academy of Natural Sciences; they represented Peale's longest and most connected written exposition on natural history. Yet they do not reflect his contributions adequately because they were auxiliary to the three-dimensional specimens from which he talked. Words were

Fig. k. An announcement for the Peales' "Magic Lanthorn," appearing in *Poulson's American Daily Advertiser*, November 3, 1821

120. GERARD TROOST (before restoration). 1823–24

Peale's Museum, through its influence on and involvement with the leading physical and natural scientists of the day, played an important role in professionalizing the study of natural history. Dutch-born geologist Gerard Troost was a founder and first president of the Academy of Natural Sciences in Philadelphia. When this portrait was painted, he was also professor of mineralogy at Peale's Museum. In 1821, he had given a course of lectures at the museum, using both the museum's geological collection, much of which he had donated, and his own collection of some five thousand specimens, the finest in private possession at that time. Troost, in his later years, followed Peale's example by establishing at the University of Nashville one of the most authentic and valuable of the western natural history museums. (*Academy of Natural Sciences of Philadelphia*)

157

121. C.B.J.F. de Saint-Mémin. CAPTAIN MERIWETHER
LEWIS. 1807

The museum enjoyed special relationships to several
federal government exploring expeditions, beginning
with Lewis and Clark in 1804. Meriwether Lewis and
Peale had a particularly close and warm association,
and Lewis gave many items of interest to the museum,
including the ermine-skin mantle he is wearing in this
watercolor. Presented to Lewis by Cameahwait, chief
of the Shoshoni nation in Idaho, the mantle was featured in a museum exhibit that emphasized a favorite
theme of Peale's—the importance of peace among
nations. It was draped on a wax portrait statue of the
explorer that has long since been lost, and which,
unlike this watercolor, showed him holding a peace
pipe. The museum label included a plea for peace that
Peale believed represented Lewis's sentiments at the
meeting. In this "speech," Lewis urged that the Indian
chief "bury the Hatchet deep in the ground never to be
taken up again—and that henceforward you may smoke
the *Calmut* of Peace and live in perpetual harmony, not
only with each other, but with the white men, your
Brothers, who will teach you many useful Arts." Peale
described the exhibit and label in a letter to Thomas
Jefferson written on January 19, 1808, concluding that
"I am pleased when I give an object which affords a
moral sentiment to the Visitors to the Museum."
(*The New-York Historical Society*)

never the primary medium of this conspicuously visual thinker. Just as talking about his
art can even today approach it only distantly, so what he said while showing his
specimens is but a hint of what was important in the presentation.

With conspicuous understanding of good education, Peale sought to associate leading
scientists and students of natural history with the museum. This was apparent in the
membership of his Board of Visitors appointed in 1792. Public figures predominated,
with Jefferson, as president, through Alexander Hamilton, James Madison, and the
governor of Pennsylvania, Thomas Mifflin, but the leading Philadelphia scientists were
also included. These ranged from physical scientists Rittenhouse and Patterson, to the
leading academic naturalists Caspar Wistar, James Hutchinson, and Benjamin Smith
Barton. One of Peale's first acts after resuming management of the museum in 1822 was
the appointment of a "faculty" to offer lectures in the museum. All were naturalists close
both to the museum and to the Academy of Natural Sciences, and productive in their
own right. John D. Godman held down physiology, Richard Harlan comparative
anatomy, Thomas Say zoology, and Gerard Troost (No. 120) mineralogy. Only Godman
and Troost actually gave lectures. Say's additional appointments as university professor

of natural history and as curator at the philosophical society may have removed him from museum service, but at the same time, they underlined the educational network in which Peale placed his museum.

The museum also became part of another important network, that of government exploration. Both Washington and Jefferson had made donations to the museum before becoming major figures in the new government under the Constitution. Their favorable attitude continued. When Jefferson became president, he predictably sent items from the Lewis and Clark Expedition to the museum. Meriwether Lewis donated others, including his own clothing, which Peale exhibited on a wax likeness—holding a peace pipe.[51] Specimens as well as sketches from the Long Expedition of 1818–21 came even more directly to the museum since Titian had participated in that (Nos. 129, 130).

Yet in Peale's mind, this was only a step toward the kind of relationship the federal

122. PLAINS HORNED LIZARD. c. 1806

A "Plains Horned Toad" was included in the earliest shipment from the Lewis and Clark Expedition sent to Peale by Jefferson. Peale replied, on July 24, 1804: "I am greatly obliged to you for the curious Lizard of Louisiana, which it certainly is, and not a Toad. . . . I have not yet had time to examine authors to know if it has been described, if not, I mean to give a drawing of it to the Philosophical Society for their next Volume." Although the drawing is inscribed in the hand of Titian Ramsay Peale II, the artist's son, as "Drawn by CW Peale from a specimen brought by Lewis & Clark," it is not absolutely certain that this is Peale's drawing. It may have been done by another artist, Pietro Ancora, who was working in Philadelphia at the time with Benjamin Smith Barton. (*American Philosophical Society*)

Louisiana Tanager.
From a Specimen obtained on Lewis & Clarks Expedt
Drawn for Captn M Lewis (1806?)

CWP. del.

123. LOUISIANA TANAGER.
c. 1806

The Lewis and Clark Expedition
sent many specimens to Peale for
his museum, a number of which
were new discoveries. As a grateful return, Peale planned to
contribute illustrations to the explorers' journal. Lewis was in
some financial difficulties, and
this gesture, Peale hoped, would
"give considerable profit to the
bold adventurer." To ensure the
correctness of the drawings, Peale
did them himself. Only four have
survived: this Louisiana tanager,
the mountain quail and Lewis's
woodpecker (No. 124), and the
horned lizard (No. 122). They
were preserved in an album kept
by his naturalist son, Titian
Ramsay Peale II.
    Peale's drawing was undoubt-
edly made from a museum specimen. Alexander Wilson, who
introduced the bird to the public
in *American Ornithology*, noted
that its "frail remains . . . [were]
set up by Mr. Peale in his
Museum." Wilson was able to
examine three skins of this species
at the museum in order to prepare
his published drawing. (*American
Philosophical Society*)

government ought to have with his museum. He tried several times to move the institution under the permanent patronage of the federal government—he saw it as "a design that [might] grow into a great national museum."[52]

His major objective was permanence, conscious of the national museums other countries maintained and depressed by the demise and dispersal of the influential Leverian Museum in London, which had remained private. He had spent more than half his adult life walking the difficult tightrope on which balance between science and popular appeal was essential. He realized fully that his successors would be incapable of this—as indeed they soon proved following his death.

Peale failed to make his a national museum in a developing nation not yet ready to assume such responsibilities. Years later a very peculiar bequest made possible the establishment of the Smithsonian Institution, a collection of museums which followed, whether consciously or not, many of Peale's pointers and justified his concepts. More broadly, natural history museums throughout the country were patterned on his pioneering successes and carried some of his unsuccessful forays on to success.

Drawn for Capt M Lewis
(1806?)
by CW Peale

124. MOUNTAIN QUAIL AND LEWIS'S WOODPECKER. c. 1806

This is another drawing Peale did for Lewis's journal (see No. 123). The intended use as an illustration is reflected in the style and composition of the drawing; the birds are arranged in a vertical, carefully balanced composition, clearly outlined, and finished in a monochromatic gray.

Lewis first saw the mountain quail on April 7, 1806, above the mouth of the Washougal River. He discovered the Lewis's woodpecker near Helena, Montana, on July 20, 1805. A skin of Lewis's woodpecker, which had been in Peale's Museum and is now in the Museum of Comparative Zoology, Harvard University, may be the only example to have survived from the entire zoological collection gathered on the Lewis and Clark Expedition. Peale's specimen of the woodpecker also served as the model for Alexander Wilson's drawing (No. 87) for his *American Ornithology*. (*American Philosophical Society*)

125. Mandan Indian Robe

This painted buffalo robe depicting an Indian warrior's account of a battle was first recorded in the invoice of articles sent by Lewis and Clark to Jefferson on April 7, 1805: "1 Buffalow robe painted by a mandan man, representing a battle which was fought 8 years ago since [1797] by the sioux and Recaras, against the Mandans, Me Ni Tarras & Ah Wah Har Ways." It is the earliest such painting presently conserved and the most important relic of the Lewis and Clark exploring party. Jefferson had it on the wall at Poplar Forest for at least ten years. How it came to be in the museum collection is not clear. Jefferson may have eventually sent it to the museum, or it may have been purchased after Jefferson's death by a Pennsylvanian who presented a painted buffalo robe that fits this description to the museum in 1828. (*Peabody Museum, Harvard University*)

126. Peace Pipe

This may be one of at least twelve calumets from the Lewis and Clark Expedition deposited in Peale's Museum by President Jefferson. Of the two clusters of feathers on this pipe, the lower represents the female element, the upper, the male. The tufts on the feathers in the upper group represent scalps taken in battle. (*Peabody Museum, Harvard University*)

Peale's science and technology reflected the same strengths in visual thinking and conceptual design that made him an outstanding artist. He thought three-dimensionally and he lived with the "open book of nature," convinced that the only fundamental sources for the life and earth sciences were the living things and the minerals to which everyone had open access. By collecting, arranging, and exhibiting them, according to the best current understanding, he advanced science primarily by providing source materials and encouraging their use. He educated and stimulated an uncounted number of men, women, and children in the realities, beauty, and order of nature. Always he looked to the future and he gave to it contributions of continuing value.

opposite:

127. Plains Hunting Shirt

Painted and ornamented with porcupine quills, this may be the piece identified by a Peale Museum label as "Indian Hunting Shirt made of Buffalo skin. This was formerly owned and worn by Capt. Clark in his Exploring Expedition. Presented to Peale's Museum by Capt. Lewis and Clark." (*Peabody Museum, Harvard University*)

128. Ojibwa Feather Flag

An Ojibwa chief once carried this flag of fowl feathers. William Clark came into possession of it, and he in turn presented it to the museum. (*Peabody Museum, Harvard University*)

129. Major Stephen H. Long. 1819

Peale painted the explorer Stephen Long for the museum's gallery of distinguished men in March of 1819 at Philadelphia, just before Long left to explore the country between the Mississippi and the Rocky Mountains. Peale was delighted that his son Titian Ramsay II had been appointed to the post of assistant naturalist on Long's expedition, and not only painted Long but Titian Ramsay (No. 130), Thomas Say (No. 90), and several other members of the group, saying, "if they did honour to themselves in that hazardly expedition that they might have the honour of being placed in the Museum and if they lost their skalps, their friends would be glad to have their portraits." The exploration was a huge success, and Long was honored by having the highest peak of the Rocky Mountains named after him.

When the expedition returned, Rubens Peale, then manager of the museum, wrote to Major Long requesting the loan of some of the specimens found on the journey. On March 20, 1821, nearly one hundred exhibits, including a wild turkey cock, six squirrels, and four wolf specimens were deposited in the museum, as were over a hundred drawings made on the trip by Titian Ramsay Peale (Nos. 131, 132). (*Independence National Historical Park Collection*)

130. TITIAN RAMSAY PEALE II. 1819

Charles Willson Peale painted this portrait of his son, Titian, the second of that name, just before
he left to serve as assistant naturalist on Major Long's exploring expedition to the Rocky Mountains.
The tall, handsome young naturalist in the elegant uniform worn by the civilian members of
the expedition undoubtedly fluttered the hearts of the young ladies of his circle before
he set off into the unknown interior of the continent.

Titian Ramsay II was born in 1799, the year after the first Titian had died of yellow fever. He
was a keen hunter, an excellent taxidermist, and a meticulously accurate painter. He early flowered
into the most competent naturalist in the family. At the age of eighteen he was elected a member
of the Academy of Natural Sciences. He traveled on a number of important exploring expeditions,
including the Wilkes Expedition to the South Seas from 1838 to 1842, and contributed drawings
to many significant studies of natural history, including the first and fourth volumes of Charles-
Lucien Bonaparte's *American Ornithology*, Thomas Say's *American Entomology*, and John D.
Godman's *American Natural History*. But at the end of his life, when he looked back, it was as an
explorer that he saw his life's accomplishments. (*Private collection*)

Dusky Wolf — E Nubilus Sa[...]
type spec[...] killed & drawn at
Engineer cantonment by TRP
1820

131. Titian Ramsay Peale II. Dusky Wolf Devouring a Mule Deer Head. 1820

Specimens brought back from the Long Expedition were used to create a museum mount similar to this drawing made by Titian Ramsay Peale while on the expedition. Edwin James in his *Account of an Expedition from Pittsburgh to the Rocky Mountains* (1823) described their hunt for the previously undescribed black-tailed or mule deer. "Verplank killed one of this description, on the afternoon of the first of August, near enough our camp to call for assistance and bring it in entire. They did not arrive until dark, and we had such pressing necessity for the flesh of the animal, that we could not defer dressing it until the next morning. The dimensions were accordingly taken, and a drawing made by Mr. Peale, by the light of a large fire." By the time the specimen reached Peale's Museum on March 20, 1821, the skin, according to James, was "so much injured by depredating insects that it has not been judged proper to mount it entire. The head has therefore been separated from the remaining portion of the skin, and may be seen in the Philadelphia Museum, placed under the foot of a prairie wolf." (*American Philosophical Society*)

opposite:

133. Titian Ramsay Peale II. American Antelope. c. 1820

This drawing is probably one of the finished watercolors made by Titian Ramsay Peale from sketches and specimens collected on the Long Expedition. The pronghorn antelope had only recently been discovered and was of special interest to naturalists of that day. Titian would have been familiar with this species: there was a mounted specimen in the museum (see No. 91) sent there by Lewis and Clark, and members of the Long Expedition killed several in June of 1820. The plants shown in the foreground—the beardtongue and the prickly pear cactus—are characteristic of the antelope's environment. (*American Philosophical Society*)

132. Titian Ramsay Peale II. Two Gray Squirrels. c. 1820

This is one of the drawings done by Titian Ramsay Peale while he served as assistant naturalist on the Long Expedition of 1819–20. These and almost one hundred other drawings were deposited in Peale's Museum on March 20, 1821, by Major Long. A half-dozen squirrels are also listed among the "Zoological Specimens" which entered the museum at the same time.

Charles Willson Peale was particularly charmed by the squirrel, describing it in his lecture series during the winter of 1799–1800 as "a beautiful little animal . . . equally admirable for the neatness and elegance of its formation, as for its liveliness and activity." He went on to describe its habits in his usual anthropocentric way: "The spring is the season of love with squirrels; at that time the males pursue the females, and exhibit wonderful proofs of agility, whilst the latter, as if to make a trial of the constancy of their lovers, seem to avoid them by a variety of entertaining sallies, and, like true coquets, feign an escape, by way of enhancing the value of the conquest." (*American Philosophical Society*)

AMERICAN ANTELOPE.
Antilocapra Americana Ord.

Charles Willson Peale:

A LIFE OF HARMONY AND PURPOSE

LILLIAN B. MILLER

III

The life of Charles Willson Peale was marked by the pursuit of harmony during a period in history unusually troubled by turmoil, social and political upheaval, and violent change. Energetic, creative, and assertive—especially when issues of justice and equity were at stake—Peale was drawn into the maelstrom of British-American conflict during the last half of the eighteenth century and became a revolutionary, a soldier, a politician, and a propagandist. But Peale was foremost an artist, impelled by his sense of design in nature to create forms that were harmonious, rhythmical, and proportioned. He required order in his life to meet his sense of order in nature. Thus, throughout the turbulent times and despite the conflicting demands made on him, he continued to search for ideas and values that would define his experiences and provide meaningful social and moral goals. In this sense, Peale mirrored the century in which he lived, sharing its values and ideals even as he participated in its disorders and confusions.

The eighteenth century was not as harmonious a period as its artistic achievements may suggest. Particularly during the latter half of the century, a steady movement of people from western Europe to the New World, the disruption of the great British empire through revolution, and the dethronement of the French king created a sense of disorder and instability. Intellectually and artistically, however, the eighteenth century asserted the primacy of such classical values as harmony, balance, symmetry, reason, patience, benevolence, and wisdom; and these values influenced its art and architecture, determined the content and form of its poetry, and stimulated its search for scientific principles. The systematic organization of all human knowledge became the purpose behind the French philosopher Diderot's *Encyclopédie*, Linnaeus's system of classification, and Peale's Museum. Despite the wrenching dislocations that marked the century, or perhaps because of them, men's minds, like Peale's, sought principles and visions of order, and dreamed of peace, progress, and harmony.

Peale's early life had been troubled by change. Fatherless by age nine, he witnessed his mother's "excess grief" which prevented her from taking "any measure to assist herself

134. SELF-PORTRAIT IN UNIFORM.
1777–78

Peale, who described himself as "a thin,
spare, palefaced man," is depicted here
in the brown uniform coat of his Pennsylvania militia regiment, the gold braid
loop on his hat the insignia of the captain's rank which he held at the battle of
Princeton. Peale bought the material for
his "Regmantles" on October 9, 1776,
and had them made by a Philadelphia
tailor. According to Silas Deane (No. 18),
the prevailing uniform was "dark brown
(like our homespun coat), faced with red,
white, yellow, or buff, according to their
different battalions, white vest and breech-
es, white stockings, half boots, and black
knee-garters. The coat is made short . . .
which shows the size of a man to a great
advantage." (*American Philosophical
Society*)

and Children." When she and her children were forced to abandon the little schoolmaster's
house in Chestertown and move to the busy town of Annapolis, the young Charles's
security must have been shaken by fear of poverty and worry about the alteration in the
family's status. His mother took up "manteau-making" to support herself and her
children, and Charles had to leave school at age thirteen to become a saddler's apprentice.

Hard work did not bring the expected rewards to the eager apprentice. Peale's
master refused to abide by their agreement under which the youth would be granted an
early discharge from his indentures in exchange for helping to manage the business.
When finally free, Peale felt as if he had made "a long and lonesome journey through a
desert, fearfull wilderness." Thus Peale's youthful experiences, so filled with uncertainty
and the humiliation of "bondage," as he called it, surely were responsible in some
measure for his later insistence on the necessity for harmony and order in human
relations and the need to "Let love and not fear be the mover to good works."[1]

Insecurity continued to haunt the young Peale. He was burdened by debts incurred
in establishing his saddlery; and his financial situation deteriorated even further when
his partner absconded with "all the monies." Unable to meet the pressures of his
creditors—pressures which became more urgent after he joined the radical Sons of
Freedom—Peale was forced to flee Annapolis or face debtors' prison. His debts finally
settled, he was able to return to the "Bosom of his family," but he had been absent for an
entire anxiety-ridden year. And he was not to remain settled for long. A few months
later "a new scene was about to take place," and Peale would again leave Annapolis and

his family for the noise and confusion of urban London—and exciting experiences and opportunities in the studio of Benjamin West.[2]

The American Revolution brought about another dramatic transformation in Peale's life. Now in Philadelphia, he witnessed the casting off of the shackles of colonialism by the newly united states. To protect his home and family against the threat of the approaching British and Hessian troops, as well as to share the agonies of his countrymen in their "struggles for liberty," Peale enlisted in the militia (No. 134).[3] Although his participation in the actual fighting of the Revolution was brief, lasting not more than a year, he experienced sufficient violence and bloodshed at Princeton (January 3, 1777) and in skirmishes around the occupied city of Philadelphia to realize the horrors and turbulence of war. Much later, after years of reflection, he expressed his sense of war's terrors in a historical painting (now lost) depicting the *Retreat Across the Delaware, 1776* (1819–20). A night landscape that purported to show "the most hellish scene I have ever beheld," Peale's painted sermon against war included not only the retreating army and its leaders, but images of "the young and thoughtless" volunteers for liberty as well as the distressed women and children who were the innocent victims of war's violence.[4] Perhaps he was remembering his own reckless enthusiasm when he joined the militia,

135. GENERAL WASHINGTON OVERLOOKING THE RARITAN RIVER AND THE ADVANCE OF THE BRITISH ARMY. 1777

Peale sketched this scene in his diary on June 26, 1777. Walking out from camp, he climbed a height, where he found General Washington and an aide observing the British under General Howe advancing from Amboy, New Jersey, and being met by Lord Stirling's Continentals. (*American Philosophical Society*)

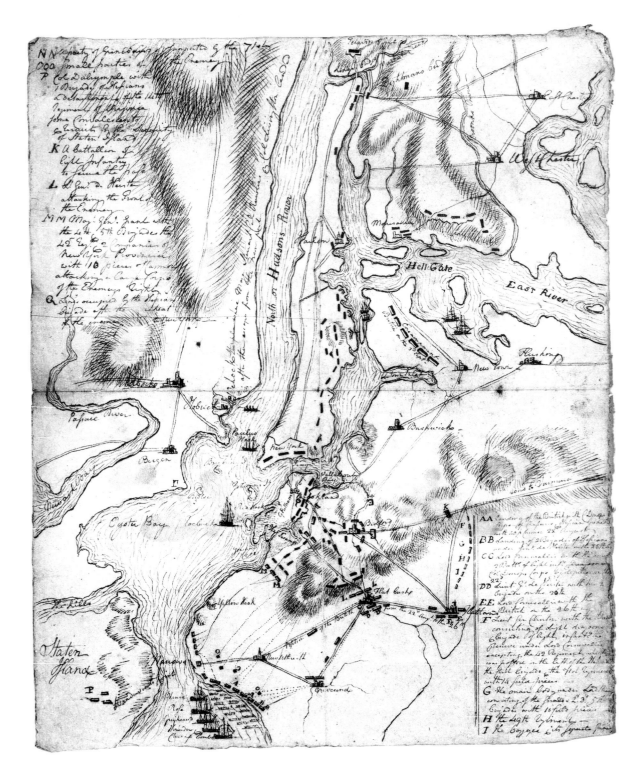

136. MAP OF NEW YORK. 1776

Maps were scarce and hard to come by during the war for independence. Peale made his copy of a map of New York on November 4, 1776, a month before his regiment marched for Trenton on December 5. The reason for the map is not known, nor is the source. The latest date found on it, designating the various positions of British forces, is September 3. The battle of Long Island took place on August 27. The defeated American forces withdrew to Manhattan Island (as seen on the map) on the night of August 29–30, 1776. Peale may have been attempting to follow the battles in New York, where his brother and brother-in-law were engaged in active service. (*American Philosophical Society*)

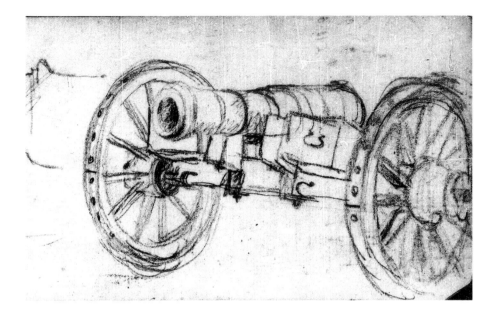

an act which had branded him as a revolutionary and sent him into hiding when the British eventually occupied Philadelphia. As a result of his radical associations, his family, too, had been forced to flee their home and find refuge from Tory persecution in the safer countryside.

Agitation also marked revolutionary politics in Pennsylvania. In Philadelphia again between military campaigns, the impetuous militia captain found himself once again in a "dangerous and troublesome . . . Sea, subject to like troubles by every blast, and very often in contrary directions."[5] He had become a member of the Whig Society —Philadelphia's radical political group known as the "Furious Whigs"—whose major purpose was to preserve the radical Pennsylvania constitution of 1776. He served on important committees in the society and, early in 1777, became its chairman. During these years, the "Furious Whigs" were embroiled in intense conflict with Philadelphia's more conservative leaders—highly respected merchants and legislators—whom they accused of excessive profiteering and escalating of prices. When the two political groups confronted each other at the home of the conservative lawyer James Wilson, in the so-called Fort Wilson riot, violence occurred. Peale suffered great discomfort at having been involved in such a turbulent episode; and he was even more embarrassed by his assignment as a militia captain to arrest or detain prominent Philadelphians accused of British sympathies.

Why he accepted an appointment as agent for confiscated estates is difficult to say; perhaps he needed the income for the support of his family. In any case, this softhearted artist found himself engaged in the even more unpleasant activities of seizing the homes and property of Philadelphia's Loyalists or Tories and preparing them for sale at auction. This was, he later wrote, the "most disagreeable part of his life (except that where he had the apprehensions of a Gaol)." He participated in these radical activities, he explained, in the hope that his efforts would "promote the common cause of America."[6]

Peale was forty-two years old when peace finally came to the United States. Up to this time his life had been marked by an occupational shift, from artisan to artist; by physical dislocations that uprooted him from the small town of Chestertown and transported him to bustling Annapolis, Yankee Boston, cosmopolitan London, and tumultuous Philadelphia; by war and violence that sent him slogging through the battlefields of New Jersey and Pennsylvania; by social and political conflict; by domestic happiness and sorrow, as he experienced marriage, births and deaths, separation and return; and by large national fluctuations, as the country went from colony to nation, from monarchy to republic.

Yet even in peace, the United States would continue to be disturbed by political and social unrest, while the government wrestled with problems of representation, individual liberties, and international rivalries. The ratification of a new constitution did not allay the intensity of political passions, as its proponents had hoped. The Whiskey Rebellion pointed up the discontent in the western settlements; and the formation of antagonistic Federalist and Republican parties contributed to a continuing sense of uncertainty and instability. Many Americans seriously began to believe that the nation could not maintain itself long as an independent republic.[7]

The troubled times must surely have revived in Peale the anxieties he had earlier experienced in both his personal and public life. But his was a sanguine temperament, inclined to optimism and high expectations. Even more important, the prevailing political and social ideology offered conceptions and purposes which provided intellectual and emotional support for coping with turmoil.

During his early years, Peale had accepted a fairly simple republican ideology based upon the Whig tradition of dissent and asserting the importance of individual freedom and national independence. These ideas had appealed to the zealous young artist, who was eager to apply his artistic talents to a worthy cause. Marching with Annapolis's Sons of Freedom in opposition to Maryland's Proprietary officeholders in 1764, he had observed how banners could be used "to designate the freedom of Tradesmen." Perhaps he had even participated in the preparation of these banners. A few months later, while in exile in Newburyport, Massachusetts, he assisted the citizens of that town in making "emblematical Ensigns" designed to indicate "with what unanimity of detestation" they regarded the Stamp Act.[8]

What these designs were we do not know, but it is likely that he used traditional allegorical images similar to those that appear in his later portraits of *William Pitt, John Beale Bordley*, and *Conrad Gérard*. These images were available in America at that time through prints, book engravings, newspaper mastheads, engraved coats of arms, and imported stereotypes. Peale might have seen them in the numerous editions of Cesare Ripa's *Iconologia*, first published in 1593 (Fig. l); in late-seventeenth-century publications of French pattern sheets and ornaments prepared for jewelers and clockmakers; or in the collections and adaptations of designs created between 1759 and 1764 by the Florentine artist John Baptist Cipriani on commission from the British art patron and radical Whig, Thomas Hollis V.[9]

In London, Peale's sense of his Americanism and republicanism was sharpened. When the king's carriage passed him on the street, he refused to doff his hat, as a protest

Fig. l. An adaptation of a plate from Cesare Ripa's *Iconologia* by George Richardson in *Iconology; or A Collection of Emblematical Figures*, 1779. Library of Congress, Washington, D.C.

against Parliament's suspension of New York's charter. For the same reason, he denied himself the pleasure of buying English clothing for his return trip. It seems quite probable that as tensions between the mother country and her colonies increased, and as Peale continued to learn something about art and its many uses, this liberty-loving, impressionable artist determined to make his own art a means for advancing America's cause.[10]

Thus, when Edmund Jenings, a Marylander who had made England his home, commissioned Peale to paint a portrait of William Pitt, earl of Chatham (see No. 3), as a gift for the gentlemen of Westmoreland County in Virginia, Peale was quite prepared to turn the portrait into an allegory of freedom. The two heroic portraits that followed the Pitt—*John Beale Bordley* (No. 5) and *Conrad Gérard* (No. 28)—were accorded similar treatment.

All three portraits are allegorical paintings that warn nations of their fate if the liberty of their subjects is disregarded. In their treatment of the standing figure, they remind us of the full-length portrait of Charles Calvert, fifth Lord Baltimore (Fig. m), which hung at the time in the Statehouse in Annapolis and which Peale may have studied before sailing for London. Similar symbols are used: a column signifying

Fig. m. Attributed to Herman Van der Myn. CHARLES CALVERT, FIFTH LORD BALTIMORE. 1730. Oil on canvas. The Peale Museum, Baltimore

firmness, a dog representing faithfulness, an Indian denoting America.[11] These are images adapted from Ripa by Cipriani, whose entire roster of symbols would probably have been available in the prints and books owned by Peale's teacher, Benjamin West, or by Joseph Wilton, the sculptor from whose statue of Pitt Peale derived his own image of the hero. The most important of these symbols, and one which Peale continued to use in his later civic designs, was Cipriani's rendition of *Brittania-Libertas*, a woman seated on a throne or large globe and accompanied by an oval shield. In her left hand she holds a trident or staff (*hasta*) topped by a liberty cap (*pilleus libertas*), while her right hand extends either an olive branch or some other significantly symbolic object (Fig. n). Other images possibly borrowed from the Cipriani group included the civic crown (in the *Pitt*), "consecrated to *that* MAN who preserved his Fellow-Citizens and Subjects from Destruction";[12] the perpetual flame of the sacred cause of liberty; cornucopias (in the *Bordley* and *Gérard*) representing fruitfulness and plenitude; massed clouds contrasting with blue skies as forecasts of the storm ahead and the eventual emergence of peace.

Although in their allegorical references these portraits reflect Peale's commitment to the revolutionary cause and contain warnings against trifling with America's traditional liberties, at the same time they reveal his deep hope for a peaceful settlement of the colonial controversy and his conviction that ultimate prosperity depended upon a resolution of national differences. Peale's *Pitt* attempts to persuade through oratory; the *Bordley* emphasizes agrarian prosperity and the rising glory of pastoral America; while in the *Gérard* the fasces overlaid with a cornucopia and the cannon with the lyre symbolize the harmony of nations that share the goals of peace and prosperity.

During the war, Peale continued to make his art serve the cause of American independence by painting three outright propaganda pieces. Two were battle flags, one for the Independent Company of Baltimore and one for a company of Norfolk volunteers. Both featured "LIBERTY trampling upon TYRANNY, and putting off SLAVERY who is approaching with hasty strides, and taking hold of DEATH, which is represented by a SKELETON on the right hand side." In these, also, Peale inserted symbols of strength achieved through peace: a column "to denote STABILITY, and an extent of country." [13] His third creation on behalf of the radical cause was directed to a particular political situation. The two-faced effigy of the traitor Benedict Arnold was constructed for a political parade planned by the "Furious Whigs," who were attempting to throw fear into suspected Tories or conservatives who opposed the democratic gains made by the new constitution of the state of Pennsylvania. In this parade (No. 138), the effigy of the traitor, prodded and tormented by a Devil, was borne on a cart to a bonfire, escorted by a large and noisy crowd of soldiers and citizens.

Peale participated in this rowdy affair, he said, out of patriotism, and because he was "always ready to give his aid to keep up with the spirit of the times, and in those periods, when the disasters of war might damp the spirits of those most anxious for our

Fig. n. Francesco Bartolozzi after John Baptist Cipriani. Design of *Brittania-Libertas*. Date unknown. The Metropolitan Museum of Art, New York City

A REPRESENTATION of the FIGURES exhibited and paraded through the Streets of PHILADELPHIA, on *Saturday,* the 30th of *September* 1780.

DESCRIPTION of the FIGURES.

A STAGE raised on the body of a cart, on which was an effigy of General ARNOLD sitting; this was dressed in red coat and had two faces, emblematical of his traiterous conduct, a mask in his left hand a letter in his right from Belzebub, telling him that he had done what mischief he could do, and now he must hang himself.

At the back of the General was a figure of the Devil, dressed in black robes, shaking a purse of money at the general's left ear, and in his right hand a pitchfork, ready to drive him into hell as the reward due for the many crimes which the thirst of gold had made him commit.

In the front of the stage and before General Arnold, was placed a large lanthorn of transparent paper, with the consequences of his crimes thus delineated, i. e. on one part, General Arnold on his knees before the Devil, who is pulling him into the flames—a label from the General's mouth with these words, "My dear Sir, I have served you faithfully;" to which the Devil replies, "And I'll reward you". On another side, two ropes from a gallows, inscribed, "The Traitors reward". And on the front of the lanthorn was wrote the following:

"MAJOR GENERAL BENEDICT ARNOLD, late COMMANDER of the FORT WEST-POINT. THE CRIME OF THIS MAN IS HIGH TREASON. "He has deserted the important post WEST-POINT, on Hudson's River, committed to his charge by His Excellency the Commander in Chief, and is gone off to the enemy at New-York.

"His design to have given up this fortress to our enemies, has been discovered by the goodness of the Omniscient Creator, who has not only prevented his carrying it into execution, but has thrown into our hands ANDRE, the Adjutant-General of their army, who was detected in the character of a spy.

"The treachery of this ungrateful General is held up to public view, for the expedition of infamy; and to proclaim with joyful acclamation, another instance of the interposition of bounteous Providence.

"The effigy of this ingrate is therefore hanged (for want of his body) as a Traitor to his native country, and a detester of the laws of honour."

The procession began about four o'clock, in the following order:
Several Gentlemen mounted on horse-back.
A line of Continental Officers.
Sundry Gentlemen in a line.
A guard of the City Infantry.
Just before the cart, drums and fifes playing the Rogues March.
Guards on each side.

The procession was attended with a numerous concourse of people, who after expressing their abhorrence of the Treason and the Traitor, committed him to the flames, and left both the effigy and the original to sink into ashes and oblivion.

'TWAS *Arnold's* post, Sir *Harry* fought,
Arnold ne'er enter'd in his thought,
How ends the bargain? let us see,
The fort is safe, as safe can be,
His favourite *per force* must die,
His view's laid bare to ev'ry eye;
His money's gone—and lo! he gains
One scoundrel more for all his pains.
ANDRE was gen'rous, true, and brave,
And in his room, he buys a knave.
'Tis sure ordain'd, that *Arnold* cheats
All those, of course, with whom he treats.
Now let the *Devil* suspect a bite
Or *Arnold* cheats him of his right.

Mothers shall still their children, and say---Arnold!---
Arnold shall be the bug-bear of their years,
Arnold!---vile, treacherous, and leagued with Satan.

138. BENEDICT ARNOLD AND THE DEVIL. 1780

The parade carrying Peale's two-faced effigy of the traitor Benedict Arnold through the streets of Philadelphia was not "a frolick of the lowest sort of people," as Quaker observer Samuel Rowland Fisher had at first thought, but rather "the Act of some of the present Rulers here. . . ." The "Rulers" were Pennsylvania's "Furious Whigs," who had succeeded in persuading Pennsylvanians to adopt a radical constitution. Ostensibly a parade to express "the people's hatred of a traitor," the exhibition was also intended to serve as a warning to Loyalists and conservatives not to meddle with the Radicals' achievement. (*The Metropolitan Museum of Art*)

independence."[14] His participation brought unforeseen political consequences: ten days later, Peale, along with other radicals, lost his bid for re-election to the state legislature. He then determined never again to be caught in such violent political activities, which were so contrary, in any case, to his essentially peace-loving disposition. He decided to foreswear politics and "follow diligently his profession of Portrait painting . . . a profession in which he could not make any enemies and which most probably would be much more profitable as well as most satisfying to his feelings."[15] Yet, given the temper of the times and Peale's propensity for involving himself in public affairs, such a decision was almost impossible to carry out. Although he never again ran for political office or joined a specifically political party, Peale could not resist using his "pencil," as his English patron Edmund Jenings had urged, to "perpetuate the Revolution."[16]

Peale found an especially effective way to promote republican ideals in the large transparencies he painted for public celebrations that took place between 1781 and 1824. The evocation of nationalism was enormously important during these years, when the country seemed hopelessly divided and disunited. Especially before the adoption of the federal Constitution in 1787, the bickerings among the states, the threats of a mutinous army, and the complaints of a disaffected ally endowed public pageantry with a crucial purpose. Philadelphia, as the seat of the federal as well as the state government, and the center of radical protest, seemed a particularly appropriate place for public demonstrations on behalf of national unity.

Beginning with the festivities marking the surrender of Cornwallis at Yorktown in October, 1781, Peale actively participated in these celebrations. His artistic skills were called upon to mark the triumphant arrival of commander in chief George Washington in Philadelphia late in November, 1781, the birth of the French dauphin in May, 1782,

139. WASHINGTON AND HIS GENERALS AT YORKTOWN. c. 1781

In this history painting, Peale celebrated the American and French victory over the British forces at the battle of Yorktown, Virginia, in October of 1781.

The officers who stand with General Washington on the bank of the York River are (front row, left to right) the Marquis de Lafayette, Count Rochambeau, and Tench Tilghman, Washington's aide and a member of Maryland's landed aristocracy. The men standing behind have been tentatively identified as the Marquis de Chastellux, who later published an account of his travels in the United States, and either General Nathanael Greene or General Benjamin Lincoln.

Peale traveled to Yorktown to sketch the scene of the battle for the background of the full-length portraits of Washington at Yorktown that he was painting for the states of Virginia and Maryland. The reality of the devastation, particularly the masts of sunken British transports projecting above the water and the beach strewn with dead horses, indicates the artist's firsthand observation of the battle's aftermath. This painting may have been done in preparation for these two public commissions. (*Maryland Historical Society*)

the birthday of Louis XVI in August, 1782, and the ratification of the peace treaty in January, 1784. Later, he would take part in ceremonies honoring the ratification of the Constitution (July 4, 1788), the "crowning" of Washington at Gray's Ferry on his way to his first inaugural (April, 1789) (see No. 61), the Louisiana Purchase (May, 1804), and the visit of the Marquis de Lafayette (September, 1824).

Transparencies were made of varnished paper or window-shade cloth primed with wax and turpentine, on which designs or images were drawn in India ink and colored washes or paint. They were then illuminated from behind. This was not a new technique: in the fourteenth century, German artists had produced linen transparencies which were hung in rooms as tapestries. Other European artists had also experimented with illuminated tinted and varnished prints as well as with painting on glass. Peale may have observed the preparation of such paper and lamps in Benjamin West's studio. In 1769, just before Peale departed for America, West and his fellow Royal Academicians were occupied in preparing transparencies for the celebration of the king's birthday on June 6.[17]

Peale had utilized the method in a small way in the Arnold parade, in which he included a lantern that set forth in words and pictures the traitor's misdeeds. But he was undoubtedly inspired to make his large transparencies celebrating the victory at Yorktown after seeing the decorations created by Alexandre-Marie Quesnay, chevalier de Beaurepaire (1755–1820), a French drawing and dancing master living at the time in Philadelphia. On the first night of the festivities, Quesnay had decorated his windows with brightly illuminated designs that featured thirteen stars (representing the thirteen states), each aiming a ray or virtue toward the name of "His Excellency General Washington," which encircled a quiver. The thirteen virtues exemplified republican ideals associated with the hero: wisdom, justice, strength, temperance, faith, charity, hope, courage, religion, love, wise policy, friendship, and consistency. Three fleurs-de-lis, symbol of France, surrounded the name of the Comte de Grasse, admiral of the French fleet that had prevented the British from escaping from Yorktown by sea. The whole was topped by the motto "HUZZA" which in turn sent "three rays of joy towards the said thirteen states." Quesnay illuminated a second window with a drawing of Washington, lance in hand, trampling underfoot the crown of Britain; above the motto "BRITISH PRIDE" he again showed the three fleurs-de-lis and the name of the Comte de Rochambeau, the French commander. Another "HUZZA" diverging three rays of joy toward Rochambeau completed the image.[18]

Peale was not to be outdone. The following evening, according to the newspaper account, his house was "most beautifully" illuminated.[19] On the first floor appeared the ship of state under full sail, "CORNWALLIS" emblazoned on her stern and flying the French flag over the British—"emblematic, first of the assistance of the fleet of our great Ally; second, the taking of a fine ship is justly compared to the glorious conquest of Cornwallis; and third, her fast sailing, to his rash and precipitate movements in some of the southern states." At the middle window on the second story appeared busts—"good likenesses"— of Washington and Rochambeau, with rays of glory emanating from them, while over their heads appear two interlaced laurel crowns, the whole encircled with palms and the motto, "SHINE VALIANT CHIEFS." Across the entire front of the third story were hung in large letters the words "FOR OUR ALLIES, HUZZA! HUZZA! HUZZA!" all in transparent painting.[20]

This exuberant display set the tone for the celebrations that followed, with Peale's designs growing more elaborate and more pointed as he warmed to his role as propagandist. When Washington arrived in Philadelphia late in November to appeal to Congress for sufficient funds to maintain the army in the field until the war was officially over, not only did Peale want to demonstrate his "respect and gratitude to the conquering Hero," but he was anxious to aid Washington in his mission. What Washington and Peale feared was that the army would mutiny if salaries and the promised bounties were not paid.[21] To avoid such a crisis and to remind Congress and the people of the importance of the army in the long fight for national freedom, Peale added new transparencies to those he had created for the previous celebration.

For one window he created a three-story, dome-topped Temple of Independence crammed with symbols that narrated the history of the recent conflict. The foundations of the temple rested on the names of the odious measures passed by the British that had led to the colonial protest. On the temple itself were listed the famous battles of the Revolution, starting with Lexington and Bunker Hill and culminating in the final victory at Yorktown. The first story of the temple, which represented THE VOICE OF THE PEOPLE, featured thirteen columns supporting a frieze called ILLUSTRIOUS SENATORS, while the pediment above the columns featured BRAVE SOLDIERY. Rays of light emanating from the senators to the soldiers symbolized the necessary Congressional support of the army. To thrust home his message, Peale added a statue of Justice replete with scales, flaming sword, and thirteen stars; Hope, with her anchor; and Industry, with her beehive.

The temple's second story designed in the Doric order showed the heroes fallen in battle, a reminder again to Congress that independence rested on the blood shed by the nation's soldiery. The gains of independence were symbolized on the third story, where Peale painted images of Agriculture holding a sheaf of wheat and a sickle, with a plough at her feet; Painting with a palette, pencils, and picture, a golden chain and medal around her neck marked IMITATION; Sculpture with a mallet, chisel, and bust ornamented with laurels; Architecture displaying a plan of elevation and a square and plummet; and Commerce with a globe and prow of a ship. Atop the dome of the temple was the figure of Fame blowing her trumpet to the east, proclaiming to the Old World what the New World had wrought.

As if the message of this window were not convincing enough, Peale decorated still another with symbols of republicanism. Peace and virtue were embodied in "a handsome female figure, the bigness of life, cloathed in white and bound by a purple sash bearing the word VIRTUE," and representing "the genius of America." Around her head was bound a fillet that bore the word PERSEVERANCE, and her striped banner proclaimed EQUAL RIGHTS. A hand rested on a globe marked UNIVERSALITY, while Discord, snakes in his hair, held a torch "the flame of which turns down on himself."[22]

These images were to appear again and again in Peale's celebratory works (Fig. o). They represented peace, virtue, prosperity, and freedom, and they proclaimed America as the home of agriculture, commerce, and the arts, and also as an example to the rest of the world of a harmonious state based upon justice, equality, and freedom. In terms of

Fig. o. Peale's design for the title page of the *Columbian Magazine* shows America fostering the arts while a youthful Agriculture plows the earth. Commerce is symbolized by a ship with flying banners. (*Library of Congress, Washington, D.C.*)

the immediate situation, they demonstrated to the people and the leaders of the nation the glorious results of wise policy; they constituted both a warning and a promise.

In 1782, Peale created two displays in honor of America's French allies. The American-French alliance was shaky as a result of the French fear that the United States would attempt to make a separate peace with Great Britain and thus ignore France's interests. To remind Americans of their obligations to the French, who had sent money, supplies, a fleet, and an army to help them in their fight with Britain, the French minister Conrad Gérard persuaded Congress to celebrate two important events: the birth a few months earlier of the French heir to the throne and the birthday of Louis XVI. Peale used these opportunities to express again republican sentiments. He had always had a strong affection for the French; Enlightenment philosophers—Diderot, Rousseau, and Voltaire—had provided him with many of his ideas about society, education, and the family. In the 1760s he had even arranged French lessons for himself and his family. Now his enthusiasm for the country's wartime partner found an outlet in elaborate illuminations, each of which became an extended symbol.

The theme running through the transparency celebrating the birth of the dauphin was "Liberty is our brightest light," and the dauphin was heralded as "A New Sun beams on the Earth." For the king's birthday, Peale chose to emphasize the idea of loyal friendship: the king and queen were praised as "Friends to mankind," and the colors of the two nations were interlaced to indicate the closeness of the alliance. Peale featured here "An ass heavy laden with plunder, driven with the point of a fixed bayonet by a British soldier," a design reminiscent of the mule loaded with American wool being driven away by an American farmer that appears in the portrait of *Bordley* (see No. 5). But the illuminated scene's meaning was quite different: to point up the miseries of "DEPENDENCE," Peale added to this image peasants and a log hut and made the whole a symbol of enslavement.[23]

Peale's most elaborate masterpiece, the Triumphal Arch, honoring the ratification of the peace treaty in January, 1784, climaxed public interest in these artistic displays (Fig. p). "A popular and patriotic throng" crowded into Lombard Street to view his illuminated windows, and then strolled on to the official residence of the president of Pennsylvania, where the spectacle was to take place. Peale's earlier Temple of Independence provided the model for the arch, but Peale planned it on a much larger scale, adding to the illumination a gigantic figure of Peace, who would descend from the top of the arch accompanied by goddesses and with her lighted torch set off a burst of hundreds of rockets which would soar colorfully into the sky.[24]

The disaster that met the Triumphal Arch would have dulled the enthusiasm of almost any one other than Peale. A precipitously lit rocket struck one of the paintings, and the massive arch, 56½ feet wide and 40 feet tall, broke into open flame, igniting the remaining rockets, which roared into the air and down upon the expectant onlookers. Peale himself suffered injuries and burns, as did many members of the crowd. With an apology to the public and an appeal for funds, he began almost immediately to reconstruct the arch—this time without rockets. For over three months he labored; and on May 4, the transparency was once again put on display before an admiring populace.

Peale's transparencies were hugely successful; the crowds filling the street in front of his house were so packed that he later wrote that not even a basket would have found "a vacancy" if it had been thrown out among them.[25] Although his appeal for funds to help rebuild the Triumphal Arch brought few contributions, Peale felt sure there was an audience for such spectacles. Soon after the second exhibition of the arch, he read descriptions in the newspapers of "moving pictures" created by the British stage designer Philippe de Loutherbourg. Here was a new way to reach the public that his experiences with transparencies and his technical skills made feasible. And, because of the large crowds who had come to witness his displays, Peale was convinced that he would receive the patronage of the citizenry. He immediately set to work creating his own "moving pictures."

Peale's *Perspective Views with Changeable Effects; or, Nature Delineated, and in Motion* contained five scenes and lasted about two hours. *Night* portrayed buildings in the countryside, which were gradually illuminated with the coming of dawn. *A Street* reversed the process: opening at twilight, the scene moved to darkness, and then lighted lamps revealed the pavement and houses. Peale's third scene, *A Grand Piece of*

Fig. p. Lester Hoadley Sellers. A Reconstruction of Peale's transparent Triumphal Arch of 1783–84

To celebrate the general sense of joy felt by Pennsylvania at the news of peace, on December 2, 1783, the General Assembly of the state commissioned Peale to erect a Triumphal Arch embellished with "illuminated paintings and suitable inscriptions" and to prepare "some fireworks . . . for the occasion." When the opening salvo of rockets went off too close to the highly inflammable structure, the entire arch was suddenly blown upward in a roaring fire that killed the artilleryman in charge and seriously burned others, including Peale. Peale reconstructed the paintings, and five months later, in May, 1784, the arch was illuminated without fireworks to a huge and expectant crowd.

   The paintings were stored in the library of the Statehouse (Independence Hall), but afterwards moved by the artist Robert Edge Pine to the steeple when Pine was given the privilege of using the space as his painting room. This was done "without the knowledge of Peale," according to the dismayed artist, who later found his paintings in the steeple, "totally destroyed." Sellers's drawing is based on descriptions in contemporary newspapers and in Peale's autobiography. (*American Philosophical Society*)

Architecture, utilized his Temple of Independence, now transformed into a Roman edifice around which raged a thunderstorm, followed by a rainbow and returning sunshine. His fourth scene dramatically climaxed the show. Taking his subject from Milton's *Paradise Lost*, Peale created a fire-and-smoke-filled vision of *Pandaemonium* and then arranged to have Milton's verses chanted along with some of his own composition in a musical accompaniment that added to the terror and sublimity of the experience. To close on a tranquil note, the artist painted a pastoral scene of *Vandering's Mill*, a well known and picturesque area located near the Falls of the Schuylkill, the tumbling waterfall and placid river conveying a sense of good cheer and optimism. Later, Peale added a naval battle that honored the exploits of the daring American commander John Paul Jones and his *Bonne Homme Richard* in conflict with the British vessel the *Serapis*. This appeared after *Pandaemonium*, in order to maintain the high level of excitement before the final unwinding of tension with *Vandering's Mill*.

Peale continued to show his moving pictures from 1785 to 1787, and then intermittently. In 1790, when interest in them had diminished and he himself began to concentrate his efforts on his museum, he sold the panels to a traveling showman. The moving pictures had not brought the income Peale had hoped for but they had served a purpose. His painting room and gallery had now become popular attractions in Philadelphia, and the way was prepared for his museum enterprise. What was important for Peale himself, the moving pictures—what he later called "the management of light"—had given him important experience in reaching the public that would add immeasurably to his success as a museum proprietor.[26]

In 1782, Peale built a long gallery onto his house in order to provide exhibition space for his portraits of "distinguished characters in the revolutionary war." By this time, Peale had found a new—and more significant—purpose for his collection, a purpose derived from the changing nature of republican ideology. During the war, as American statesmen had become involved in the writing of state constitutions and the establishment of governments that would "preserve our liberties inviolate," they began to debate questions involving the nature of representation and the sources of power. An important idea that emerged from this debate was the conviction that the success of a self-governing state lay in the character and spirit of the people, in their capacity for virtue and benevolence. Republican rhetoric began to call not for individual freedom so much as for the sacrifice of self-interest for the larger good, and it established service to the public as the highest contribution of the individual. Prescribing such values as frugality, moderation, industry, and simplicity, this new civic republicanism looked forward to a harmonious society based on benevolence and good will, and offered as the reward for disinterested service and virtuous behavior the approval of posterity. Such ideas were grist to Peale's mill: they fired his idealism and appealed to his preference for peace and his desire to serve his country.[27]

Peale came to believe that his portraits served the national interest. The men he portrayed were, he was convinced, visual embodiments of republican ideals; in their public service they had demonstrated the important republican principle that the happiness of the individual is attached to the happiness of mankind, and that man is under obligation to exert himself for the general good because his own depends on it. By presenting portraits of these eminent men to the public and providing models for emulation, Peale believed that he was sowing "the seed of Virtue" and influencing the development of a "benevolent" national character.[28] So that viewers would come to know "the history that produced . . . such distinction," he affixed biographical labels to his portraits. From such a recitation of the deeds of men of "superior endowments & deserving of high estimation, not only for their talents, but also for their having raised themselves, even from obscurity to their present high standing," visitors would also learn "benevolence"—the mutual concern that citizens of a republic must feel for each other and that theorists posited as essential to the success of republican government.[29] Peale did not limit his roster of great men to Americans. Always cosmopolitan in his interests, he included portraits of deserving Europeans—statesmen, writers, artists, and scientists.

Peale's gallery portraits are painted in a simple neoclassic style on the assumption that the sitters' virtues were apparent in their physical features. The sitters were representative types: *Benjamin Franklin* (No. 140), the versatile and practical scientist and diplomat, very much of this world; *George Washington* (No. 141), the civilian leader, noble and dignified, unblemished, and absolutely virtuous, stern, serious, but kindly; *Thomas Jefferson* (No. 142), the energetic thinker, hair electric with the intellectual energy that Peale perceived in him in this first sitting; *Baron von Steuben* (No. 29) and *(Baron) Johann de Kalb* (No. 31), strong and determined military geniuses; *Major Stephen H. Long* (No. 129), *Meriwether Lewis* (1807; Independence National Historical Park Collection), *William Clark* (1810; Independence National Historical Park Collection), and *Zebulon Pike* (1808; Independence National Historical Park Collection), intrepid and youthfully eager explorers of America's unknown frontiers; *William Bartram* (No. 144), kindly naturalist and investigator into nature's secrets; *Charles-Alexandre Lesueur* (No. 76), *Thomas Say* (No. 90), and *Gerard Troost* (No. 120), young and dedicated scientists; *Baron von Humboldt* (1805; College of Physicians of Philadelphia), aristocratic explorer of the South American wilderness; and *John Adams* (No. 143) and his son *John Quincy Adams* (No. 67), exemplars of republican statesmanship. In Peale's scheme of things, these were superior men whose capacity to create a civilization revealed the "wisdom and goodness of Beneficent God." "I love the art of painting," Peale wrote to Thomas Jefferson, "but the greatest merit of execution on subjects that have not a virtuous tendency lose all their value in my estimation."[30]

Peale's portrait gallery fulfilled his desire to be of service to his country while earning a livelihood. Republican idealism helped him to transform his youthful radicalism into a positive course of action; and in turning his art in the direction of public utility, Peale was able to justify to himself his role as an artist in the new republic. Now, as Peale turned to the study of natural history, he encountered still a new set

opposite:

140. BENJAMIN FRANKLIN. 1785

Peale first met Franklin in London in 1767 and always remained a respectful admirer. Over the years, Franklin aided Peale in a variety of ways. He was appreciative of Peale's personal efforts as an artist, and he enthusiastically supported the museum. Indeed, he was one of the first to present a specimen—the carcass of an angora cat. Franklin's stamp of approval long remained a silent encouragement to both American and European contributors to the museum.
Earlier Peale had copied David Martin's 1767 portrait of Franklin, but in 1785 he added a life portrait of the wise old man to his gallery of illustrious personages. Having concluded peace negotiations with Great Britain, Franklin arrived in Philadelphia on September 14, world famous, sick, old, very frail but with many great services to his country still to come. The portrait that Peale painted that autumn has the frankness and immediacy of Peale's documentary work. (*The Pennsylvania Academy of the Fine Arts*)

141. GEORGE WASHINGTON. 1795

In September, 1795, seventeen-year-old Rembrandt Peale was commissioned by the retiring director of the United States Mint, Chancellor Henry William De Saussure, to paint a portrait of the president. The elder Peale, wanting to assist his son in his first important commission, made arrangements with Washington for the sitting. Peale then joined Rembrandt and Washington in the painting room at Philosophical Hall in order to maintain a conversation with the president and ease the way for his shy son. Later, other Peales were admitted to the sittings: James Peale, who worked on a miniature; Raphaelle Peale, who took a profile drawing; and the young Titian Ramsay Peale I. The scene of the Peales painting in a circle around the famous man gave rise to Gilbert Stuart's pun that Washington was being "Pealed all round."

The elder Peale's idealized portrait of Washington the civilian leader, shown here, reflects the artist's increased awareness of Washington's meaning for the new republic. The contrast with Rembrandt Peale's more realistic portrait made at the same sitting is striking (Fig. q). Not so much concerned with accuracy, Charles Willson Peale has caught here Washington's restraint and intelligence. His portrait is a classic and forceful expression of republican virtues. (*The New-York Historical Society*)

142. THOMAS JEFFERSON. 1791

Peale painted Thomas Jefferson's portrait for the museum in December of 1791. "I have a great desire to exert my best abilities in this portrait," he wrote in arranging the sitting, and with this informal, lively pose, Peale reflects much of his deep feeling for the man. Jefferson, as Secretary of State, then resided in Philadelphia, where he gave important support to Peale's Museum as chairman of its Board of Visitors. The two men saw each other occasionally, at American Philosophical Society meetings for example, and laid the foundation of a continuing friendship. When he became president of the United States, Jefferson arranged that important western specimens be placed in the museum. On January 26, 1802, in response to an inquiry from Peale asking whether the U.S. would provide for the establishment of his museum in Washington, Jefferson wrote: "No person on earth can entertain a higher idea than I do of the value of your collection nor give you more credit for the unwearied perseverance and skill with which you have prosecuted it, and I very much wish it could be made public property." Disappointingly he held little hope for Peale's plans. (*Independence National Historical Park Collection*)

143. JOHN ADAMS. 1791–94

The exact date of Peale's portrait of the brilliant, yet difficult, New England lawyer who left a permanent impression on the early history of the American republic is unknown. This painting shows him as vice-president during George Washington's two administrations, from 1788 to 1796. While serving as a delegate to the Continental Congress, Adams visited Peale's painting room in August, 1776. He described the artist to his wife, Abigail, as "a tender, soft, affectionate Creature. . . . He has a Variety of Portraits—very well done. But not so well as Copeleys Portraits. Copeley is the greatest Master, that ever was in America. His Portraits far exceed Wests. . . . He [Peale] is ingenious. He has Vanity—loves Finery—Wears a sword—gold lace—speaks French—is capable of Friendship, and strong Family Attachments and natural Affections." (*Independence National Historical Park Collection*)

144. WILLIAM BARTRAM. 1808

At a later stage of history, William Bartram would have been a botanist on the staff of a great agricultural or horticultural institute, but in Bartram's time none such existed, at least in America. He derived his botanical training from his father, John Bartram, whom he accompanied on travels in East Florida. From 1773 to 1778 he traveled widely in the southern colonies and his account of these experiences, published in 1791 as "Travels through North and South Carolina, Georgia, East and West Florida, the Cherokee Country, the extensive Territories of the Muskogee or Creek Confederacy, and the Country of the Choctaws," was an early romantic masterpiece that profoundly impressed his generation and those to come.

Peale was indebted to Bartram for providing specimens to the museum, and it is surprising that this portrait of the grand old man of botany was not added to the gallery of distinguished men until 1808. The flower in Bartram's lapel, long a subject of speculation, has been identified as *Jasminium officinale*, a white flowered vine of the South. (*Independence National Historical Park Collection*)

of ideas and ideals that expanded his social thought while providing him with exciting intellectual discoveries.

Peale was fifty years old in 1791 when he revived his earlier plan of transforming his picture gallery into a museum and creating therein "A world in Miniature." In fact, the initial idea of forming a museum was accidental: the seed had been planted by his brother-in-law, Nathaniel Ramsay, who admired Peale's drawings of fossil bones. The museum developed gradually, from a simple display of these sketches and a dried paddlefish to a more elaborate exhibition of stuffed birds, minerals, and mammals. As the number of specimens increased, Peale found it necessary to learn more about natural history. He had, in particular, to find an organizing scheme for the arrangement of his specimens.

The artist, characteristically unfazed by his ignorance of the field of natural history and the enormousness of the task he had undertaken, set about learning all he could absorb from available literature. He ransacked the shelves of the Library Company of Philadelphia and the American Philosophical Society, to which he had been elected in 1786. He incorporated his newfound world of nature into his domestic life: animals, plants, and minerals lodged with his large family in the same building; his honeymoon with his second wife, Elizabeth DePeyster, became a bird-hunting expedition; the museum became his children's school. His study of natural history strengthened his desire for harmony in the conduct of life, pointed out the best way to achieve health and domestic happiness, and influenced him as a social philosopher, a landscape gardener, and a public educator. When Peale returned to painting, it was with renewed enthusiasm for the intricacies as well as the beauties of nature. His art profited from this new interest: he now painted some of his most beautiful portraits; he created a highly imaginative historical work based upon his discoveries in natural history—*The Exhumation of the Mastodon* (No. 54); and he discovered the delight of painting landscapes. The study of nature also alerted Peale to the possibilities of American culture and transformed him into a citizen of the world.

In 1799, Peale offered a series of lectures on natural history (No. 145). In these, he explained his conception of the civic significance of a museum and his attitude toward current theories concerning the creation of the world, the organization of the great chain of being, and the condition of species. He expected that his lectures would entice patrons into his exhibition; but, as in all Peale enterprises, the practical was mixed with the idealistic. By teaching the uses and beauties of nature and illustrating through examples from nature how society could organize itself properly, he also hoped to be "useful to mankind."[31]

Peale was convinced that harmony and order ruled in nature, and would rule in human society once man learned nature's principles. "To shew the harmony of Creation, Manifested in the particular construction of such a variety of Creatures, so wonderfully and happily adapted to their several stations in life, and to draw from them and their economy, such moral reflections as may help to correct our errors," lectured Peale, "is certainly deserving the countenance and aid of every denomination of Men—political and religious."[32]

Peale's method was to describe animal life in terms of human characteristics—a

145. Peale's draft for an introductory lecture on natural history. 1799. (*Academy of Natural Sciences of Philadelphia*)

Introductory Lecture

With an ardent desire of rendering myself useful to my Country, I undertake works perhaps of greater magnitude than may be thought perfectly prudent for an Individual of my years; — means of support; — and mental powers.

But when is felt so much pleasure in the contemplation of the wonderful works of an all-wise Creator! — Can I leave any difficulty untryed to display those beauties which in every step we take, unfold scenes that ought to lead us to adore that finger which directs a Universe?

Grant thou divine architect strength to these nerves; — light to this mind enabling

common approach to zoology in the eighteenth century. "The female Bear and the She Wolf," he explained, "are both cowardly Animals, yet when they have their young, affection . . . is so powerful, that no Animal can exceed their intrepidity to defend, or care to support their offspring."[33] Similar parental concern was also ascribed to the bat, the wolf, the sea lion, and various species of monkeys. The dog he described as "constant in his affections, friendly without interest, and grateful for the slightest favors . . . his only hope to be serviceable, his only terror to displease."[34] The orangutan "possessed a considerable share of modesty," and was temperate ("spontaneously left its [wine] for milk, tea, or other mild liquors"); "gratitude" was the most prominent feature in the character of the elephant;[35] and the talapoin monkey had "extremely gentle manners . . . may indeed by called a handsome Monkey." The sight of the animal, however, encouraged him to reflect on the "blessings " of "gentle Manners," which "whether joined to a handsome figure or not . . . not only gives peace and comfort to the Possessor, but distributes happiness to all around; it disarms the passionate; puts an end to strife and its baneful consequences, and *sometimes* arrests the direful purposes of *Madmen*."[36]

The study of animal life meant more to Peale than simply a means of teaching people how to live, although that, of course, was a major purpose behind his lectures. By comparing animal development and behavior he became aware, he said, of how they were all part of "the same chain . . . extended by such small gradations from Animal to Animal throughout the Earth, Sea, and Air, and even from animal to vegetable beings, and still a further continued series from thence throughout all Nature's productions; manifesting the most perfect *order* in the works of a great *Creator*—who's ways are wisdom, her paths are peace, harmony and Love."[37]

Peale believed this "scale of connection" was very important: recognition of it and of the "variety and progression which reign in the Universe" elevated the mind and revealed the perfection of God.[38] Admitting that an understanding of nature's processes was valuable to the farmer, the merchant, and the mechanic for practical reasons, Peale insisted that the most important lessons man could derive from nature were moral. He reiterated again and again that man had to learn from animals, whether from the "perfect harmony" that prevailed within species which did not wage war against their own kind, or from the "models" animals provided "of friendship, constancy, parental care, and every other social virtue."[39]

In the conduct of his own family life, Peale did not need the lessons animals provided. He had always felt strongly about family harmony and the importance of shared interests. Sometime in the early 1770s, he had begun a group portrait (No. 146) which reflected these sentiments. In *The Peale Family* he pictured his desire to share his artistic skills with other members of the family, an effort that ultimately succeeded in launching his brother James Peale (No. 147) on a fairly prosperous career as a miniature painter. Peale also patiently taught the sons of his first wife painting and preserving techniques, educating them in the two areas of his greatest competence. While he demonstrated, he worked alongside them to show the way and serve as model. Indeed, to help Rembrandt succeed in his first commission—a portrait of President Washington (Fig. q)—he joined the seventeen-year-old artist in the painting room, maintaining conversation with the great man so that the awestruck boy could continue with his work. Rubens's interest in botany made him the perfect candidate for museum work, as did Titian Ramsay I's interest in insects; while Raphaelle's artistic genius was constantly encouraged despite the young man's wayward nature and propensity for alcohol.

By the time Peale was faced with the raising of his second family, he had begun to define parental concern as a dictate of nature. Parents, he now believed, were obligated to train their children for life in the same way that the cat, the monkey, the sea lion, and other mammals prepared their offspring for independent existence. Although the actual effect of this insight on the training and deportment of his children does not seem to have been much different from that which had followed his earlier, more spontaneous, program, his new understanding made it possible for him to place his parental anxieties within a manageable framework.

Rather than simply absorbing his younger sons into his own artistic and scientific enterprises, as he had the older boys, Peale now planned their education more deliberately. He decided that each should receive a different kind of training to avoid competition with each other; and "to make them good and useful members of society"—a goal that involved for Peale moral as well as practical education—he apprenticed them to a manufacturer of machinery in the belief that machines offered the best opportunities for young men in the new republic.[40] When Franklin and Linnaeus were ready to establish their own enterprise—a cotton factory—he assisted them by providing them with a building and land at "Belfield," his retirement farm. He even traded a portrait for raw cotton to help them get started. Unfortunately, the Peale cotton manufactory could not produce sufficiently cheap cotton to compete successfully, although Peale boasted that the yarn the young men manufactured was of the highest quality.[41] This training was not wasted on Franklin who, as chief coiner in the United States Mint at a later date, eventually profited from it. Linnaeus's career, however, took a disappointing direction. The rebellious son joined the United States Cavalry much against his father's pacifist principles, and later engaged in local politics on behalf of Andrew Jackson's democracy.

Peale's plans for Titian Ramsay Peale II, his youngest son, were more in line with his own interests, but that was because the young man shared them. Recognizing Titian's artistic and scientific talents, his father encouraged him both to assist in the museum and to develop his career as an illustrator (see Nos. 84, 93). To this younger son, Peale poured out his philosophy of nature and the moral good to be derived from observation of natural phenomena. "The true Naturalist," he wrote Titian, now far away from home with the Long exploring expedition, if he gave his attention to "the sustenance afforded millions of organized beings" would not want piety, "not with all these Monitors before his Eyes in all places. Certainly not, if possessing reasoning faculties."[42]

Peale did not neglect his daughters' education either. He was convinced that women

overleaf:

146. THE PEALE FAMILY. c. 1770–73 and 1808

The largest and most ambitious of Peale's conversation pieces, this group was begun in Annapolis for exhibition in Peale's gallery. John Adams admired it when he visited Peale's painting room in Philadelphia on August 20, 1776, finding in the family faces "a pleasant, a happy cheerfulness" and "a familiarity in their air towards each other." Unable to complete the work at that time, Peale retained it until 1808, when he decided to finish it and incorporate it into the museum collection.
    The theme is the warm affection uniting the family. The actual subject is a drawing lesson which Peale is giving to his brother, St. George. In the group portrait, Charles, standing at his easel, bends over St. George to see the drawing his brother is making of their mother, who sits across the table and holds Peale's young daughter Eleanor (1770–c. 1772). Next to St. George is James Peale and beside him is Charles's wife, Rachel Brewer, holding on the table before her baby Margaret, born in January, 1772, and destined to die before the year was out; at the right is Peale's sister, Elizabeth Digby. Standing next to Charles is another, older sister, Margaret Jane (Jenny), while at the right is the family's old beloved nurse, Peggy Durgan. In the revisions of 1808, Peale united the three central figures more clearly, added the dog Argus, and thinking the design sufficient to explain the theme, painted out the words *Concordia Animae* which he had formerly written on the canvas. The busts on the shelf behind, inscribed from left to right *B. West*, *C. W. Peale*, and *E. Jenings*, were sculpted by Peale while in London. (*The New-York Historical Society*)

147. James Peale Painting a Miniature. 1795

Throughout his life, Charles Willson Peale maintained a protective attitude toward his brother James, a gentle and somewhat retiring artist. James, like his brother, had been trained as a saddler, and later became a framemaker. When Charles returned from his studies in England, he taught James the art of painting in miniature. In 1786, the two brothers decided to divide the Philadelphia market between them, Charles to paint portraits in oil and James to work in miniature. A broadside circulated throughout Philadelphia announced their prices. Although this division of labor was not strictly adhered to, James did tend to specialize in miniature painting after 1786. This portrait of him by Charles recognizes James's proficiency in the art and his well-established reputation in what once had been Charles Willson Peale's favorite branch of painting. (*Amherst College, Mead Art Museum*)

possessed capacities of a greater depth and intensity than men and were capable of brilliant achievement if their minds were not occupied by "affairs which allow no time for them to devote to the arduous pursuits of science."[43] He warned his daughter Elizabeth when she went off to school in Wilmington, "never to return an injury for an injury" and to ignore the unpleasant behavior of others toward her if she were not responsible for it. Calling her attention to vegetable and animal creation, which "becomes luxurent and fine for use" and "strait and beautiful . . . with kind usage," he compared the cultivation of her talents with the cultivation of natural objects, urged modesty and industry, and encouraged her to "do the best you can according to your abilities."[44]

Peale's desire to educate others in the lessons he had absorbed from his study of natural history extended beyond his family. "Visiting a friend in the City," he reminisced in his autobiography, "he [Peale] observed that he [the 'friend'] had been too often at the side-board, and that his wife seemed rather careless in her attentions to him, and under the impression that some advice to her might have a tendency to make her change her manners . . . and by practising a more tender and affectionate marriage, be the means of some reform in him, he thought that by writing a letter of some length to her that it would be a more effectual mode to induce her to think more seriously on their situation. . . ."[45]

That letter turned into *An Essay to Promote Domestic Happiness*, which he distributed to his friends and sold in the museum. The pamphlet, wrote Thomas Jefferson to the author, "is full of good sence and wholesome advice, and I am making all

Fig. q. Rembrandt Peale. GEORGE WASHING-TON. 1795. Oil on canvas. National Portrait Gallery, Smithsonian Institution, Washington, D.C.

my grandchildren read it, married and unmarried, and the story of farmer Jenkins will I hope remain on their minds through life."[46]

Where Peale obtained the Farmer Jenkins poem that he included in the *Essay* is not clear; in the spirit of Thomas Heywood's *A Woman Killed with Kindness* (1603), the humorous verses told the story of the farmer and his wife who argued over "the very silliest of things in life"—in this case, whether the starling was a thrush—even though they knew that "it was idle and absurd/To wrangle so about a bird." In essence, the poem summarized the *Essay*'s message: that marriage is "a social bond" which had to be conducted as any other social activity designed to promote "harmony, industry, and the wealth of the nation"; that it requires patience and prudence and good humor, and in particular, love, to succeed. Peale warned married couples against indulgence in alcohol, which produced the greatest amount of unhappiness and degraded the individual "below the brutes," and advised that the wife of a drunkard should treat her husband as a sick person if he was to reform. After pointing out the duties of husband and wife toward each other, he recommended for a happy marriage good society, cheerful manners, interesting conversation, prudent living, healthy living, industry, and sensible dress. "Being happy ourselves," he concluded, "we shall rejoice in the happiness of others."[47]

Peale enjoyed finding examples of such domestic happiness in the family pictures he was asked to paint. Mr. and Mrs. James Gittings (No. 149), he was pleased to report, were so fond of each other that he decided to paint the old couple holding hands. The scene is completely integrated: the grandparents' affection for their grandchild is related to nature through the squirrel which the child holds and through their relation to the stretch of land extending from themselves into the distance. The "happy slaves" harvesting the wheat in a sunny and peaceful landscape carry out the idea of "great order and quiet" that Peale sensed existed "in the government of the family."[48] The portrait, in effect, symbolizes the contentment and harmony emanating from domestic happiness.

The Peale Family (No. 146), *Self-Portrait with Angelica and a Portrait of Rachel* (No. 153), *Mrs. Charles Peale with Her Grandchildren* (No. 154), *Thomas McKean and His Son* (No. 155), *William Smith and His Grandson* (No. 156), the *Robert Goldsborough Family* (No. 157), *Mrs. John Nicholson and Son* (No. 158), and *Mrs. Alexander Robinson and Her Daughter* (No. 160)—all reflect this same idea of harmony derived from mutual love and respect. The theme is most clearly revealed in *The Peale*

opposite:

148. Titian Ramsay Peale I. PAPELIO [BUTTERFLY]. 1796

Titian Ramsay Peale I (1780–1798) was the fourth surviving child of Charles Willson Peale and his first wife, Rachel Brewer Peale. The boy early demonstrated interest and skill in natural history and art, and became his father's close companion. He assisted his father at the museum and accompanied him on bird-hunting expeditions. In 1796 the young Titian began a work called "Drawings of American Insects," for which he drew in watercolor illustrations such as this butterfly. He died of yellow fever in September, 1798, in New York. (*National Agricultural Library*)

149. Mr. and Mrs. James Gittings and Granddaughter. 1791

One of Peale's most delightful family portraits, this work was painted on commission from
Colonel Gittings's son, Richard, whose wedding portrait Peale had painted in 1788. Museum
affairs and the death of Peale's wife Rachel in 1790 and his mother in May, 1791, prevented him
from fulfilling the commission; but after his second marriage, he completed the work. Now
steeped in his own newfound happiness, he was sensitive to the "apparent fondness of this old
couple," which gave him "the thought of this point of the action": the grandparents hold hands
while their grandchild plays with a ground squirrel. Mr. Gittings's grist mill and extensive wheat
fields appear in the view on the left, suggesting the "rich valley where [Mr. Gittings] has all the
blessings that a country life can afford." Even the slaves harvesting the wheat share in the
contentment of the farm, which emanates from its "great order and quiet." (*The Peale Museum*)

Family, which Peale had originally called *Concordia Animae*. Indeed, he had included
the words in the painting, removing them only to allow "the design to tell the object."[49]
"Happiness," Peale wrote in his autobiography in commenting on his second marriage,
"is a plant of tender growth."[50] Peale's sense of the organic nature of family life—the
relation between family affection and nature—is apparent in these family pieces and
particularly in his paintings of *The Stewart Children* (No. 162) and *The Stoddert
Children* (No. 163), where landscape flows naturally around and extends from the
children, becoming the binding element in the composition.

Peale's study of nature also provided him with ideas concerning health and prompted
him to devise or adapt inventions for adding comfort or physical well-being to man's
experiences. In 1803, he published a slim pamphlet called *An Epistle to a Friend, on the
Means of Preserving Health, Promoting Happiness; and Prolonging the Life of Man to*

its Natural Period. Being a Summary View of Inconsiderate and Useless Habits that Derange the System of Nature, thereby causing Premature Old Age and Death. With Some Thoughts on the Best Means of Preventing and Overcoming Disease (No. 164). The publication had begun as a letter to President Thomas Jefferson and was originally intended to suggest to the president, whom Peale had learned was "indisposed," how he should take care of himself in his "new building" in Washington, which might not be as dry and warm as was necessary for good health. "A logg-hut," advised Peale, "is better than a new Pallace." As his letter advanced, however, Peale found the subject more and

150. THOMAS JOHNSON FAMILY. 1772

Thomas Johnson was one of Maryland's leading spirits in opposing parliamentary efforts to tax the colonies. Together with Charles Carroll, Barrister (No. 1), Samuel Chase, and William Paca (No. 7) he argued for colonial autonomy and helped form a "Bill of Rights" for Maryland. As a member of the Continental Congress, he served on three of its most important committees and nominated George Washington as commander in chief of the army. John Adams wrote of him that he had a "clear and cool Head, and possessed an extensive Knowledge of Trade as well as Law." In 1777, he was elected the first governor of the state of Maryland and in 1791, a justice of the Supreme Court.

Peale's portrait, painted before these active years, shows the successful lawyer with his wife, Ann Jennings, and their three eldest children, Thomas, Ann, and Rebecca, who died in childhood. This may be the only time in colonial portraiture that a man was painted wearing clothes popular at the time in England—the Van Dyck costume. (*Private collection*)

151. MRS. SAMUEL CHASE AND HER DAUGHTERS MATILDA CHASE AND ANNE CHASE. 1772–75

Anne Baldwin (c. 1743–1778) married the fiery and impetuous lawyer and politician, Samuel Chase, on May 21, 1762. She is shown here with her two daughters, Matilda and Anne, who takes a peach from the basket held by her older sister. (*Maryland Historical Society*)

152. Mrs. James Smith [Mrs. Patrick Campbell] and Grandson. 1776

Although Peale referred to her in his portrait lists and diary as Mrs. James Smith (b. 1719), she had already married her second husband, Patrick Campbell, when Peale began her portrait on September 15, 1776. His commission came from her son William Smith—which undoubtedly accounts for the artist's confusion about her name. The young boy, Campbell Smith (1768–1804), whose name honored his step-grandfather, later became an officer in the Philadelphia city cavalry (1792–1802); here he is portrayed studying "Hamlet's Soliloquy" in the popular manual of oratorical training, *The Art of Speaking*.

The portrait does not reveal Peale's anxieties at the time concerning reports of an engagement between British troops and Americans in New York, nor his fears of a possible British invasion of Philadelphia. Instead, its emphasis on parental affection and the peaceful art of literature bespeaks his constant interest in familial harmony and shared pleasures. (*National Museum of American Art, Smithsonian Institution*)

153. Self-Portrait with Angelica and a Portrait of Rachel. c. 1782–85

Peale's self-portrait with his wife and daughter was designed to be symbolic as well as sentimental. Angelica, who had painted as a young girl, is shown taking the brush from her father's hand while she points upward to heaven, the source of her beauty and talent. He has made her here the embodiment of the concept of posterity that was so important to Peale and his contemporaries: Angelica is portrayed as the beneficiary of her mother's beauty and character and her father's artistic talent. (*The Museum of Fine Arts, Houston*)

154. The Artist's Mother, Mrs. Charles Peale, with Her Grandchildren. c. 1783

No portrait illustrates more clearly than this the distance that Peale had traveled artistically from the preceding generation of portrait painters in America. John Wollaston and John Hesselius (see Fig. a) left us images of impersonal dignity in stiff, formal poses. In this charming group portrait, Peale presents, in an easy and informal way, his sense of a vibrant life and of the relationship between childhood and age. The children are absorbed in their own world of play; the enfolding affection of the grandmother belongs to another world of feeling. The children are traditionally identified as Raphaelle (at upper left), Angelica (in dark blue), and Rembrandt (in yellow). (*Private collection*)

155. THOMAS MCKEAN AND HIS SON, THOMAS, JR. 1787

Statesman, signer, lawyer—this tall, forceful, hot-tempered man played a dominant role in Pennsylvania for nearly half a century; and such was the uncertainty of American society that at one time he represented Delaware in Congress while serving as Chief Justice of Pennsylvania. When this portrait was painted, he was a member of the Constitutional Convention and a strong advocate of the new federal government. Later, he supported Jefferson and served as governor of Pennsylvania during the Virginian's presidency.

Still under the influence of the imagery of his various transparencies, Peale could not resist adding to this double portrait the symbol of Justice with scales and sword, teetering on the edge of a rooftop; beside the Chief Justice may be found the papers and law books of his profession. As in so many of Peale's family pictures of this period, the son represents both the tender sentiment of parental affection and posterity. (*Philadelphia Museum of Art*)

more "interesting" and, as he wrote, was "naturally led to reflections that were not necessary to communicate to the person it was intended for."

Nature, Peale wrote, dictated simplicity in living habits, temperance, and exercise as the basis for good health. "Wantonly to destroy our intellects" by overindulgence "was a crime." Yet, despite all that has been said or written on the subject, "some men will be thus mad." His essay, then, was to "inform [those] that are disposed to think, and thus do good."[51]

Peale's "inventions" for improving health were as practical as his publications. Not entirely original with him, most of his devices were adaptations of inventions he had either read about in newspapers or of which he had seen models. His fertile mind, however, and his unremitting industriousness, combined with an imagination that immediately perceived the uses to which machinery could be put, urged him on to develop these devices and make them available to friends and relatives who might profit from them. "Anything," he reported in his autobiography, "which he conceived would be beneficial or conducive to health, he has never regarded the cost or trouble to have executed."[52] Thus, the vapor or steam bath was suggested to him by Dr. Joseph Priestley, who had seen one in a London hospital (No. 165); the fan chair was the invention of the "very Ingenious Mr. Cram (Musical Instrument Maker)"; the Draisiana —a bicycle without pedals—was invented by a German named Drais and adapted by a Baltimore musical instrument maker named Stewart (No. 166); the kitchen equipment had been developed by Count Rumford (Benjamin Thompson); but to all of these, Peale added his own ingenious constructions and somehow made them his own.

The fan chair (No. 167), for instance, he had undoubtedly suggested to Cram, who developed it for him. The idea of the chair reflects the simplicity and ingenuity of his inventive mind and also his sense of how "very useful" it could be to "the studious and others that are oblig'd to sitt at their Imployments, for while their hands are busily imployed, a small motion of the foot will moove the fan in such manner as to keep them cool and with some cutings of paper fastened to the fan will prevent the flies from being troublesome." This simple machine, he pointed out to the members of the American Philosophical Society, to whom he submitted a drawing of Cram's design, would be "conducive to the health of the sedentry . . . and relieve the distress's of humane nature."[53]

The Draisiana, or velocipede, provided exercise and facilitated movement over long distances without "incuring much fateague." Peale called it a "fast walker" and experimented with the materials out of which it was constructed as well as its design in order to lighten the load so that it would "go without labour uphill" and to improve its management so as to prevent accidents.[54]

Peale developed the kitchen equipment after reading of the experiments of Count Rumford, who had attempted to break down the large open fireplace into many small and easily regulated stoves and who had also refined the design of cooking pots to make them more efficient. Peale had always been concerned with the wastefulness of the large American fireplace, with its inefficient use of fuel.[55] Stimulated by the newspaper articles announcing Rumford's work, he designed and built a similar stove for his own use. "To prepare our food for giving the most nourishment," he wrote to President Jefferson; "to construct the cooking utensil with such forms as will lessen labours, ward

off danger, ensure cleanlyness, command the power of fire, and economise fuel, are certainly aspects of no little consequences to the Citizens of America." [56] Soon afterward, he offered to design and build such a stove for the Pennsylvania Hospital, actually designed a fireplace and kitchen stove for the New York Alms House, and continued to urge his model on the many visitors who frequented his kitchen to see "the ease and economy of our cooking." [57]

Perhaps Peale's most original adaptation of inventions for health involved his experiments with the making of porcelain false teeth. From middle life on, he had been concerned with the making of artificial teeth for himself and his family and had tried different materials—ivory, sea-cow teeth, sea-horse teeth. Finding that these were subject to quick decay "and thus become offensive besides the great loss of time," he searched for a harder substance, trying the teeth of horses, cows, and hogs, which he cut down and fitted to the human mouth. Since all animal substances were liable to decay, however, he decided to try porcelain. He read as much about the process of manufacturing porcelain as he could and visited nearby potteries in Philadelphia, where he received advice and instruction as well as materials. For two years, Peale experimented with different materials, glazes, and fuels for the furnace, working at the process until he

opposite:

156. WILLIAM SMITH AND HIS GRANDSON. 1788

The portrait of William Smith, a successful Baltimore merchant, and his grandson was painted on commission from Gen. Otho Holland Williams, Smith's son-in-law (No. 30). Both men were active supporters of the constitution in Maryland, and in the autumn of 1788, Smith was elected to represent the state in the first Congress of the United States. To symbolize Smith's role in the founding of the new government, Peale painted him seated before a stately classical structure. Smith was also a devoted family man, who asked to be painted with his two-year-old grandson, Robert Smith Williams. The little boy is shown holding a peach from Smith's farm and a hat with a great ostrich feather. The double portrait represents the ideal of parental affection as well as Peale's concept of posterity. Smith's other interests are indicated on the marble-topped table: a peach-tree branch, a pruning hook, and several books: *Gardening*, James Thomson's *Seasons*, John Milton's poetry, and James Beattie's *Essays on Trust* (1770).

The scene is Smith's country seat, "Eutaw," named for the battle of Eutaw Springs where General Williams at a critical moment led his regiment in a bayonet charge that won the victory. In his diary, Peale tells of riding out to "Eutaw" with General Williams to make drawings with his "painter's quadrant" (No. 56), and this view of an eighteenth-century Maryland farm and mill is the result. (*Virginia Museum*)

overleaf:

157. ROBERT GOLDSBOROUGH FAMILY. 1789

This family portrait is one of Peale's most complex, elegant, and decorative paintings. Judge Robert Goldsborough of "Myrtle Grove," Talbot County, Maryland, is shown with his wife (née Mary Emerson Trippe), thirteen-year-old daughter Elizabeth Greenberry, and ten-year-old son Robert Henry, later a United States Senator. The portrait is dated December 8, 1789. On July 26, 1791, the artist returned to "Myrtle Grove" to repaint the flesh tones, which had faded as a result of the turpeth mineral color Peale had experimented with. On this return trip, Peale probably added the bust of President Washington that looks down over the family group in the background —a symbol, perhaps, of the judge's strong admiration for the first president. (*Private collection*)

opposite:

158. MRS. JOHN NICHOLSON AND SON JOHN, JR. 1790

This young woman, shown holding her lively baby boy, was born Hannah Duncan. She was married to Philadelphia businessman John Nicholson, who from 1782 to 1794 was comptroller general of Pennsylvania. During this period, Nicholson was one of the wealthiest men of the day, owning about 3,700,000 acres of land in Pennsylvania. Later, as a partner of Robert Morris in disastrous speculations, Nicholson failed and was sent to debtor's prison, where he died in 1800. His widow was left with eight children and debts of more than $4,000,000. She moved to New Orleans with the son shown in this portrait to begin a new life. (*The Art Institute of Chicago*)

159. ALEXANDER ROBINSON AND HIS WIFE, ANGELICA PEALE. 1795

In 1794, Angelica Kauffman Peale, the artist's daughter, married Alexander Robinson, an English-born businessman who was stiff, vain, and snobbish and who disliked everything about his father-in-law—his picture-painting, bird-collecting, and museum-keeping.

This portrait was painted shortly before the birth of the couple's first child. Peale's diary account of the sitting reflects the antagonism between the artist and his son-in-law: ". . . the situation of Angelica required that no time should be lost, as it was daily expected that she would be *in the straw*. . . . I had no difficulty with the portrait of my daughter, yet I found much with Mr. Robinson's portrait.

"I may say that I never found a more disagreeable business, altho' the object was certainly as much to oblige him as myself, yet he sat with a bad grace, and with very much labor I at last completed the original and made a copy unfinished and the face of Mr. Robinson not quite equal to the first, and was contented to have it so rather than plague a man who seemed to have so little disposition to give me a chance of doing justice to my reputation as a painter." (*Private collection*)

160. MRS. ALEXANDER ROBINSON AND HER DAUGHTER. 1818

To Peale's great unhappiness, his daughter Angelica's marriage cut her off from her family.
Although the Robinsons had settled in nearby Baltimore, Angelica rarely visited "Belfield"; but
when she did, her father painted portraits of her marked by an unusual tenderness, as if he felt the
separation keenly. Here she is shown with her thirteen-year-old daughter, Charlotte Ramsay,
already ill and fated to die the following year. The picture was hung in the seventh annual exhibition of the Pennsylvania Academy of the Fine Arts (1818) as "Portrait of a mother caressing her
convalescent child." The mood is tender, and the face of the child is one of Peale's most sensitive
and perceptive. (*Private collection*)

161. REMBRANDT PEALE. 1818

Rembrandt Peale, depicted here at the age of thirty, was Peale's third surviving child by his first wife, Rachel Brewer. A prolific and innovative artist in his own right, Rembrandt had developed a "new system of coloring for portrait and landscape painting" that Peale readily adapted when he actively resumed painting during the summer of 1818. Peale's absorption with this new discovery inspired him to rework a portrait he had earlier begun of Rembrandt. On August 9, 1818, Peale wrote to his son that by using orange and green hues to lighten his palette, he had eliminated the portrait's dark background, and now had decided to depict a "warm horizon and distant mountain and . . . a river and a cascade." No doubt reflecting his excitement over these promising techniques and thus his confidence in Rembrandt's artistic future, Peale described the revised portrait to his son as a "Prophetic Picture . . . emblematical that the evening of your days will be brighter than on former times." (*National Portrait Gallery, Smithsonian Institution*)

162. THE STEWART CHILDREN. 1770–75

Isabella and James Stewart were the children of Anthony Stewart, Tory owner of the brig *Peggy Stewart*, which he burned in Annapolis harbor just prior to the Revolution to prevent its capture by the rebellious Americans. The painting, one of a small group of conversation pieces that Peale executed during this period, probably accompanied the family in its exile to London, where it was recently discovered and identified. (*Thyssen-Bornemisza Collection*)

163. THE STODDERT CHILDREN. 1789

Benjamin Stoddert, officer in the Revolution, secretary to the Board of War under the Continental Congress, and later first Secretary of the Navy under President Adams, lived in a house overlooking the Potomac River in Georgetown, a village which he helped develop.

Peale probably visited the Stodderts in order to deliver to Mrs. Stoddert a miniature he had made of her mother, Elizabeth Tasker Lowndes. Mrs. Lowndes was mortally ill and had asked the artist to paint seven miniature portraits of her as parting gifts to her children. When he arrived at the Stoddert house on September 9, 1789, Stoddert and his wife commissioned a portrait of their three children—Benjamin, age seven, Elizabeth, age five, and Harriet, a baby five months old. The variety of age and size puzzled the artist at first, but he solved the problem by one of his most ingenious compositions. Benjamin is putting the baby in a go-cart, while Elizabeth, holding the pole, looks toward her brother; the whole forms a happy group united in a moment of fun. (*The National Society of The Colonial Dames of America*)

produced a satisfactory plate of porcelain teeth. The difficulty of making them and the time required concerned his children, who urged their elderly father to "do other works of less trouble, more pleasant, and more profitable." But Peale could not be stopped; he knew, he explained, "the vast advantage" of his manufactured teeth, and he found it "pleasant" to be able to assist others in the enjoyment of food and sweet breath. "Experience in overcoming difficulties in a variety of cases will ultimately free the road to perfection with less labor," he wrote. "Yet if he is to receive money as a reward, he will not be satisfied with that only, he claims their thanks in addition."[58]

Peale's desire to "improve" extended to other areas of human activity. The physiognotrace, an invention of the Englishman John Hawkins (No. 116), took profiles "in less than a minute." When the machine was lodged in Peale's Museum, however, Peale gave it a greater—an educational—significance: "Very few persons possess more than confined ideas of the lines of the faces even of their most intimate acquaintance," he wrote in the *Aurora* on July 11, 1803; "but by this happy contrivance, each individual can gain a critical knowledge of the lines composing the profiles of friends and acquaintances. To contemplate the immense variety of character in a collection of profiles taken with this machine, is a feast to the physiognomist and philosopher."[59]

The polygraph—another of Hawkins's inventions (No. 115)—appealed to the artist as a labor-saving device and convenience that rendered life "more comfortable," especially since it might encourage communication among family members, thereby promoting domestic harmony. Thus, he "neither spared labour or expense to *simplify the machinery*" so that it would be easily understood by all people "on the first sight of it." Capable of "multiplying copies of Writing or of Musick, etc.," the polygraph facilitated correspondence and business transactions.[60] Peale sold the machine to Jefferson and to Benjamin Henry Latrobe, the architect, among others. But Peale was particularly concerned that the ma-

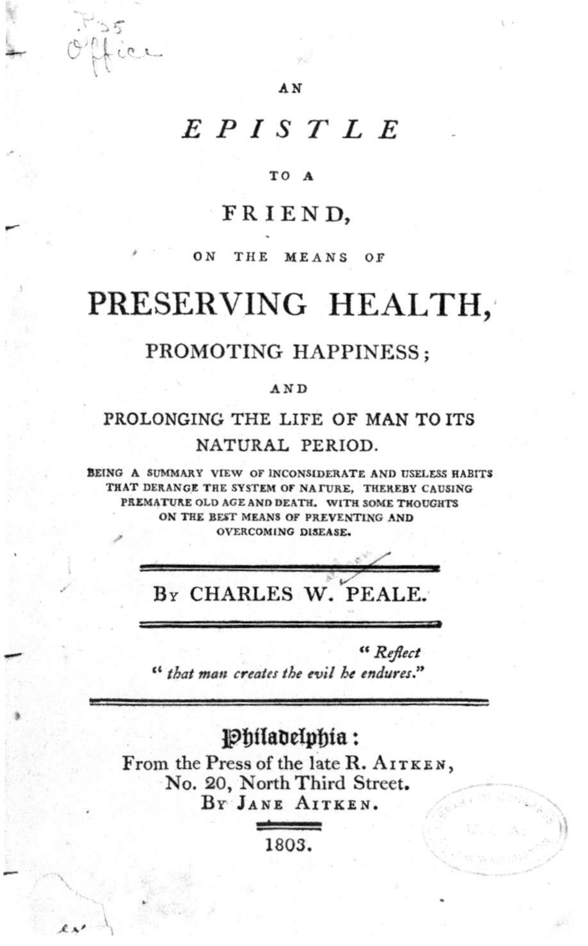

AN

EPISTLE

TO A

FRIEND,

ON THE MEANS OF

PRESERVING HEALTH,

PROMOTING HAPPINESS;

AND

PROLONGING THE LIFE OF MAN TO ITS
NATURAL PERIOD.

BEING A SUMMARY VIEW OF INCONSIDERATE AND USELESS HABITS
THAT DERANGE THE SYSTEM OF NATURE, THEREBY CAUSING
PREMATURE OLD AGE AND DEATH. WITH SOME THOUGHTS
ON THE BEST MEANS OF PREVENTING AND
OVERCOMING DISEASE.

By CHARLES W. PEALE.

" *Reflect*
" *that man creates the evil he endures.*"

Philadelphia:
From the Press of the late R. Aitken,
No. 20, North Third Street.
By Jane Aitken.

1803.

164. *An Epistle to a Friend.* 1803. Library of Congress

165. Drawing and description of the vapor bath. 1801

Peale developed his patent portable steam bath, or vapor bath, on the suggestion of Dr. Joseph Priestley, a politically radical English chemist who described to Peale how a similar apparatus was being used in London hospitals. Peale "invented sundry important improvements" on which he obtained a patent. The bath was recommended for all occasions calling for simple medication and cleanliness: fevers, infection, general pain and discomfort. Peale particularly recommended it as a custom that Americans should adopt, especially in "our Cities." It was a mode of maintaining health, he wrote in *An Epistle to a Friend* (1803), "simple, and so easy as to be in the reach of every one at all times." (*American Philosophical Society*)

chine not fall "amongst fools and knaves," but rather "into the hands of good men as I wish to work only for such, & I do believe there is enough of that class to take all I can do."[61]

Peale's eagerness "to make labour easey" found an outlet at "Belfield," his farm in Germantown where he had retired "to muse away the remainder of my life" (which for Peale was, of course, impossible).[62] When Jefferson described the moldboard of his plow to the newly established farmer, Peale reciprocated the interest, making a model of Jefferson's device and then ordering a copy of it from "the best Plow maker in the vicinity." He continued to improve Jefferson's plow in order to meet such problems as exposure to sun and rain or breakage on stony ground. The problems of farming excited his imagination: he produced a two-story mill to utilize the power of the streams that ran through his property, a windmill with sails to pump water, and such labor-saving devices as a butter churn, tool grinder, hominy beater, clothes washer, turn bench, and milk machine (No. 168).

As with most of Peale's contrivances, this latter invention served a number of purposes. He had discovered, he wrote to Jefferson, that "Milk food . . . contributed to cure my Lunges [of Phlegm]." Providing drink as well as food, milk was "perfection in the Country but shamefully spoiled by the retailers of it in the City." Especially "in the hot weather this Summer [city dwellers] could not get milk at any price." A machine to carry milk from nearby farms to Philadelphia came immediately to his inventive mind. The milk carrier that resulted was so constructed with strainers and pivots that the tub swung on wheels and maintained its level, thus preventing spillage as the milk was conveyed in carriages over the bumpy roads. And again, in characteristic fashion, Peale decided to make all his farming utensils in his workshop, for the sake of economy, but also for educational purposes: "My present labourers are all young men, and teaching them the use of Carpenters tools may be of some importance to them hereafter."[63]

Belfield Farm became the place where Peale's feelings for nature and his instinct for artistic improvement reached full expression. He shaped his world not only with tools, but with actual manipulation of the landscape; his effort was dedicated to carving a segment out of the land and transforming it into a work of art. The desire to endow his environment with artistic and intellectual significance impelled Peale to create a garden that was, in effect, another museum (No. 169).[64]

166. THE PEDESTRIAN'S HOBBY-HORSE. c. 1819

Peale was just turning seventy-eight when he learned of an invention by the German Baron von Drais, a two-wheeled device by which a foot traveler could move at undreamed-of speeds. It was propelled by one's feet on the ground but at an easily accelerated pace, and one could lift one's feet for a flying dash down a hill. Peale had one made for himself immediately—delighted by the amazement it caused as it sped along country lanes or city streets, and concerned also with adapting it to useful purposes such as the measuring of distances. His ink-and-wash sketch is based on an illustration of the machine in the *Analectic Magazine* of 1819. (*American Philosophical Society*)

Explanation. A a frame to be fastened to the bottom and
uppermost part of the Chair, of such convenient height,
with the fan hanging down, as will admit a person to sit
upright beneath it.   B a Treadle which acts as a lever
working by an axis, the pivots of which enter into the pieces
c, c, fastened to the front legs of the Chair.   D the fan, made of
paste-board; to which are fastened two spring catches that
go into mortices in the mooving axis at e, e. This axis has
a pulley, to which are fastened two pieces of leather, to moove
it in reverse directions, as may be better understood by the
figure F, each piece of leather after being once turned round
the pulley are fastened into the piece G at the holes h, h, and
needs no other fastning to the frame above; at the bottom
the end i, is hinged to the treadle B at the extremities k.

167. FAN CHAIR. 1786

Peale had a special interest in devices that would enhance comfort and physical well-being. This
chair would not only cool the sitter but drive away flies, all through a small action by the foot. On
being elected to the American Philosophical Society in July of 1786, Peale submitted to its president, Dr. Benjamin Rush, this drawing and description "of the Fan Chair which the very
ingenious Mr. John Cram Musical Instrument Maker Invented and made for me." (*American
Philosophical Society*)

(29)

for liking the farmers life, is yet to be told. For many years before I came to this place, my lungs was not sound; salt phlegm troubled me, and I seldom could get into sound sleep before I had thrown off that Phlegm — By using a great deal of exercise in the open air, with hilly grounds, fine water and temperate eating I am more than paid for the cost of the farm, by strong health. It is true that I had experienced considerable benefit by an abridgment of my solid food, before I left the city, I had been relieved from coliths and head-aches; from that time I had read M.r John Sinclears code of Longevity, about the time my son Rembranet went to France. Milk food may also have contributed to cure my lungs; it serves for drink as well as food, and we have it perfection in the country but shamefully spoiled by the retailers of it in the city.

The last line gives one the thought of a Machine to carry milk to market, like one I contrived to take my milk from the cow pen to the Spring House, which saves a great deal of labour — as short description of it may be acceptable, I got a large ceder Tub of an oval form made with care to it, a little below the top pegs to rest a strainer on, a wire to make to fit its place, a broad hem to run the wire through, to prevent the wire from rusting, I varnished it. A frame to let the Tub move freely in, with pivots in opposite direction to those in the Tub, and thus it swings like the mariners compass. The carriage has 3 wheels, the hind wheels with a crook axle tree to let the carriage be low. The strainer prevents the splashing of the Milk from perpendicular jolts. The pivots of the Tub so as admit it be tilted to pour into a pan set on the fore part of the carriage, having a lip to the Tub to prevent the spilling the Milk. The fore wheel with a swivel, and the tongue embraces the axle tree to turn the wheel to the right or left — altho' my drawing is very slight, yet with the description sufficient for your comprehension, Such a carriage on a larger scale to be drawn by a horse would be good to carry milk to the city, and the profits will pay for the trouble. In the hot weather this summer, they could not get milk at any price, at least for a few days. A grass farm gives the least trouble and most profit near to the city — I shall endeavor to obtain such, but time is necessary for this as well as perfectioning of Fruit Trees. I don't want fruit Trees to make cyder, I consider it a pernicious liquor, as cau-ing

168. Letter from Charles Willson Peale to Thomas Jefferson, with drawing of the milk cart. 1811

Of all Peale's agricultural inventions, none attracted more attention than the milk cart, which he described to Jefferson in this letter of September 9, 1811. In it, the principle of the balanced mariner's compass was adapted to the transportation of milk from barn to house. Peale believed the cart could be used for longer distances and help to make fresh milk more easily available to city dwellers. (*American Philosophical Society*)

169. Letter from Charles Willson Peale to Rembrandt Peale, with sketches of Belfield Farm. 1810

Peale first called his retirement home "Farm Persevere," but after two years changed it to "Belfield." "Belfield" soon became a popular place of "rational amusement" and learning, dedicated to innovative scientific agriculture and linked by personal correspondence to Jefferson's Monticello. It took the place of the museum in Peale's heart for awhile and became, in effect, his outdoor museum. He took delight in sharing his plans, as he did in this letter, with his son Rembrandt, to whom he was especially obligated for new insights into the use of colors and varnishes. His landscape designs at "Belfield," whether created in actuality or painted on canvas, he wrote, "pleased himself, and they gave pleasure to others, and they offended none, being perfectly innocent." (*American Philosophical Society*)

Peale had written to Jefferson that "Your garden must be a museum to you."[65] Along with flowers and vegetables, Peale's museum-garden contained works of art—allegories that added "moral sentiment" to the garden's "utility." Such a sentiment was required, Peale believed, for the garden was being visited by an ever-increasing number of visitors who came to see Peale's improvements and applaud his ingenuity.[66]

In the design of his garden, Peale transformed a toolbox into a garden seat; he made the front of the box also serve as a gateway, its top becoming both a step and a bench. Above the box, "to try his art of Painting," Peale drew more steps "representing a passage through an arch beyond which was represented a western sky, and to ornament the upper part over the arch, he painted several figures on boards cut to the outlines of said figures as representing statutes [*sic*] in sculpture."[67] This description of his painting in his autobiography recalls Peale's *Staircase Group* of 1795 (No. 55), a *trompe l'oeil* work which featured an actual step connected to painted steps in order to add to the realism and deceptive quality of the painting. The painting of a distant landscape and the statues cut out of board symbolizing America "with an even ballance—as justifying her acts" recall his earlier republican transparencies and their allegorical messages. How familiar is his description of the statue representing Congress as being "*upright*, as that body ought to be, with wisdom its base, designated by the owl"! Once again, Peale resorted to such symbols as the beehive of industry supported by Truth and Temperance on one side and Industry with her distaff and cornucopia on the other to describe the effects of good government; in this later allegory, he added images of children as emblems of posterity. Above the whole arrangement, Peale proclaimed the pacifistic maxim: "A wise Policy will do away with wars. Hence Mars is fallen."

Peale also built a summer house in his garden, designed in the "Chinese taste, dedicated to meditation." On its facade, he inscribed the message:

Meditate on the Creation of *worlds*, which perform their evolutions in proscribed periods! on the changes and revolutions of the *Globe* which we inhabit:—on the wonderful variety of animals inhabiting the earth, the air and the waters: their immence number and diversity; their beauty and delicacy of structure . . . Then let me ask *myself, why am I here?* am I blessed with more profound reason than other Animals, if so, *Lett me be thankful: Let me meditate on the past, on the present, and on the future.*

At the end of a walk behind the house, Peale erected an obelisk, on the pedestal of which he inscribed on all four sides still further aphorisms:

Never return an injury, it is a noble triumph to
overcome evil by good.
Labour while you are able, it will give health to the
body, and peaceful content in the mind.
He that will live in peace and rest, must hear and see
and say the best, oy, voy, & te tais, si tu veux, vivre en paix.
Neglect no duty.

To instruct visitors in American history, he erected a pedestal inscribed with ninety memorable events in the nation's past, beginning with the first discovery of the continent and ending with the battle of New Orleans. Thus, as Peale and his family, or visitors to his farm, strolled around the garden "for exercise or amusement," they were reminded of what he considered "sacred Laws"; and whenever he placed some new object in his garden, he continued to combine it with a written message—"all of a moral tendency."[68]

Essentially Peale was an educator, a man who sought order and organization in his own life and felt impelled to teach others the important lessons he had learned. His lessons were derived from nature, which to Peale was beneficent and life-enhancing. Peale's nature was not the alien wilderness feared by seventeenth-century theologians, nor the transcendental Revelation asserted by nineteenth-century poets and artists. Rather, like many of his contemporaries who were nurtured as he was on the poetry of Pope and Thomson and the treatises of Rousseau and Diderot, Peale regarded nature as a creation from the hand of God. In that sense, nature was a revelation, not so much of God, but of His plan for the universe and mankind. To the eighteenth-century mind, nature possessed an innate order reflecting its Maker, and was therefore susceptible to human organization and intellectual exploration. Nature was domesticated, rational, and intelligible. The natural world remained constant; it had been created full and persisted in its fullness. Peale accepted the prevailing view that species were permanent and could never become extinct, although toward the end of his long life, after his discovery of the mastodon, he was forced to confront evidence that this was not so. But permanence meant that in an unchanging physical world, man could concentrate his desire for progress on the improvement of the less perfect social environment.

Like other educated men in the eighteenth century, Peale did not possess a theory of progress so much as a program for progress.[69] An activist, he believed that improvement of man's lot would emanate from the establishment of educational institutions based upon natural principles, and progress would result from the knowledge gained. Behind the founding of his museum, the Columbianum Society, and the Pennsylvania Academy of the Fine Arts (No. 170), then, lay Peale's conviction that institutions of "rational entertainment" possessed "a tendency to improve the morals of the people" and provided the "virtuous education" necessary for the maintenance of "republican government" and "the liberties of the people."[70]

In 1812, the liberties of the Quakers of Philadelphia appeared to be threatened by a law requiring all citizens either to enlist in the militia or pay a fine. The city was facing possible invasion by the British army in the new war between Great Britain and the United States, and the law was stringently applied. Because of their religious principles, Quakers refused to obey the law; they would neither enlist nor pay the fine. As a result, their shops were frequently entered by zealous militiamen who seized "articles of value" as security against the payment of the fine and then sold these for "a comparative trifle." In some instances, militia officers were the purchasers of these valuable goods. Peale was incensed at the brutal and dishonest behavior of the militia. In an article destined for publication but never actually published called "A Voice in Behalf of the Oppressed" Peale lashed out at the law and the militia. He argued that America had always been a

170. Letter from Charles Willson Peale to Robert Fulton, with drawing of Peale's plan for an exhibition at the Pennsylvania Academy. 1807

Peale and his son Rembrandt were among the founders of the Pennsylvania Academy of the Fine Arts, and took a strong interest in its affairs. Peale particularly wanted to develop its school and its exhibitions of contemporary art. With the completion of a building in 1808, he mounted an exhibition of Benjamin West's paintings owned by the artist and inventor Robert Fulton. Here was a chance to impress the town as never before: they were "wonderful works of art," he wrote to Fulton on November 15, 1807. "We shall now feel the Pulse of the Citizens of Philad.ª with the effect of a grand Exhibition. I long very much to hear what will be said by the *Friends*, and other denominations of X^ans." (*American Philosophical Society*)

refute for those who sought "freedom of mind," and in this country religious differences were to be respected and protected. The artist's pen, as he wrote his argument, seems to have raced furiously across the page, the letters hardly completed and the words increasing in size. Friends were good citizens of the Commonwealth, he insisted, always ready to perform their "civic duty" in times of distress. Could good Christians stand by and see others molested for carrying out their beliefs? he asked with much agitation. Not a Friend himself, Peale declared that it was his duty to speak out "for the sufferings of the oppressed and the sacred liberty of CONSCIENCE."[71]

By this time, Peale had come to conceive of his role as that of a teacher. In his two self-portraits painted toward the end of his life—*The Artist in His Museum* (No. 75) and *The Exhumation of the Mastodon* (No. 54)—he presented himself in that image. The artist in the museum becomes a lecturer on a stage as he opens the curtain to show that "he had given to his country a sight of natural history in his labours to form a Museum."[72] The objects around him constitute the subject matter for his lectures, while the light falling on him from behind provides illumination that clarifies knowledge. The artist in the field who directs the search for the mammoth bones is also a lecturer, on the outdoor stage this time. With outstretched arm, he points to the relationship between

Fig. r. THE EXHUMATION OF THE MASTODON (detail of the family group). 1806–8

Peale was eager to include portraits of members of his family in his large history painting, as
Benjamin West had done many years earlier in his *Penn's Treaty with the Indians*. To integrate
the family into the picture's meaning, Peale made them represent posterity. The older children—
Rembrandt, Rubens, and Raphaelle—listen attentively to their father's explanation, while Peale's
young daughter, Sybilla Miriam, points upward to heaven as she explains God's plan for the
universe—the meaning of the discovery—to her small sister Elizabeth. (*The Peale Museum*)

his drawing of the bone—the object of the search—the open pit where it was discovered,
and the stormy sky, which threatened to undo his investigations into nature's secrets.
The picture commemorates a discovery which for Peale proved the existence of a chain
of creation and added to man's knowledge of the natural world as God had planned it.
But Peale could not resist including a scene of domestic harmony in this historical
painting: the family group—the symbol of posterity—stands before the open pit as if in
a Greek frieze, concentrating on the father's lecture, while his young daughter Sybilla
points upward to heaven as she explains to her younger sister Elizabeth the meaning of
the discovery (Fig. r).[73]

Peale's purpose as a teacher was to contribute to good citizenship and a moral
society, a worthwhile aim for this American and one that he enjoyed and worked hard at
achieving. He had begun his life as a young radical parading for independence. He had
fought for independence on the battlefield and in the legislative halls of his state. He had
used his talents as an artist to advance his society's political values and to ensure that
republican ideals would be communicated to the people through artistic symbols to

which they could respond. His training was in portraiture, and he practiced it for his livelihood; but as soon as it was economically feasible, he turned that talent also to what he believed were the needs of his country and made his portraits of eminent Revolutionary and republican heroes representations of the "benevolent" national character he wished so much to influence.

When he finally turned his attention to natural history and immersed himself in his museum, he immediately perceived the educational advantages of his new interest. He accepted the prevailing ideas about nature because they satisfied his essential tidiness, his basic instinct for harmony and order, and his passion for organization. He delighted in the classical Linnaean system because it established a method by which he could organize a variety of natural specimens in a meaningful way, "so that the mind may not be confused and distracted in viewing such a multitude of objects." For the same reason, the conception of a "chain of creation" was attractive to him, because it enabled him to proceed "step by step" in good didactic fashion "to trace the beauties which we shall find that each [species] possesses, in its relative situation to other beings."[74]

In all of his efforts, Peale had his country's future in mind. He had made the beginning, he wrote to Jefferson, "and posterity may build on it to magnificence."[75] Peale had a strong sense of himself as a founding father, a member of that initiating generation that had established the structure of government, society, and culture upon which future generations of Americans would continue to build. When he thought of making copies for the corporation of the city of Baltimore of the portraits of six Maryland governors which he had painted at an earlier time, he did so, he wrote, for a motive that was "in some measure selfish": he wished to be "the founder of a collection of Portraits, which has promise of becoming a rich and highly valuable Gallery of distinguished men elected to the highest office in a free Government."[76] And he justified his neglect of portrait painting, which would "probably have produced him more wealth," with the insistence that his museum was a work that would be of great use to posterity "if judiciously managed" and could become "equal to any undertaking of the kind in Europe."[77]

Peale's life was filled with diverse and important accomplishments, and yet, like his vision of the world, it was a harmonious whole. Incessantly active, indefatigable in his pursuits, moral in his aims, he embodied the highest ideals of the revolutionary generation. His life was as much an achievement as his art.

NOTES

All manuscripts cited herein may be consulted in the microfiche edition of *The Collected Papers of Charles Willson Peale and His Family*, ed. Lillian B. Miller, 3 vols. (Millwood, N.Y., 1980).

PART I

1. Rembrandt Peale, "Reminiscences," *The Crayon* I (1855), pp. 81–83.

2. Charles Willson Peale, Autobiography, Peale-Sellers Papers, American Philosophical Society (hereafter cited as Autobiography, APS).

3. Charles A. Barker, *The Background of the Revolution in Maryland* (New Haven, 1940), p. 314.

4. Chase showed in this campaign the fiery temper that made him a Whig leader; later, when appointed to the Supreme Court of the United States, he continued to be so outspoken in his Federalist opinions that he was impeached, though not convicted.

5. Charles Carroll, of the Protestant branch of the Maryland Carrolls, was educated at Cambridge and read law at the Temple; but returning to Maryland in 1756 he had turned his energies to public affairs and to business. His business correspondence, published in the *Maryland Historical Magazine* (Vols. XXXI, 1936, and XXXII, 1937), makes one understand the frustrations and vexations of doing business through an agent three thousand miles away from London.

6. Autobiography, APS.

7. Ibid.

8. Carroll's letter, in the Library of Congress, is quoted in full in Charles Coleman Sellers, *The Artist of the Revolution: The Early Life of Charles Willson Peale* (Hebron, Conn., 1939), p. 62.

9. Autobiography, APS.

10. Rembrandt Peale, "Reminiscences," p. 82.

11. Quoted in William Dunlap, *History of the Rise and Progress of the Arts of Design in the United States* (New York, 1834), p. 137.

12. Robin Robernier, abbé, *Nouveau Voyage dans l'Amérique Septentrionale, en l'année 1781; et Campagne de l'Armée de M. le Comte de Rochambeau* (1782).

13. Peale to John Beale Bordley, written before 1770, APS. This appeal to Titian as a realist may sound odd but it reflects the opinion of Italian idealist critics from Vasari to Mengs (West's mentor). Titian was criticized by Vasari for not studying the antique and not working out his compositions first in preliminary drawings, "though he imitated natural things, as best he could, coloring them like life," as Vasari said. This rather disparaging Florentine opinion held that the Venetian painters who did not study the antique in Rome were obliged to conceal their ignorance of good *disegno* by splendor of color. Peale was appealing to Titian's example as authority for his own practice of painting direct from nature.

14. Peale letter of 1772, APS. Spelling modernized.

15. Michael Ayrton, *Giovanni Pisano* (London and New York, 1969), p. 34.

16. Peale, Diary 3, APS.

17. Peale to Benjamin West, April, 1783, APS.

18. Peale to Edmund Jenings, 1783, APS.

19. Peale to West, November 17, 1788, APS.

20. There had, of course, always been collectors. Philadelphia had an interesting one. A French Swiss named Pierre Eugène du Simitière, after traveling for some years in the West Indies, settled at Philadelphia in 1767. He was an omnivorous collector of historical notes, natural curiosities, drawings, prints, and coins. In 1782, taking advantage of an unusual number of visitors to the city, he

advertised (*Pennsylvania Gazette*, May 1) that he would show his collection three days a week to "lovers of the fine arts, naturalists, or [the] curious in general." He died in 1784 and his collections were scattered. All that he may have left to Peale was an idea and the name by which he had advertised his collection, AMERICAN MUSEUM.

21. Autobiography, APS.

22. George Gaylord Simpson, "The Beginnings of Vertebrate Paleontology in North America," in *The Early History of Science and Learning in America* (Philadelphia, 1942), pp. 130–88.

23. *Annales du Musée d'Histoire Naturelle* (Paris), VIII (1806), p. 312.

24. J. Mordaunt Crook, *The British Museum* (London, 1972), p. 53.

25. Cecil Gould, *Trophy of Conquest: The Musée Napoléon and the Creation of the Louvre* (London, 1965), p. 26.

26. The inscription was adapted from a now-forgotten drama, Beller's "Injured Innocence," according to Titian R. Peale (Notebook 1, APS).

27. On Peale's Museum as an educational instrument see Charles Coleman Sellers, "Peale's Museum and the New Museum Idea," in *Proceedings of the American Philosophical Society* (1979), and *Mr. Peale's Museum* (New York, 1980).

28. Nicholas B. Wainwright, *Colonial Grandeur in Philadelphia: The Home and Furniture of General John Cadwalader* (Philadelphia, 1964), p. 47.

29. Peale to John Cadwalader, March 22, 1771, APS.

30. Karol A. Schmiegel, "Encouragement Exceeding Expectation: The Lloyd-Cadwalader Patronage of Charles Willson Peale," *Winterthur Portfolio* XII (Charlottesville, Va., 1977), pp. 87–102.

31. Peale to Edmund Jenings, July 10, 1771, APS.

32. The first mention of this drawing instrument is in a letter to John Beale Bordley, March 29, 1772, APS. I do not know exactly what the term means— some kind of *camera obscura*, but what kind? We do not know.

PART II

1. Brooke Hindle, *Emulation and Invention* (New York, 1981), pp. 50–56, 85–107.

2. Ibid., pp. 135–42.

3. Charles Willson Peale, Autobiography, Peale-Sellers Papers, American Philosophical Society (hereafter cited as Autobiography, APS).

4. Frank D. Prager, ed., *The Autobiography of John Fitch* (Philadelphia, 1976), pp. 52–54.

5. Autobiography, APS.

6. Ibid.

7. Peale to Thomas Jefferson, February 17, 1807, APS.

8. Autobiography, APS.

9. Ibid.

10. Ibid.

11. "Memorial to The City Commissioners of Public Revenue," *Poulson's American Daily Advertiser*, August 15, 1816, cited by Charles Coleman Sellers in *Charles Willson Peale* (New York, 1969), p. 213n.

12. Charles Coleman Sellers, *Mr. Peale's Museum* (New York, 1980), pp. 24–25.

13. Brooke Hindle, *The Pursuit of Science in Revolutionary America* (Chapel Hill, N.C., 1956), pp. 11–35.

14. Peale, Lecture 1, APS.

15. Peale, Lectures 16, 4, and 10, APS.

16. Philadelphia, n.d.

17. Philadelphia, 1796.

18. Peale to Palisot de Beauvois, July 14, 1802, APS.

19. Peale and Beauvois, *A Scientific and Descriptive Catalogue of Peale's Museum*.

20. Brooke Hindle, *David Rittenhouse* (Princeton, N.J., 1964), p. 281.

21. *Medical Repository* IV (1801), pp. 211–14, cited by Sellers in *Mr. Peale's Museum*, p. 113.

22. Peale, Autobiography, typescript copy, pp. 311–12 (hereafter cited as Autobiography [TS], APS).

23. Autobiography (TS), APS.

24. Peale to Georges Cuvier, July 16, 1802, APS.

25. Rembrandt Peale, *Account of The Skeleton of the Mammoth* (London, 1802).

26. Hindle, *Pursuit*, pp. 269, 328.

27. Peale, *Introduction to a Course of Lectures on Natural History . . .* (Philadelphia, 1800).

28. Peale to Beauvois, June 16, 1799, APS; Peale to Cuvier, April 21, 1808, APS.

29. Peale to Zaccheus Collins, January 7, 1822, Parker Papers, Columbia Historical Society.

30. Peale to Samuel Mitchill, January 21, 1809, APS.

31. Sellers, *Mr. Peale's Museum*, pp. 205–6.

32. W.S.W. Ruschenberger, *A Notice of the Origin, Progress, and Present Condition of the Academy of Natural Sciences of Philadelphia* (Philadelphia, 1860), pp. 65–67.

33. Jeannette E. Graustein, *Thomas Nuttall, Naturalist: Explorations in America 1808–1841* (Cambridge, Mass., 1967), pp. 115–16.

34. Peale, *Gentleman, I Thank You . . .*, Broadside, Philadelphia, 1792.

35. *Guide to the Philadelphia Museum* (Philadelphia, 1805), p. 3.

36. Ibid., pp. 2–3.

37. Peale, "The Bow," *American Museum* VI (1789), pp. 205–6.

38. *Guide*, p. 4.

39. Peale to The Honorable Legislature of Pennsylvania, APS.

40. Autobiography (TS), APS.

41. Peale, drawing, July 17, 1786. MS Communications No. 10, APS.

42. Autobiography (TS), APS.

43. C.W. Peale and his son Raphaelle, "Description of some Improvements in the common Fire-places accompanied with Models, offered to the consideration of The American Philosophical Society," *Transactions of the American Philosophical Society* V (1802), pp. 320–24.

44. Peale, "Description of the Stove lately built by Mr. Charles Willson Peale . . . ," *The Weekly Magazine* II, No. 25 (July 21, 1798), pp. 353–54.

45. Peale, *A Descriptive Catalogue of Mr. Peale's Exhibition of Perspective Views with Changeable Effects; or Nature Delineated, and in Motion*, Broadside, Philadelphia, 1785.

46. Peale to Thomas Jefferson, July 17, 1803, APS; Peale to Jefferson, February 1, 1826, Massachusetts Historical Society.

47. Peale to Jefferson, January 10, 1803, APS.

48. Autobiography (TS), APS.

49. Hindle, *Emulation*, p. 15; Peale to Timothy Matlock, March 15, 1802, APS.

50. Peale, Lecture 2, APS.

51. Jefferson to Peale, October 6, 1805, Hanley Collection, University of Texas at Austin.

52. Peale, *To the Citizens of the United States of America*, Broadside, February 1, 1790, Massachusetts Historical Society.

PART III

1. Charles Willson Peale, Autobiography, typescript copy, p. 3, Peale-Sellers Papers, American Philosophical Society (hereafter cited as Autobiography [TS], APS).

2. Autobiography (TS), APS, pp. 14, 19, 29.

3. Peale to Thomas Allwood, August 30, 1775, APS.

4. Peale to Thomas Jefferson, August 21, 1819, and Peale to Charles Peale Polk, January 9, 1820, APS.

5. Autobiography (TS), APS, p. 48.

6. Ibid., p. 53.

7. See John R. Howe, Jr., "Republican Thought and the Political Violence of the 1790's," *American Quarterly* XIX, No. 2, pt. 1 (Summer 1967), pp. 147–65.

8. Autobiography (TS), APS, pp. 19, 40.

9. See Mario Praz, *Studies in Seventeenth Century Imagery* (Rome, 1964); Rosemary Freeman, *English Emblem Books* (London, 1948); Peter M. Daly, *Literature in the Light of the Emblem* (Toronto, 1979); Ronald Paulson, *Hogarth: His Life, Art, and Times*, 2 vols. (New Haven, 1971), Vol. I, pp.

49–50, 514; Frank H. Sommer, "The Metamorphoses of Brittania," in *American Art 1750–1800: Towards Independence*, eds. Charles F. Montgomery and Patricia E. Kane (Boston, 1976), pp. 40–49; Caroline Robbins, "The Strenuous Whig," *William and Mary Quarterly*, 3d ser., VII (July 1950), pp. 406–53; Beverly Orlove, "Charles Willson Peale and American Civic Pageantry," paper delivered at the Peale Conference, October 23, 1981, National Portrait Gallery, Washington, D.C.

10. Autobiography (TS), APS, p. 40.

11. 1730; attributed to the Dutch artist Herman Van der Myn. See Roger B. Stein, "Charles Willson Peale's Expressive Design: *The Artist In His Museum*," *Prospects: The Annual of American Cultural Studies* VI (1981), p. 145. Late in life, Peale exchanged copies of his portraits of six Maryland governors for this painting, which was owned by the Corporation of the City of Baltimore. To silence criticism, he presented the portrait to Rembrandt Peale's Baltimore Museum (The Peale Museum, Baltimore), where it has remained. See Peale to John Boyle, July 1, 1824, APS.

12. [Peale], *A Description of the Picture and Mezzotinto of Mr. Pitt, done by Charles Willson Peale, of Maryland*, Broadside, Library of Congress, Rare Books Division, Broadside Collection.

13. Peale to John Pinckney, January or February 25, 1775, APS; *Purdie's and Dixon's Virginia Gazette*, February 23, 1775.

14. Autobiography (TS), APS, pp. 84–85.

15. Ibid., p. 78. See also Peale, *Introduction to a Course of Lectures on Natural History . . . November 16, 1799* (Philadelphia, 1800), pp. 21–22; and Peale to Samuel Chase, November 23, 1784, APS.

16. Peale to Edmund Jenings, December 10, 1783, APS.

17. For transparencies, see Thomas John Gulick and John Timbs, *Painting Popularly Explained* (London, 1859), pp. 9–10; for West and the celebration of the king's birthday, see Robert C. Alberts, *Benjamin West: A Biography* (Boston, 1978), p. 102. Also see Kenneth Silverman, *A Cultural History of the American Revolution* (New York, 1976), pp. 75–80.

18. *Pennsylvania Packet*, November 1, 1781.

19. *Freeman's Journal*, October 31, 1781.

20. *Pennsylvania Packet*, November 1, 1781. *Freeman's Journal*, October 31, 1781, described Peale's illuminations with a few minor differences. Instead of palm branches encircling Washington and Rochambeau, the *Journal* indicated "flowers de luce"; and instead of SHINE VALIANT CHIEFS, the *Journal* gave the motto: LIVE VALIANT CHIEFS.

21. See James Thomas Flexner, *Washington: The Indispensable Man* (Boston, 1969), pp. 165–66.

22. *Pennsylvania Packet*, December 4, 1781; *Freeman's Journal*, December 12, 1781.

23. *Pennsylvania Packet*, August 29, 1782.

24. *Pennsylvania Packet*, January 17 and 24, 1784.

25. Autobiography (TS), APS, p. 85.

26. Charles Coleman Sellers, *Charles Willson Peale* (New York, 1969), pp. 204–5, 211.

27. See Robert E. Shalhope, "Toward a Republican Synthesis: The Emergence of an Understanding of Republicanism in American Historiography," *William and Mary Quarterly*, 3d ser., XXIX (1972), pp. 49–80; Gordon S. Wood, *The Creation of the American Republic, 1776–1787* (Chapel Hill, N.C., 1969), p. 128. Wood's entire work discusses in detail the changing nature of republican theory from its origins in the Whig tradition of dissent to its development as a prescription for the organization of government.

    Posterity was an important eighteenth-century concept. As the French philosopher Diderot remarked, "What posterity is for the philosopher, the other world is for the religious man" (quoted in Peter Gay, *The Enlightenment: An Interpretation*, Vol. II: *The Science of Freedom* [New York, 1978], p. 90). A "passion for secular immortality," according to the historian Douglass Adair, lay behind the patriots' efforts to create a viable Republican state: "The pursuit of fame, they had been taught, was a way of transforming egotism and self-aggrandizing impulses into public service; they had been taught that public service nobly (and selfishly) performed was the surest way to build 'lasting monuments' and earn the perpetual remembrance of posterity" ("Fame and the Founding Fathers," in *Fame and the Founding Fathers*, ed. Edmund P. Willis [Bethlehem, Pa., 1967], p. 32; see also pp. 27–52).

28. Peale to Governor Joseph Reed, June 12, 1780, Pennsylvania Archives, Ser. 1, 10, p. 163.

29. Peale to Count Rumford, January 21, 1809, APS.

30. Peale to Thomas Jefferson, July 3, 1820, APS.

31. Peale, *Introduction to a Course of Lectures . . .*, p. 1.

32. Peale, Lecture 39, APS.

33. Peale, Lecture 5, APS.

34. Peale, Lecture 3, APS.

35. Peale, Lecture 10; Lecture 2, APS.

36. Peale, Lecture 1, APS.

37. Ibid.

38. Ibid.

39. Peale, *Discourse Introductory to a Course of Lectures on the Science of Nature . . . November 8, 1800* (Philadelphia, 1800), pp. 9–10.

40. Peale to John DePeyster, February 19, 1804, APS.

41. Autobiography (TS), APS, p. 397.

42. Peale to Titian Ramsay Peale, February 20, 1820, APS.

43. Peale, Lecture on Natural History and the Museum (1823), p. 20, APS.

44. Peale to Elizabeth DePeyster Peale, October 30, 1814, APS.

45. Autobiography (TS), APS, pp. 387–88.

46. Thomas Jefferson to Peale, April 17, 1813, Hanley Collection, University of Texas at Austin.

47. Peale, *An Essay to Promote Domestic Happiness* (Philadelphia, 1812), p. 22.

48. Autobiography (TS), APS, pp. 167–68.

49. Peale to Angelica Peale Robinson, June 16, 1808, APS.

50. Autobiography (TS), APS, p. 323.

51. Peale, *An Epistle to a Friend . . .* (Philadelphia, 1803), pp. 3–4; Autobiography (TS), APS, p. 324.

52. Autobiography (TS), APS, pp. 276–77.

53. Peale to Benjamin Rush, July 31, 1786, APS.

54. Peale to Titian Ramsay Peale, July 30, 1819, APS.

55. Sidney Hart, "'To Encrease the Comforts of Life': Charles Willson Peale and the Mechanical Arts," paper delivered at the Peale Conference, October 23, 1981, National Portrait Gallery, Washington, D.C.

56. Peale to Thomas Jefferson, March 8, 1801, APS.

57. Peale to the Managers of the Pennsylvania Hospital, April 2, 1801, APS.

58. Autobiography (TS), APS, pp. 443–45, 476–77.

59. *The Aurora General Advertiser* (Philadelphia), July 11, 1803.

60. *The Aurora General Advertiser* (Philadelphia), October 6, 1803.

61. Peale to Benjamin Henry Latrobe, November 3, 1803, APS.

62. Autobiography (TS), APS, p. 386; Peale to Thomas Jefferson, September 9, 1811, APS.

63. Peale to Thomas Jefferson, September 9, 1811, APS.

64. Sellers has noted that the garden at "Belfield" took "the place in [Peale's] heart that the Museum had filled." See his *Peale* (1969), p. 366.

65. Peale to Thomas Jefferson, March 13, 1812, APS.

66. Autobiography (TS), APS, pp. 391–92.

67. Ibid., pp. 390–91.

68. Ibid., pp. 391–92.

69. See Gay, *The Enlightenment*, pp. 99–100.

70. Peale, Lecture on Natural History and the Museum (1823), APS.

71. Peale, "A Voice in Behalf of the Oppressed," 1812, APS.

72. Autobiography (TS), APS, p. 446. See Stein, "Charles Willson Peale's Expressive Design" for an extended analysis of this painting.

73. See Lillian B. Miller, "Charles Willson Peale as History Painter: *The Exhumation of the Mastodon*," *American Art Journal* XIII (Winter 1981), pp. 47–68, for an extended analysis of *The Exhumation*.

74. Peale, *Discourse Introductory*, p. 33.

75. Peale to Thomas Jefferson, January 1, 1824, APS.

76. Peale to John Boyle, July 1, 1824, APS.

77. Autobiography (TS), APS, p. 168.

SELECTED BIBLIOGRAPHY

BOOKS

Adair, Douglass. "Fame and the Founding Fathers," in *Fame and the Founding Fathers*, ed. Edmund P. Willis (Bethlehem, Pa., 1967).

Barker, Charles A. *The Background of the Revolution in Maryland* (New Haven, 1940).

Barker, Virgil. *American Painting: History and Interpretation* (New York, 1950).

Bell, Whitfield J., Jr. "Science and Humanity in Philadelphia, 1775–1790," Ph.D. dissertation, University of Pennsylvania, 1947 (University Microfilms Publication no. 2499).

Boyd, Julian P., ed. *The Papers of Thomas Jefferson* (Princeton, 1950–).

Bridenbaugh, Carl and Jessica. *Rebels and Gentlemen: Philadelphia in the Age of Franklin* (New York, 1942).

Brunhouse, Robert L. *The Counter-Revolution in Pennsylvania, 1776–1790* (Philadelphia, 1942; reprint 1971).

Butterfield, Lyman H., ed. *Letters of Benjamin Rush.* 2 vols. (Princeton, 1951).

Cincinnati Art Museum. *Paintings by the Peale Family* (Cincinnati, 1954).

Crook, J. Mordaunt. *The British Museum* (London, 1972).

Daly, Peter M. *Literature in the Light of the Emblem* (Toronto, 1979).

The Detroit Institute of Arts. *The Peale Family: Three Generations of American Artists* (Detroit, 1967).

Dunlap, William. *History of the Rise and Progress of the Arts of Design in the United States* (New York, 1834).

Faxon, Walter. *Relics of Peale's Museum* (Cambridge, Mass., 1915).

Flexner, James Thomas. *America's Old Masters: First Artists of the New World* (New York, 1939).

———. *Washington: The Indispensable Man* (Boston, 1969).

Freeman, Rosemary. *English Emblem Books* (London, 1948).

Gay, Peter. *The Enlightenment: An Interpretation.* Vol. II: *The Science of Freedom* (New York, 1978).

Gould, Cecil. *Trophy of Conquest: The Musée Napoléon and the Creation of the Louvre* (London, 1965).

Graustein, Jeannette E. *Thomas Nuttall, Naturalist: Explorations in America 1808–1841* (Cambridge, Mass., 1967).

Greene, John C. *The Death of Adam: Evolution and Its Impact on Western Thought* (Ames, Iowa, 1959).

Gulick, Thomas John, and John Timbs. *Painting Popularly Explained* (London, 1859).

Harris, Neil. *The Artist in American Society: The Formative Years, 1790–1860* (New York, 1966).

Hindle, Brooke. *David Rittenhouse* (Princeton, 1964).

———. *Emulation and Invention* (New York, 1981).

———. *The Pursuit of Science in Revolutionary America* (Chapel Hill, N.C., 1956).

Hoffman, Ronald. *A Spirit of Dissension: Economics, Politics, and the Revolution in Maryland* (Baltimore, 1973).

Honour, Hugh. *Neo-Classicism* (Harmondsworth, England, 1968).

Hunter, Wilbur Harvey. *The Peale Family and Peale's Baltimore Museum, 1814–1830* (Baltimore, 1965).

———. *Rendezvous for Taste: An Exhibition Celebrating the 25th Anniversary of the Peale Museum* (Baltimore, 1956).

Labaree, Leonard W., ed., Vols. I–XIV; William B. Willcox, ed., Vols. XV–XX. *The Papers of Benjamin Franklin* (New Haven, 1959–).

Land, Aubrey C.; Lois Green Carr; and Edward C. Papenfuse, eds. *Law, Society, and Politics in Early Maryland* (Baltimore and London, 1977).

Miller, Lillian B. *The Collected Papers of Charles Willson Peale and His Family: A Guide and Index to the Microfiche Edition* (Millwood, N.Y., 1980).

———. *Patrons and Patriotism: The Encouragement of the Fine Arts in the United States, 1790–1860* (Chicago, 1966).

Morse, John D., ed. *Prints in and of America to 1850* (Charlottesville, Va., 1970).

Oberholtzer, Ellis P. *Philadelphia: A History of the City and Its People . . .* (Philadelphia and Chicago, 1912).

Papenfuse, Edward C. *In Pursuit of Profit: The Annapolis Merchants in the Era of the Revolution, 1763–1805* (Baltimore, 1975).

Paulson, Ronald. *Hogarth: His Life, Art, and Times.* 2 vols. (New Haven, 1971).

The Pennsylvania Academy of the Fine Arts. *Catalogue of an Exhibition of Portraits by Charles Willson Peale and James Peale and Rembrandt Peale* (Philadelphia, 1923).

Poesch, Jesse. *Titian Ramsay Peale, 1779–1885, and His Journals of the Wilkes Expedition* (Philadelphia, 1961).

Prager, Frank D., ed. *The Autobiography of John Fitch* (Philadelphia, 1976).

Praz, Mario. *Studies in Seventeenth Century Imagery* (Rome, 1964).

Richardson, Edgar P. *Painting in America* (New York, 1956).

Ruschenberger, W.S.W. *A Notice of the Origin, Progress, and Present Condition of the Academy of Natural Sciences of Philadelphia* (Philadelphia, 1860).

Scharf, J. Thomas, and Thompson Westcott. *History of Philadelphia.* 3 vols. (Philadelphia, 1884).

Sellers, Charles Coleman. *Charles Willson Peale* (New York, 1969).

———. *Charles Willson Peale with Patron and Populace: A Supplement to Portraits and Miniatures by Charles Willson Peale* (*Transactions of the American Philosophical Society*, n. s. LVI, pt. 3, Philadelphia, 1969).

———. *Mr. Peale's Museum: Charles Willson Peale and the First Popular Museum of Natural Science and Art* (New York, 1980).

———. *Portraits and Miniatures by Charles Willson Peale* (*Transactions of the American Philosophical Society*, 1952).

Silverman, Kenneth. *A Cultural History of the American Revolution* (New York, 1976).

Simpson, George Gaylord. "The Beginnings of Vertebrate Paleaontology in North America," in *The Early History of Science and Learning in America* (Philadelphia, 1942).

Sommer, Frank H. "The Metamorphoses of Brittania," in *American Art 1750–1800: Towards Independence*, eds. Charles F. Montgomery and Patricia E. Kane (Boston, 1976).

Wainwright, Nicholas B. *Colonial Grandeur in Philadelphia: The Home and Furniture of General John Cadwalader* (Philadelphia, 1964).

Wood, Gordon S. *The Creation of the American Republic, 1776–1787* (Chapel Hill, N.C., 1969).

MAGAZINE ARTICLES

Egbert, Donald Drew. "General Mercer at the Battle of Princeton as Painted by James Peale, Charles Willson Peale, and William Mercer," *Princeton University Library Chronicle* XIII (1952).

Ellis, Richard P. "The Founding, History, and Significance of Peale's Museum in Philadelphia, 1785–1841," *Curator* IX, No. 3 (1966).

Howe, John R., Jr. "Republican Thought and the Political Violence of the 1790's," *American Quarterly* XIX, No. 2, pt. 1 (Summer 1967).

Miller, Lillian B. "Charles Willson Peale as History Painter: *The Exhumation of the Mastodon*," *American Art Journal* XIII (Winter 1981).

Robbins, Caroline. "The Strenuous Whig," *William and Mary Quarterly*, 3d ser., VII (July 1950).

Schmiegel, Karol A. "Encouragement Exceeding Expectation: The Lloyd-Cadwalader Patronage of Charles Willson Peale," *Winterthur Portfolio* XII (Charlottesville, Va., 1977).

Sellers, Charles Coleman. "Charles Willson Peale as Sculptor," *American Art Journal* II (Fall 1970).

———. "Indians as Symbols of Peace in the Art of Charles Willson Peale," *American Art Journal* VII, No. 2 (Fall 1975).

———. "Peale's Museum and the New Museum Idea," in *Proceedings of the American Philosophical Society* (Philadelphia, 1979).

Shalhope, Robert. "Toward a Republican Synthesis: The Emergence of an Understanding of Republicanism in American Historiography," *William and Mary Quarterly* 3d ser., XXIX (1972).

Stein, Roger B. "Charles Willson Peale's Expressive Design: *The Artist in His Museum*," *Prospects: The Annual of American Cultural Studies* VI (1981).

PEALE FAMILY
PUBLISHED WRITINGS

Peale, Charles Willson. "The Bow," *American Museum* VI (Philadelphia, 1789).

———. "Description of the Stove lately built by Mr. Charles Willson Peale . . . ," *The Weekly Magazine* II, No. 25 (July 21, 1798).

———. *Guide to the Philadelphia Museum* (Philadelphia, 1805).

———. *Introduction to a Course of Lectures on Natural History . . .* (Philadelphia, 1800).

Peale, Charles Willson, and A.F.M.J. Palisot de Beauvois. *A Scientific and Descriptive Catalogue of Peale's Museum* (Philadelphia, 1796).

Peale, Charles Willson and Raphaelle. "Description of some Improvements in the common Fire-places accompanied with Models, offered to the consideration of The American Philosophical Society," *Transactions of the American Philosophical Society* V (1802).

Peale, Rembrandt. *An Historical Disquisition on the Mammoth, or, Great American Incognitum, An Extinct, Immense, carnivorous Animal whose Fossil Remains have been found in America* (London, 1803).

———. "Reminiscences," *The Crayon* I (1855).

CATALOGUE

The items in this catalogue are reproduced and are included in the exhibition unless otherwise noted. The references are arranged chronologically, with one exception: the publications by Charles Coleman Sellers, the authority on Charles Willson Peale, are listed first. His catalogue raisonné *Portraits & Miniatures* precedes all other citations.

REFERENCE ABBREVIATIONS

Coues: Elliott Coues, *History of the Expedition under the Command of Lewis and Clark*. 4 vols. (New York, 1893).

Cutright, *History* (1976): Paul Russell Cutright, *A History of the Lewis and Clark Journals* (Norman, Okla., 1976).

Cutright, *Lewis and Clark* (1969): Paul Russell Cutright, *Lewis and Clark: Pioneering Naturalists* (Urbana, Chicago, and London, 1969).

Faxon: Walter Faxon, *Bulletin of the Museum of Comparative Zoology at Harvard College* LIX (July 1915), pp. 120–39.

Jackson: Donald Jackson, ed., *Letters of the Lewis and Clark Expedition with Related Documents 1783–1854* (Urbana, Chicago, and London, 1962).

James: Edwin James, comp., *Account of an Expedition from Pittsburgh to the Rocky Mountains*. 2 vols. (Philadelphia, 1823).

Poesch: Jesse Poesch, *Titian Ramsay Peale, 1799–1855, and His Journals of the Wilkes Expedition* (Philadelphia, 1961).

Sellers, *Early Life* (1939): Charles Coleman Sellers, *The Artist of the Revolution: The Early Life of Charles Willson Peale* (Hebron, Conn., 1939).

Sellers, *Later Life* (1947): Charles Coleman Sellers, *Charles Willson Peale: Later Life*. Vol. II: *1790–1827* (Philadelphia, 1947).

Sellers, *Mr. Peale's Museum* (1980): Charles Coleman Sellers, *Mr. Peale's Museum: Charles Willson Peale and the First Popular Museum of Natural Science and Art* (New York, 1980).

Sellers, *Peale* (1969): Charles Coleman Sellers, *Charles Willson Peale* (New York, 1969).

Sellers, *Portraits & Miniatures*: Charles Coleman Sellers, *Portraits and Miniatures by Charles Willson Peale* (1952); issued as Vol. XLII, pt. 1, of the Transactions of the American Philosophical Society held at Philadelphia for Promoting Useful Knowledge, Independence Square, Philadelphia; numbers preceded by the letters "SP" refer to Charles Coleman Sellers, *Charles Willson Peale with Patron and Populace: A Supplement to Portraits and Miniatures by Charles Willson Peale with a Survey of His Work in Other Genres* (1969), issued as Vol. LIX, pt. 3, of the Transactions of the American Philosophical Society.

Stauffer: David McNeely Stauffer, *American Engravers upon Copper and Steel* (New York, 1964).

Thwaites: Reuben Gold Thwaites, *The Original Journals of the Lewis and Clark Expedition*. 8 vols. (New York, 1904).

Frontispiece. SELF-PORTRAIT
1821
Oil on canvas, 66 × 55.9 cm. (26 × 22 in.)

Reference: Sellers, *Portraits & Miniatures*, No. 635.

Provenance: Probably sent by Charles Willson Peale to the Baltimore Museum, which was then being managed by Rubens Peale; to Mary Jane Peale; to James Burd Peale; to Mrs. Rebecca Burd Peale Patterson, great-granddaughter of the artist; to Elise Peale Patterson; to Kennedy Galleries; to private collection.

(*Not in exhibition*)

1. CHARLES CARROLL, BARRISTER (1723–1783)
c. 1770–71
Miniature on ivory, set in gold as a pin, 4.8 × 2.7 cm. (1⅞ × 1⅛ in.)

References: Sellers, *Portraits & Miniatures*, No. SP12; Michael F. Trostel, *Antiques* CXI (1979), pp. 342–51.

Provenance: Mrs. Charles Henry Hart, 1914; Mrs. Jean B. Hart, 1958; Herman M. Ellis, 1969, to Israel Sack, Inc., New York City; to Kennedy Galleries; to private collection.

2. MATTHIAS AND THOMAS BORDLEY
1767
Watercolor on ivory, 9.2 × 10.8 cm. (3⅝ × 4¼ in.)
References: Sellers, *Portraits & Miniatures*, No. 67; National Portrait Gallery, Smithsonian Institution, Washington, D.C., *Benjamin West and His American Students*, catalogue by Dorinda Evans (1980), pp. 39–40.
Provenance: Bordley family descent to Mr. and Mrs. Murray Lloyd Goldsborough, Jr.; to National Museum of American Art, Smithsonian Institution, Washington, D.C., 1974 (1974.113).
(*Not in exhibition*)

3. WILLIAM PITT (1708–1778)
1768
Mezzotint, 58.1 × 37.5 cm. (22⅞ × 14¾ in.)
Inscribed at lower right: *Cha⁵ Willson Peale, pinx. et fecit./ Worthy of Liberty, M' Pitt scorns to invade the Liberties of other People.*
References: Sellers, *Portraits & Miniatures*, No. 695; Sellers, *Early Life* (1939), p. 86.
The Pennsylvania Academy of the Fine Arts, Philadelphia (1876.9.415)
(*Not in exhibition*)

4. *A Description of the Picture and Mezzotinto of Mr. Pitt, done by Charles Willson Peale, of Maryland*
1768
Broadside, 41 × 24.8 cm. (16⅛ × 9¾ in.)
Reference: Sellers, *Peale* (1969), pp. 67–69.
Library of Congress, Washington, D.C., Rare Books Division
(*Not in exhibition*)

5. JOHN BEALE BORDLEY (1727–1804)
1770
Oil on canvas, 214.5 × 148.6 cm. (84⁷⁄₁₆ × 58½ in.)
Signed and dated on rock at bottom right: *C. Peale Pinx./maryland/1770.*
References: Sellers, *Portraits & Miniatures*, No. 61, No. SP8; Sellers, *Later Life* (1947), pp. 81–82; Sellers, *Peale* (1969), pp. 83–85; Sellers, *Pharos VII* (1969), pp. 20–25.
Provenance: Painted for Edmund Jenings, London; LeRoy Highbaugh and Stetson University College of Law, Deland and St. Petersburg, Florida, after 1952; to Kennedy Galleries; to The Barra Foundation, Inc.; on loan to National Gallery of Art, Washington, D.C., 1978.

6. MORDECAI GIST (1742–1792)
1774
Oil on canvas, 76.2 × 63.5 cm. (30 × 25 in.)

References: Sellers, *Portraits & Miniatures*, No. 299; The Fine Arts Museum of San Francisco, *American Art: An Exhibition from the Collection of Mr. and Mrs. John D. Rockefeller 3rd*, catalogue by E.P. Richardson (1976), No. 12.
Provenance: Gist family descent to Mrs. H. Cavendish Darrell; Mrs. F. LaMotte Smith and Ruth Gist Dickens, great-great-granddaughters of the sitter, by 1949; Mr. and Mrs. Lawrence Fleischman, by 1960; Mr. and Mrs. John D. Rockefeller 3rd, by 1976; to The Fine Arts Museums of San Francisco, 1979 (1979.7.79).

7. WILLIAM PACA (1740–1799)
1772
Oil on canvas, 224.4 × 147.9 cm. (88⅜ × 58¼ in.)
References: Sellers, *Portraits & Miniatures*, No. 607; Eugenia Calvert Holland et al., *Four Generations of Commissions: The Peale Collection of the Maryland Historical Society* (1975), No. 5.
Provenance: Paca family descent to William Bennett Paca; to Peabody Institute, Baltimore; on loan to Maryland Historical Society, Baltimore, since 1924 (24.24.4).
(*Not in exhibition*)

8. WILLIAM STONE (1739–1821)
1774–75
Oil on canvas, 254 × 154.9 cm. (100 × 61 in.)
Signed and dated at lower left: *Chas Peale/pinx: 1774–75.*
References: Sellers, *Portraits & Miniatures*, No. 836; Stuart Feld, *American Paintings and Historical Prints from the Middendorf Collection*, The Metropolitan Museum of Art (1967), No. 2; Eugenia Calvert Holland et al., *Four Generations of Commissions: The Peale Collection of the Maryland Historical Society* (1975), No. 11.
Provenance: Stone family descent to J. William Middendorf, Jr., great-grandson of the sitter; to Maryland Historical Society, Baltimore, 1973 (73.83.1).

9. MRS. THOMAS HARWOOD (1747–1821)
c. 1771
Oil on canvas, 78.7 × 62.2 cm. (31 × 24½ in.)
References: Sellers, *Portraits & Miniatures*, No. 370; Bryson Burroughs, *Metropolitan Museum of Art Bulletin* XXVIII (1933), p. 138 ff.; Albert Ten Eyck Gardner and Stuart P. Feld, *American Paintings: A Catalogue of the Collection of the Metropolitan Museum of Art* I (1965), p. 59.
Provenance: Harwood family descent to Blanchard Randall, 1918; to The Metropolitan Museum of Art, New York City, Morris K. Jesup Fund, 1933 (33.24).

10. EDWARD LLOYD FAMILY
1771
Oil on canvas, 122 × 146 cm. (48 × 57½ in.)
Signed at right, on back of sofa: *C.W. Peale pinxt. 1771.*

References: Sellers, *Portraits & Miniatures*, No. 486, No. SP77; Sellers, *Later Life* (1947), p. 78; Edwin Wolf 2nd, *Winterthur Portfolio* V (1969), pp. 87–122.

Provenance: Lloyd family descent to Elizabeth Lloyd Lowndes, until 1964; to The Henry Francis du Pont Winterthur Museum, Delaware, 1964 (64.124).

11. WASHINGTON AS COLONEL OF THE VIRGINIA REGIMENT
1772
Oil on canvas, 128.3 × 105.4 cm. (50½ × 41½ in.)
Signed and dated at lower right: *Chas : W Peale, pinxt 1772.*

References: Sellers, *Portraits & Miniatures*, No. 894; William S. Baker, *The Engraved Portraits of Washington* (1880); Elizabeth Bryant Johnston, *Original Portraits of Washington* (1882), p. 5; Justin Winsor, *Narrative and Critical History of America* VII (1887), pp. 562–82; Clarence Winthrop Bowen, ed., *The History of the Centennial Celebration of the Inauguration of George Washington as First President of the United States* (1892), pp. 9, 541; Horace Wells Sellers, *Pennsylvania Magazine of History and Biography* XXXVIII (1914), pp. 257–86; John Hill Morgan and Mantle Fielding, *The Life Portraits of Washington and Their Replicas* (1931), p. 24, No. 1; Alfred Frankenstein, ed., *Washington-Custis-Lee Family Portraits from the Collection of Washington and Lee University, Lexington, Virginia* (1974).

Provenance: Mount Vernon; to George Washington Parke Custis, grandson of Martha Washington by her marriage to Daniel Parke Custis; to his daughter Mary Randolph Custis Lee, wife of Robert E. Lee; through their son George Washington Custis Lee, to his daughter, Mary Custis Lee, and his grandson's wife, Mrs. George Bolling Lee; to Washington-Custis-Lee Collection, Washington and Lee University, Lexington, Virginia, 1951 (1951.80).

12. JOHN DICKINSON (1732–1808)
1770
Oil on canvas, 124.5 × 99.1 cm. (49 × 39 in.)
References: Sellers, *Portraits & Miniatures*, No. 217; C.W. Peale, *An Historical Catalogue of Peale's Collection of Paintings* (1795); The Pennsylvania Academy of the Fine Arts, *Catalogue of an Exhibition of Portraits by Charles Willson Peale and James Peale and Rembrandt Peale* (1923), No. 41; *Pennsylvania Magazine of History and Biography* LVII (1933), p. 42; William Sawitzky, *Catalogue Descriptive and Critical of the Paintings and Miniatures in the Historical Society of Pennsylvania* (1942).

Provenance: Dickinson family descent to A. Sydney Logan, great-grandson of the sitter; to Historical Society of Pennsylvania, Philadelphia, 1926 (1926.1).

13. MRS. JOHN DICKINSON AND HER DAUGHTER SALLY
1773
Oil on canvas, 124.5 × 99.1 cm. (49 × 39 in.)
Signed and dated at lower right: *C: W: Peale. pinx. 1773.*

References: Sellers, *Portraits & Miniatures*, No. 221; The Pennsylvania Academy of the Fine Arts, *Catalogue of an Exhibition of Portraits by Charles Willson Peale and James Peale and Rembrandt Peale* (1923), No. 41; *Pennsylvania Magazine of History and Biography* LVII (1933), p. 42; William Sawitzky, *Catalogue Descriptive and Critical of the Paintings and Miniatures in the Historical Society of Pennsylvania* (1942).

Provenance: Dickinson family descent to A. Sydney Logan, great-grandson of the sitter; to Historical Society of Pennsylvania, Philadelphia, 1926 (1926.2).

14. JOHN CADWALADER FAMILY
1772
Oil on canvas, 130.8 × 104.8 cm. (51½ × 41¼ in.)
Signed and dated at lower left: *C W Peale/pinx^t 1771.*

References: Sellers, *Portraits & Miniatures*, No. 94; Sellers, *Early Life* (1939), p. 95; Sellers, *Later Life* (1947), p. 87; Sellers, *Peale* (1969), pp. 87, 103–4; Philadelphia Museum of Art, *Three Centuries of American Art* (1976), pp. 117–18.

Provenance: Descended in Cadwalader family to Capt. John Cadwalader, U.S.N.R. (Ret.).

15. JOHN PHILIP DE HAAS (1735–1786)
1772
Oil on canvas, 127 × 101.6 cm. (50 x 40 in.)
Signed and dated at lower right: *C. W. Peale pinx^t. 1772.*

References: Sellers, *Portraits & Miniatures*, No. 193; Frederic F. Sherman, *Art in America* XI (1923), p. 328.

Provenance: Mary J. Peale, granddaughter of the artist; to her sister-in-law, Mrs. Edward Burd Peale; to her daughter, Mrs. Frederick Carrier, 1922; Thomas B. Clarke, 1928; Andrew W. Mellon to 1939; Andrew W. Mellon Educational and Charitable Trust, 1939–42; to National Gallery of Art, Washington, D.C., Andrew W. Mellon Collection, 1942 (562).

16. GEORGE WASHINGTON (1732–1799)
1776
Miniature on ivory, 4.3 × 3.5 cm. (1 11/16 × 1 3/8 in.)
Reference: Sellers, *Portraits & Miniatures*, No. 897.

Provenance: Painted for Mrs. Washington; to the daughter of Dr. David Stuart, second husband of Mrs. John Parke Custis (daughter-in-law of Mrs. Washington by her first marriage); from her descendants to The Mount Vernon Ladies' Association of the Union, Virginia, 1920 (W460).

(*Not in exhibition*)

17. MARTHA WASHINGTON (1731–1802)
1776
Miniature on ivory, 4 × 3.3 cm. (1 9/16 × 1 5/16 in.)
Reference: Sellers, *Portraits & Miniatures*, No. 954, No. SP137.

Provenance: Painted for John Parke Custis, son of the sitter by her first marriage; to his daughter, Martha

Parke Custis Peter; to her daughter, Britannia Wellington Peter Kennon; to her grandson, G. Freeland Peter; to his son, G. Freeland Peter, Jr.; to The Mount Vernon Ladies' Association of the Union, Virginia, 1956 (W2102A).

(*Not in exhibition*)

18. SILAS DEANE (1737–1789)
1776
Miniature on ivory, 3.8 × 3.2 cm. (1½ × 1¼ in.)
Reference: Sellers, *Portraits & Miniatures*, No. 188.
Provenance: Deane family descent to William C. Alden, great-grandson of the sitter, 1879; estate of Frank Edward Johnson; to The Connecticut Historical Society, Hartford, 1937 ([1937] 391).

19. GEORGE WASHINGTON (1732–1799)
Probably 1779
Miniature, 3.8 × 3.3 cm. (1½ × 1⁵/₁₆ in.)
Reference: See Sellers, *Portraits & Miniatures*, "Miniatures based on full length of 1779," pp. 233–34.
Provenance: Ronald A. Lee, London, as agent, by 1969; to Kennedy Galleries, 1969; to private collection.

20. COLONEL GEORGE BAYLOR
1778
Watercolor on ivory, 3.8 × 3.2 cm. (1½ × 1¼ in.)
Reference: Sellers, *Portraits & Miniatures*, No. SP5A.
Provenance: John Walker Baylor, son of the sitter; to Fanny Baylor Horner Britton; to William R. Robins, Jr.; to Anderson House, The Society of the Cincinnati, Washington, D.C., 1967 (F1267).

21. HENRY KNOX (1750–1806)
1778
Miniature, 4.6 × 3.8 cm. (1¹³/₁₆ × 1½ in.)
Reference: Sellers, *Portraits & Miniatures*, No. 439.
Provenance: Old Print Shop, New York City; to Kennedy Galleries; to private collection.

22. GEORGE WALTON (1741–1804)
c. 1781
Miniature on ivory, 3.5 × 2.9 cm. (1⅜ × 1⅛ in.)
Reference: Sellers, *Portraits & Miniatures*, No. 892.
Provenance: Mrs. Charles Hickman (Blanche Walton), great-niece of the sitter; to Mrs. Louise Barrett; to Mrs. Mabel Brady Garvan; to Yale University Art Gallery, New Haven, 1944 (1944.74).

23. COLONEL WALTER STEWART (C. 1756–1796)
1781
Oil on canvas, 124.5 × 100.3 cm. (49 × 39½ in.)
Reference: Sellers, *Portraits & Miniatures*, No. 827.
Provenance: Philip Church, son-in-law of the sitter; to his son, John Church; Church family descent to Philip Schuyler Church; to Victor Spark and Graham Galleries; to private collection.

24. MRS. WALTER STEWART (1763–1823)
1782
Oil on canvas, 124.5 × 100.3 cm. (49 × 39½ in.)
Signed and dated at lower right: *C. W. Peale, pinx. 1782.*
Reference: Sellers, *Portraits & Miniatures*, No. 829.
Provenance: Philip Church, son-in-law of the sitter; to his son, John Church; Church family descent to Philip Schuyler Church; to Victor Spark and Graham Galleries; to private collection.

25. THOMAS ROBINSON (1751–1819)
c. 1784
Oil on canvas, 76.2 × 60.3 cm. (30 × 23¾ in.)
Reference: Sellers, *Portraits & Miniatures*, No. 748.
Provenance: Reverend Nalbro Frazier Robinson; to Independence National Historical Park Collection, Philadelphia, 1897 (13.244).

26. WASHINGTON AT THE BATTLE OF PRINCETON
1779
Oil on canvas, 238.8 × 149.9 cm. (94 × 59 in.)
References: Sellers, *Portraits & Miniatures*, No. 904; Peale Museum Catalogues (1795, 1813).
Provenance: The state of Pennsylvania until 1781, when the picture was slashed by vandals; returned to Peale for repair, but for reasons unknown the picture seems never to have been returned to the state; Peale's Museum, 1781–1854; Sale No. 151; purchase, Henry Pratt McKean, 1854; Elizabeth Wharton McKean Estate; to The Pennsylvania Academy of the Fine Arts, Philadelphia, 1943 (1943.16.2); lent in commemoration of the Tricentennial of Philadelphia.

27. HIS EXCELLENCY GEORGE WASHINGTON, ESQUIRE, COMMANDER IN CHIEF OF THE FEDERAL ARMY (1732–1799)
1780
Mezzotint, 37.6 × 26.7 cm. (14¹³/₁₆ × 10½ in.)
Inscribed: *Chaˢ Willson Peale pinx.ᵗ et fecit/His Excellency George Washington Esquire, Commander in/Chief of the Federal Army/This Plate is humbly Inscribed to the Honorable the Congress of the United States of America/By their Obedient Servant/Chaˢ Willson Peale.*
References: Sellers, *Portraits & Miniatures*, No. 916; William S. Baker, *The Engraved Portraits of Washington* (1880); Horace Wells Sellers, *Pennsylvania Magazine of History and Biography* LVII (1933), pp. 153–74; Stauffer, No. 2428; Wendy J. Shadwell, "The Portrait Engravings of Charles Willson Peale," in *Eighteenth-Century Prints in Colonial America*, ed. Joan D. Dolmetsch (1979), pp. 131, 142.
Provenance: Charles Allen Munn; to The Metropolitan Museum of Art, New York City, 1924 (24.90.5).

28. CONRAD-ALEXANDRE GÉRARD (1729–1790)
1779
Oil on canvas, 241.3 × 150.2 cm. (95 × 59⅛ in.)

References: Sellers, *Portraits & Miniatures*, No. 292,
No. SP45; Los Angeles County Museum of Art,
American Portraiture in the Grand Manner 1720–1920,
catalogue by Michael Quick (1981), pp. 110–13.

Provenance: Painted for the Continental Congress but
never delivered; Peale's Museum until 1854; Sale No.
139; purchase, city of Philadelphia, 1854; on permanent
loan to Independence National Historical Park Collection, Philadelphia, 1854 (13.083).

(*Not in exhibition*)

29. FREDERIC WILLIAM AUGUSTUS, BARON
VON STEUBEN (1730–1796)
1780
Oil on canvas, 75.5 × 62.9 cm. (29¾ × 24¾ in.)

Reference: Sellers, *Portraits & Miniatures*, No. 825.

Provenance: Judge Richard Peters; the Peters family;
Mrs. M.L.M. Peters; to The Pennsylvania Academy of
the Fine Arts, Philadelphia, 1881 (1881.1); lent in
commemoration of the Tricentennial of Philadelphia.

30. GENERAL OTHO HOLLAND WILLIAMS (1749–1794)
1782
Oil on canvas, 58.4 × 48.2 cm. (23 × 19 in.)

Reference: Sellers, *Portraits & Miniatures*, No. 986.

Provenance: Peale's Museum until 1854; Sale No. 39;
purchase, city of Philadelphia, 1854; on permanent
loan to Independence National Historical Park Collection, Philadelphia, 1854 (13.315).

31. (BARON) JOHANN DE KALB (1721–1780)
1781–82
Oil on canvas, 55.9 × 45.7 cm. (22 × 18 in.)

Reference: Sellers, *Portraits & Miniatures*, No. 431.

Provenance: Peale's Museum until 1854; Sale No. 25;
purchase, city of Philadelphia, 1854; on permanent
loan to Independence National Historical Park Collection, Philadelphia, 1854 (13.139).

32. GENERAL WILLIAM SMALLWOOD (1732–1792)
c. 1781–82
Oil on canvas, 59.7 × 49.5 cm. (23½ × 19½ in.)

Reference: Sellers, *Portraits & Miniatures*, No. 798.

Provenance: Peale's Museum until 1854; Sale No. 28;
purchase, city of Philadelphia, 1854; on permanent
loan to Independence National Historical Park Collection, Philadelphia, 1854 (13.264).

33. COLONEL JOHN EAGER HOWARD (1752–1827)
1782
Oil on canvas, 58.4 × 48.2 cm. (23 × 19 in.)

References: Sellers, *Portraits & Miniatures*, No. 389;
Joseph Loubat, *The Medallic History of the United
States of America, 1776–1876* (1967), No. 10.

Provenance: Peale's Museum until 1854; Sale No. 40;
purchase, city of Philadelphia, 1854; on permanent
loan to Independence National Historical Park Collection, Philadelphia, 1854 (13.121).

34. COLONEL WILLIAM (AUGUSTINE) WASHINGTON
(1752–1810)
c. 1782
Oil on canvas, 58.4 × 48.9 cm. (23 × 19¼ in.)

References: Sellers, *Portraits & Miniatures*, No. 958;
Joseph Loubat, *The Medallic History of the United
States of America, 1776–1876* (1967), No. 9.

Provenance: Peale's Museum until 1854; purchase,
city of Philadelphia, 1854; on permanent loan to
Independence National Historical Park Collection,
Philadelphia, 1854 (33.305).

35. GENERAL WILLIAM MOULTRIE (1730–1805)
1782
Oil on canvas, 67.5 × 57 cm. (26½ × 22½ in.)

References: Sellers, *Portraits & Miniatures*, No. 584;
James Thomas Flexner and Linda Bantel Samter, *The
Face of Liberty: Founders of the United States* (1975),
p. 176; Gibbes Art Gallery, *Selections from the
Collection of the Carolina Art Association* (1977), p. 64.

Provenance: Moultrie family descent to William Moultrie
Reid; with M. Knoedler and Co., as agent; Andrew W.
Mellon Charitable and Educational Trust; to National
Portrait Gallery, Smithsonian Institution, Washington,
D.C., 1942 (65.57) (deposited at National Gallery of
Art until 1965).

36. GENERAL JAMES WILKINSON (1757–1825)
1797
Oil on canvas, 61 × 50.8 cm. (24 × 20 in.)

Reference: Sellers, *Portraits & Miniatures*, No. 980.

Provenance: Peale's Museum until 1854; Sale No. 27;
purchase, city of Philadelphia, 1854; on permanent
loan to Independence National Historical Park
Collection, Philadelphia, 1854 (13.318).

37. NANCY HALLAM AS FIDELE IN CYMBELINE
1771
Oil on canvas, 127 × 102.9 cm. (50 × 40½ in.)

References: Sellers, *Portraits & Miniatures*, No. 342,
No. SP58; Sellers, *Early Life* (1939), pp. 97–98; Sellers,
Peale (1969), pp. 93–99, 452; George O. Seilhamer,
History of the American Theatre I (1888), pp. 270–81;
National Portrait Gallery, Smithsonian Institution,
Washington, D.C., *Portraits of the American Stage*
(1971), p. 16; National Gallery of Art, Washington,
D.C., *The Eye of Thomas Jefferson* (1976), pp. 15, 353.

Provenance: Peale's Museum until 1854; Sale No. 246;
purchase, Baird, 1854; Miss Marguerite Kumm, 1953;
to Colonial Williamsburg Foundation, Virginia, 1956
(1956.296).

38. RACHEL WEEPING
1772 and probably 1776
Oil on canvas, 94.3 × 81.9 cm. (37⅛ × 32¼ in.)

References: Sellers, *Portraits & Miniatures*, No. 645;
Sellers, *Early Life* (1939), p. 114; Sellers, *Peale* (1969),
pp. 106–8; Philadelphia Museum of Art, *Three
Centuries of American Art* (1976), p. 118; The Museums

at Stony Brook, New York, *A Time to Mourn: Expressions of Grief in Nineteenth Century America* (1980), p. 128.

Provenance: Peale family descent to Charles Coleman Sellers, until 1972; The Barra Foundation, Inc.; to Philadelphia Museum of Art, 1977 (1977.34.1).

39. Charles Willson Peale after Benjamin West
ELISHA RESTORING TO LIFE THE SHUNAMMITE'S SON
1767
Watercolor on paper, mounted on canvas, 40.6 × 61 cm. (16 × 24 in.)

Reference: Sellers, *Portraits & Miniatures*, No. S10.

Provenance: Peale family descent to Charles Coleman Sellers, to 1980; to private collection.

(*Not in exhibition*)

40. MRS. JACOB RUSH (MARY WRENCH)
1786
Oil on canvas, 83.2 × 68.6 cm. (32¾ × 27 in.)
Signed on edge of table at lower right: *C. W Peale 1786.*

References: Sellers, *Portraits & Miniatures*, No. 761; Sellers, *Early Life* (1939), pp. 100–111; Sellers, *Later Life* (1947), pp. 100–103; Peale, Autobiography, American Philosophical Society.

Provenance: Harriet Rush, daughter of the sitter; to her cousin, Mary Fullerton (Mrs. Erskine) Hazard; to her son, Albert B. Hazard; to his nephew, John Lyman Cox; to his daughter; to Kennedy Galleries; to private collection.

41. CHARLES PETTIT (1736–1806)
1792
Oil on canvas, 90.8 × 68 cm. (35¾ × 26¾ in.)
Signed and dated at lower left: *C. W Peale/painted 1792.*

Reference: Sellers, *Portraits & Miniatures*, No. 686.

Provenance: Painted for the sitter's son, Andrew Pettit; Pettit family descent to Sara Blair Pettit (later Mrs. Seth Caldwell Hetherington), great-great-granddaughter of the sitter, after 1890; with Copley Gallery, Boston, as agent, 1919; to Worcester Art Museum, Massachusetts, 1919 (1919.121).

42. GEORGE WASHINGTON (1732–1799)
1787
Oil on canvas, 60.3 × 48.2 cm. (23¾ × 19 in.)

Reference: Sellers, *Portraits & Miniatures*, No. 939.

Provenance: Peale's Museum until 1854; Sale No. 81; purchase, Joseph Harrison, 1854; to Mrs. Joseph Harrison, Jr. (Sarah Harrison); to The Pennsylvania Academy of the Fine Arts, Philadelphia, 1912 (1912.14.3); lent in commemoration of the Tricentennial of Philadelphia.

43. MRS. JAMES LATIMER (SARAH GEDDES)
1788
Oil on canvas, 91.5 × 69.2 cm. (36 × 27¼ in.)
References: Sellers, *Portraits & Miniatures*, No. 460;

Recent Acquisitions, Pennsylvania Academy of the Fine Arts, 1974–1975, No. 29.

Provenance: Latimer family descent to Robert C. Latimer; to The Pennsylvania Academy of the Fine Arts, Philadelphia, 1974 (1974.18.1); lent in commemoration of the Tricentennial of Philadelphia.

44. JAMES LATIMER (1720–1807)
1788
Oil on canvas, 89.5 × 67.3 cm. (35¼ × 26½ in.)

References: Sellers, *Portraits & Miniatures*, No. 459; *Recent Acquisitions, Pennsylvania Academy of the Fine Arts, 1974–1975*, No. 28.

Provenance: Latimer family descent to Robert C. Latimer; to The Pennsylvania Academy of the Fine Arts, Philadelphia, 1974 (1974.18.2); lent in commemoration of the Tricentennial of Philadelphia.

45. CAPTAIN JAMES JOSIAH (1751–1820)
1787
Oil on canvas, 76.2 × 63.5 cm. (30 × 25 in.)
Signed and dated at right, behind chair back: *painted by/C W Peale 1787.*

References: Sellers, *Portraits & Miniatures*, No. SP72; William Bell Clark, *Pennsylvania Magazine* LXXIX (October 1955), pp. 452–84.

Provenance: F. Woodward Earl, grandson of Susan Josiah (adopted daughter of Captain Josiah); purchased by Arthur Sussel at Freeman's Auction, 1952; to Allan Sussel.

46. HIS EXCELLENCY B. FRANKLIN, L.L.D., F.R.S., PRESIDENT OF PENNSYLVANIA (1706–1790)
1787
Mezzotint (oval), 15.2 × 12.7 cm. (6 × 5 in.)
Inscribed on outer oval border: HIS EXCELLENCY B. FRANKLIN L.L.D. F.R.S. PRESIDENT OF PENNSYLVANIA & LATE MINISTER OF THE UNITED STATES OF AMERICA AT THE COURT OF FRANCE; signed at base on inner border: *C. W. Peale pinx^t. et Fecit 1787.*

References: Sellers, *Portraits & Miniatures*, No. 280; Stauffer, No. 2423; E.P. Richardson, *Winterthur Portfolio* I (1964), p. 169; Wendy J. Shadwell, "The Portrait Engravings of Charles Willson Peale," in *Eighteenth-Century Prints in Colonial America*, ed. Joan D. Dolmetsch (1979), pp. 135, 142.

Provenance: Charles Allen Munn; to The Metropolitan Museum of Art, New York City, 1924 (24.90.52).

47. THE MARQUIS DE LAFAYETTE (1757–1834)
1787
Mezzotint (oval), 15.5 × 12.9 cm. (6⅛ × 5⁵⁄₁₆ in.)
Inscribed on outer oval border: THE MARQUIS DE LA FAYETTE MAJOR GENERAL IN THE ARMIES OF THE UNITED STATES OF AMERICA; signed at base on inner border: *C. W. Peale Pinx^t. et Fecit.*

References: Sellers, *Portraits & Miniatures*, No. 450; Stauffer, No. 2424; E.P. Richardson, *Winterthur Portfolio* I (1964), p. 171; Wendy J. Shadwell, "The Portrait

Engravings of Charles Willson Peale," in *Eighteenth-Century Prints in Colonial America*, ed. Joan D. Dolmetsch (1979), pp. 135, 142.

Provenance: Samuel P. Avery; to The Metropolitan Museum of Art, New York City, 1894 (94.1).

48. HIS EXCELLENCY G. WASHINGTON, ESQ. (1732–1799)
1787
Mezzotint (oval), 16 × 12.9 cm. (6⁵⁄₁₆ × 5¹⁄₁₆ in.)
Inscribed on outer oval border: HIS EXCEL: G: WASHINGTON ESQ: L.L.D. LATE COMMANDER IN CHIEF OF THE ARMIES OF THE U.S. OF AMERICA & PRESIDENT OF THE CONVENTION OF 1787; signed at base on inner border: *Painted & Engraved by C. W. Peale 1787.*

References: Sellers, *Portraits & Miniatures*, No. 940; Stauffer, No. 2429; E.P. Richardson, *Winterthur Portfolio* I (1964), p. 173; Wendy J. Shadwell, "The Portrait Engravings of Charles Willson Peale," in *Eighteenth-Century Prints in Colonial America*, ed. Joan D. Dolmetsch (1979), pp. 139, 143.

Provenance: Charles Allen Munn; to The Metropolitan Museum of Art, New York City, 1924 (24.90.54).

49. THE REVEREND JOSEPH PILMORE (1739–1825)
1787
Mezzotint (oval), 15.2 × 12.7 cm. (6 × 5 in.)

References: Sellers, *Portraits & Miniatures*, No. 692; Stauffer, No. 2425; E.P. Richardson, *Winterthur Portfolio* I (1964), p. 172; Wendy J. Shadwell, "The Portrait Prints of Charles Willson Peale," in *Eighteenth-Century Prints in Colonial America*, ed. Joan D. Dolmetsch (1979), pp. 136, 142.

Provenance: Charles Allen Munn; to The Metropolitan Museum of Art, New York City, 1924 (24.90.652).

50. THE ACCIDENT IN LOMBARD STREET
1787
Etching, 19.4 × 30.8 cm. (7⁵⁄₈ × 12¹⁄₈ in.)
Inscribed at left: *The pye from Bake-house she had brought/But let it fall for want of thought*; at right: *And laughing Sweeps collect around/The pye that's scatter'd on the ground./No. 1*; at center, THE ACCIDENT IN LOMBARD-STREET/PHILADᴬ. 1787 *designed & engraved by C.W. Peale.*

References: Sellers, *Portraits & Miniatures*, No. S54; E.P. Richardson, *Winterthur Portfolio* I (1964), p. 180.

The Henry Francis du Pont Winterthur Museum, Delaware (62.88)

51. Golden Pheasants
References (to the living and mounted pheasants): Sellers, *Early Life* (1939), pp. 253–54; Sellers, *Peale* (1969), p. 216; Sellers, *Mr. Peale's Museum* (1980), pp. 25, 115, 338 fn. 5; Peale letters to George Washington: December 31, 1786, George Washington Papers, Library of Congress; February 16, 1787, Feinstone Collection, American Philosophical Society; and February 27, 1787,

Peale-Sellers Papers, American Philosophical Society; Washington letter to Peale, March 13, 1787, Collection of Edward Ambler Armstrong, Princeton University Library; Faxon, pp. 126–27; Cutright, *Lewis and Clark* (1969), p. 391.

Provenance: Marquis de Lafayette, 1786; to George Washington, Mount Vernon, 1786–87; to Peale's Museum, 1787 until 1850; Moses Kimball of the Boston Museum; Boston Society of Natural History, by 1899; C. J. Maynard, Newtonville, Massachusetts, 1900; recovered by the Boston Society of Natural History, until 1914; Museum of Comparative Zoology, Harvard University, Cambridge, Massachusetts.

(*Not in exhibition*)

52. William Birch
BACK OF THE STATE HOUSE, PHILADELPHIA
1799
Engraving, 27.6 × 32.9 cm. (10⁷⁄₈ × 12¹⁵⁄₁₆ in.)
The Library Company of Philadelphia (P. 8742)

53. Charles Willson Peale and Titian Ramsay Peale II
THE LONG ROOM
1822
Ink and watercolor on paper, 35 × 52.7 cm. (14 × 20¾ in.)
Inscribed on back: *Interior of front room/Peale's Museum/State House/Philadelphia/1822/by T. R. Peale.*

Reference: Sellers, *Portraits & Miniatures*, No. S126.

Provenance: Edward Eberstadt and Sons, New York City, by 1957; to The Detroit Institute of Arts, The Founders Society; Director's Fund, 1957 (57.261).

(*Not in exhibition*)

54. THE EXHUMATION OF THE MASTODON
1806–8
Oil on canvas, 127 × 58.8 cm. (50 × 62½ in.)
Signed at lower right: *C WPeale/1806.*

References: Sellers, *Portraits & Miniatures*, No. 252; The Peale Museum, Baltimore, *Rendezvous for Taste* (1956), p. 4; Lillian B. Miller, *American Art Journal* XIII (1981), pp. 47–68.

Provenance: Peale's Museum until 1854; Lloyd Rogers; George Reuling; Bertha James (Mrs. Harry) White, 1905; to The Peale Museum, Baltimore, 1948 (48.83).

55. THE STAIRCASE GROUP: RAPHAELLE (1774–1825) AND TITIAN RAMSAY PEALE I (1780–1798)
1795
Oil on canvas, 226.1 × 100.3 cm. (89 × 39½ in.)

References: Sellers, *Portraits & Miniatures*, No. 662; *The Columbianum* (1795); Philadelphia Museum of Art, *Three Centuries of American Art* (1976), pp. 166–67.

Provenance: Peale's Museum until 1854; Sale No. 100; purchase, L.H. Newbolt, 1854; Mrs. Sabin W. Colton, Jr., great-granddaughter of the artist; Harold Sellers Colton; to Philadelphia Museum of Art, The George W. Elkins Collection, 1945 (E45.1.1).

56. EUTAW (?)
October 12, 1788 (?)
Pencil and brown ink on paper, 41.2 × 60.4 cm. (16¼ × 23¾ in.)
Inscribed at center: *Tufts of grass / intermixed with gravel*; at upper right: *a arbour / T. light seen through*; at center on lower right, in pencil: *C W Peale*; on back, below house, far right: *green*.

Reference: Sellers, *Portraits & Miniatures*, No. S66.

Provenance: Peale family; acquired by the American Philosophical Society, Philadelphia, between 1945 and present (RFB:P31 oversize No. 452).

57. James Trenchard (1747–?) after Charles Willson Peale
A N.W. VIEW OF THE STATE HOUSE IN PHILADELPHIA TAKEN 1778
1787
Engraving, 12.7 × 18.4 cm. (5 × 7¼ in.)
Inscribed: *Columb. Mag./C. W. Peale delin. J. T. Sculp./*A N.W. VIEW OF THE STATE HOUSE IN PHILADELPHIA *taken* 1778.

References: Sellers, *Portraits & Miniatures*, No. S30; Robert D. Crompton, *Art Quarterly* XXIX (1960), pp. 378–97; E. P. Richardson, *Winterthur Portfolio* I (1964), pp. 166–81.

Provenance: Engraved for the *Columbian Magazine* I (July 1787), opp. p. 513; Charles Coleman Sellers until 1980; private collection.

58. PERSPECTIVE VIEW OF THE COUNTRY BETWEEN WILMINGTON AND THE DELAWARE
1787
Engraving, 19.7 × 37.5 cm. (7¾ × 14¾ in.)
Inscribed at top: *Perspective View of the Country between Wilmington and the Delaware. Taken from the Hill S.W. of the Academy.*

Reference: Sellers, *Portraits & Miniatures*, No. S51.

Provenance: Engraved for the *Columbian Magazine* I (April 1787), opp. p. 351; the Old Shoe Gallery, Lewes, Delaware; to Robert G. Stewart, 1977.

59. James Trenchard (1747–?) after Charles Willson Peale
AN EAST VIEW OF GRAY'S FERRY, ON THE RIVER SCHUYLKILL
1787
Engraving, 20 × 35 cm. (7⅞ × 13¾ in.)
Inscribed: *C. W. Peale delin. J. T. sculp./*AN EAST VIEW OF GRAY'S FERRY, *on the* RIVER SCHUYLKILL.

References: Sellers, *Portraits & Miniatures*, No. S52; John Scharf and Thompson Westcott, *History of Philadelphia* III (1884), p. 2143; E.P. Richardson, *Winterthur Portfolio* I (1964), pp. 176–77.

Provenance: Engraved for the *Columbian Magazine* I (August 1787), opp. p. 565; The Library Company of Philadelphia (P.2283.36).

60. James Trenchard (1747–?) after Charles Willson Peale
A SOUTH EAST VIEW OF CHRIST'S CHURCH
1787
Engraving, 21.3 × 17.2 cm. (8⅜ × 6¾ in.)
Inscribed: *A South East View of Christ's Church.*

References: Sellers, *Portraits & Miniatures*, No. S56; Robert C. Crompton, *Art Quarterly* XXIII (1960), p. 383; E. P. Richardson, *Winterthur Portfolio* I (1964), p. 178.

Provenance: Engraved for the *Columbian Magazine* I (December 1787), opp. p. 839; The Library Company of Philadelphia ([1] 1525.F.22b).

61. James Trenchard (1747–?) after Charles Willson Peale
AN EAST VIEW OF GRAY'S FERRY, NEAR PHILADELPHIA, WITH THE TRIUMPHAL ARCHES, & ERECTED FOR THE RECEPTION OF GENERAL WASHINGTON, APRIL 20, 1789
1789
Engraving, 10.5 × 17.1 cm. (4⅛ × 6¾ in.)
Inscribed within border: *C. W. Peale delin.*; below: *J. Trenchard Sculp./An East View of* GRAY'S FERRY, *near Philadelphia, with the* TRIUMPHAL ARCHES, *& erected for/the Reception of General Washington, April 20, 1789.*

References: Sellers, *Portraits & Miniatures*, No. S70; Sellers, *Later Life* (1947), pp. 274–76.

Provenance: Engraved for the *Columbian Magazine* III (May 1789), frontis.; Bowdoin College Library, Brunswick, Maine.

62. Attributed to Thackara and Vallance, probably after Charles Willson Peale
VIEW OF SEVERAL PUBLIC BUILDINGS, IN PHILADELPHIA
1790
Engraving, 11.3 × 20.2 cm. (4⁷⁄₁₆ × 7¹⁵⁄₁₆ in.)
Inscribed: *View of Several Public Buildings, in Philadelphia.*

Reference: Sellers, *Portraits & Miniatures*, No. S72.

Provenance: Engraved for the *Columbian Magazine* IV (January 1790), opp. p. 25; The Library Company of Philadelphia (1525.F.39d).

63. VIEW OF WEST POINT FROM THE SIDE OF THE MOUNTAIN, in bound sketchbook entitled "Highlands of the Hudson"
1801
Pen and watercolor on paper, 15.6 × 19.3 cm. (6¼ × 7⅝ in.)

Reference: Sellers, *Portraits & Miniatures*, No. S83.

Provenance: Peale family; acquired by the American Philosophical Society, Philadelphia, between 1945 and present (8D BP. 31.8).

64. BELFIELD
1815–16
Oil on canvas, 71.1 × 92.1 cm. (28 × 36½ in.)

References: Sellers, *Portraits & Miniatures*, No. S108; Jessie Poesch, *Antiques* LXXII (1957), pp. 434–39.

Provenance: Anna Elizabeth Peale, granddaughter of the artist; to her namesake, Anna Peale Amies; to Horace Wells Sellers; to Kennedy Galleries; to private collection.

65. MILL BANK
1818
Oil on canvas, 38.1 × 53.3 cm. (15 × 21 in.)

Reference: Sellers, *Portraits & Miniatures*, No. S113.

Provenance: Charles Coleman Sellers until 1980; Kennedy Galleries, 1981; to private collection.

66. SELLERS HALL
c. 1818
Oil on canvas, 38.1 × 52.7 cm. (15 × 20¾ in.)

Reference: Sellers, *Portraits & Miniatures*, No. S114.

Provenance: Charles Coleman Sellers, until 1980; to Kennedy Galleries, New York City, 1981; to private collection, 1982.

67. JOHN QUINCY ADAMS (1767–1848)
1818
Oil on canvas, 61 × 50.8 cm. (24 × 20 in.)

References: Sellers, *Portraits & Miniatures*, No. 4; William Sawitzky, *Catalogue Descriptive and Critical of the Paintings and Miniatures in the Historical Society of Pennsylvania* (1942), p. 38; Andrew Oliver, *Portraits of John Quincy Adams and His Wife* (1970), pp. 87–89; National Portrait Gallery, Smithsonian Institution, Washington, D.C., *The Life Portraits of John Quincy Adams* (1970), No. 10.

Provenance: Peale's Museum until 1854; Sale No. 142; purchase, Charles S. Ogden, 1854; to Historical Society of Pennsylvania, Philadelphia, 1896 (1896.6).

68. HENRY CLAY (1777–1852)
1818
Oil on canvas, 61 × 50.8 cm. (24 × 20 in.)

References: Sellers, *Portraits & Miniatures*, No. 144; William Sawitzky, *Catalogue Descriptive and Critical of the Paintings and Miniatures in the Historical Society of Pennsylvania* (1942), p. 49.

Provenance: Peale's Museum until 1854; Sale No. 134; purchase, Charles S. Ogden, 1854; to Historical Society of Pennsylvania, Philadelphia, 1896 (1896.7).

69. MRS. COLEMAN SELLERS (SOPHONISBA ANGUSCIOLA PEALE) (1786–1859)
1805
Watercolor on paper (oval), 15.3 × 12.7 cm. (6 × 5 in.)

Reference: Sellers, *Portraits & Miniatures*, No. 779.

Provenance: Coleman and Sophonisba Sellers; to their daughter, Anna Sellers; to her brother, Coleman Sellers; to Jessie Sellers Colton; to his son, Harold Sellers Colton; to private collection.

70. COLEMAN SELLERS (1781–1834)
1805
Watercolor on paper (oval), 15.3 × 12.7 cm. (6 × 5 in.)

Reference: Sellers, *Portraits & Miniatures*, No. 777.

Provenance: Coleman and Sophonisba Sellers; to their daughter, Anna Sellers; to her brother, Coleman Sellers; to Jessie Sellers Colton; to his son, Harold Sellers Colton; to private collection.

71. COLEMAN SELLERS (1781–1834)
c. 1811
Oil on canvas, 73 × 59.7 cm. (28¾ × 23½ in.)

References: Sellers, *Portraits & Miniatures*, No. 778; Sellers, *Peale* (1969), pp. 322–23.

Provenance: Sellers family descent to Charles Coleman Sellers, until 1980; to Kennedy Galleries, 1981; to private collection, 1982.

72. MRS. CHARLES WILLSON PEALE (HANNAH MOORE) (1755–1821)
1816
Oil on canvas, 61 × 50.8 cm. (24 × 20 in.)
Signed and dated at center right: *C. W. Peale/painted 1816*; inscribed on reverse: *Hannah Peale aged 61 yrs. 10th July 1816/painted by Chas. W. Peale in his 76 year.*

References: Sellers, *Portraits & Miniatures*, No. 653; The Detroit Institute of Arts, *The Peale Family* (1967), pp. 45–46; Museum of Fine Arts, Boston, *American Paintings in the Museum of Fine Arts*, I (1969), p. 208.

Provenance: Hannah Moore Peale; Deborah Moore Jackson, sister of the sitter, 1821; Harriet Jackson Iddings, 1832; Mary Iddings Parker, her sister; Reverend Henry Ainsworth Parker, by 1902; Reginald Seabury Parker, his son, 1919; Mrs. Reginald Parker; to Museum of Fine Arts, Boston, 1965 (65.611).

73. SELF-PORTRAIT
1822
Oil on canvas, 74.9 × 61.6 cm. (29½ × 24¼ in.)

References: Sellers, *Portraits & Miniatures*, No. 633; The Fine Arts Museums of San Francisco, *American Art: An Exhibition from the Collection of Mr. and Mrs. John D. Rockefeller 3rd*, catalogue by E.P. Richardson (1976), No. 14.

Provenance: Painted for Peale's daughter, Sophonisba Peale (Mrs. Coleman Sellers); Peale family descent to Mrs. Sabin W. Colton, Jr., great-granddaughter of the artist; to Harold Sellers Colton; to Museum of Northern Arizona, Flagstaff, 1972; to private collection.

74. JAMES PEALE (1749–1831) BY LAMPLIGHT
1822
Oil on canvas, 68.6 × 91.4 cm. (27 × 36 in.)

Reference: Sellers, *Portraits & Miniatures*, No. 659.

Provenance: Peale's Museum until 1854; possibly Sale No. 88; Mr. and Mrs. Augustin Runyon Peale (grandson of the artist), 1854; to Augustin Runyon Peale, Jr.; to his son and daughter Herbert Raphaelle and Adele Peale Conway; to Mr. Dexter M. Ferry, Jr.; to The Detroit Institute of Arts, 1950 (50.58).

75. THE ARTIST IN HIS MUSEUM
1822
Oil on canvas, 262.9 × 203.2 cm. (103½ × 80 in.)

References: Sellers, *Portraits & Miniatures*, No. 636;
Roger B. Stein, *Prospects: The Annual of American
Cultural Studies* VI (1981), pp. 139–85.

Provenance: Peale's Museum until 1854; Sale No. 250;
purchase, Joseph Harrison, 1854; to Mrs. Joseph Harrison, Jr. (Sarah Harrison); to The Pennsylvania Academy
of the Fine Arts, Philadelphia, 1878 (1878.1.2); lent
in commemoration of the Tricentennial of Philadelphia.

76. CHARLES-ALEXANDRE LESUEUR (1778–1846)
1818
Oil on canvas, 58.4 × 48.2 cm. (23 × 19 in.)

References: Sellers, *Portraits & Miniatures*, No. 476;
Historical Society of Pennsylvania, Philadelphia, "Memoranda of the Philadelphia Museum," Peale Papers (1818),
p. 91; *Academy of Natural Sciences Proceedings* VII
(1854–55), p. 2; The Metropolitan Museum of Art,
New York City, *Nineteenth-Century America* (1970),
No. 12.

Provenance: Peale's Museum until 1854; purchase,
naturalist George Ord, 1854; to the Academy of Natural
Sciences of Philadelphia, 1854 (24).

77. DAVID RITTENHOUSE (1732–1796)
1791
Oil on canvas, 94 × 68.6 cm. (37 × 27 in.)

References: Sellers, *Portraits & Miniatures*, No. 739;
Sellers, *A Catalogue of Portraits and Other Works of
Art in the Possession of the American Philosophical
Society* (1961), p. 62; Benjamin Rush, *Eulogium Intended
to Preserve the Memory of David Rittenhouse* (1796);
Brooke Hindle, *David Rittenhouse* (1964), pp. 361–62.

Provenance: Painted for the American Philosophical
Society, Philadelphia 1791, and still in its collection
(58.P.29).

78. The White-Headed or Bald Eagle (*Falco
leucocephalus*)

References (both to the living and mounted eagle):
Sellers, *Later Life* (1947), pp. 62–63, 228; Sellers, *Mr.
Peale's Museum* (1980), pp. 89, 343 fn. 10; Alexander
Wilson, *American Ornithology* IV (1811), pl. xxxvi,
pp. 89–100; "Memoirs of Charles Willson Peale [1790
and 1826] from his Original Manuscript, with Notes
by Horace Wells Sellers" [c. 1900], p. 221, Peale-Sellers
Papers, American Philosophical Society; Faxon, pp.
134–35; Roger B. Stein, *Prospects: The Annual of
American Cultural Studies* VI (1981), pp. 160–61.

Provenance: Alexander Wilson, 1810 or 1811; Peale's
Museum by 1813 until 1850; Moses Kimball of the
Boston Museum; Boston Society of Natural History,
by 1899; C. J. Maynard, Newtonville, Massachusetts,
1900; recovered by the Boston Society of Natural
History, until 1914; Museum of Comparative Zoology,
Harvard University, Cambridge, Massachusetts
(MCZ 67.846).

79. Alexander Lawson (1773–1846) after a drawing by
Alexander Wilson (1766–1813)
WHITE-HEADED EAGLE
1811
Hand-colored engraving and etching on paper, 27.6 ×
36.8 cm. (10⅞ × 14½ in.)
Inscribed in the plate at lower left: *Drawn from Nature
by A. Wilson*; at lower center: *White-headed Eagle*; at
lower right: *Engraved by A. Lawson*.

References: Alexander Wilson, *American Ornithology*
IV (1811), pl. xxxvi, pp. 89–100; Venia and Maurice
Phillips, *Guide to the Manuscript Collections of the Academy of Natural Sciences of Philadelphia* (1963), p. 50.

Provenance: Alexander Lawson, died 1846; his daughters, Malvina Lawson and Mary Lawson Birckhead,
Philadelphia and West Chester, Pennsylvania; Academy
of Natural Sciences of Philadelphia (Collection 79,
vol. 2: 28).

80. American Wild Turkey

References (to the living and mounted turkey and its
appearance in *The Artist in His Museum* [No. 75]):
Sellers, *Portraits & Miniatures*, p. 121; Sellers, *Mr.
Peale's Museum* (1980), p. 242; James, I, p. 373;
Charles-Lucien Bonaparte, *American Ornithology; or,
The Natural History of Birds Inhabiting the United
States not given by Wilson* I (1825), pl. ix, pp. 79–105;
Faxon, p. 134; Poesch, pp. 46–47; Roger B. Stein,
Prospects: The Annual of American Cultural Studies
VI (1981), pp. 143–44, 160–61, 177 fn. 11.

Provenance: Peale's Museum until 1850; Moses Kimball
of the Boston Museum; Boston Society of Natural
History, by 1899; C. J. Maynard, Newtonville, Massachusetts, 1900; recovered by the Boston Society of Natural
History, until 1914; Museum of Comparative Zoology,
Harvard University, Cambridge, Massachusetts (MCZ
no. 67842).

81. Charles Willson Peale and A.M.F.J. [Palisot de]
Beauvois
*A Scientific and Descriptive Catalogue of Peale's
Museum*, printed by Samuel H. Smith, Philadelphia,
1796

References: Sellers, *Peale* (1969), p. 279; Sellers, *Mr.
Peale's Museum* (1980), p. 83.

American Philosophical Society, Philadelphia
(V.6, #3)

82. Rembrandt Peale (1778–1860)
WORKING SKETCH OF THE MASTODON
1801
Ink and watercolor on paper, 38.9 × 32.5 cm. (15³⁄₁₆ ×
12¾ in.)

Reference: Sellers, *Mr. Peale's Museum* (1980), pp.
141–44.

Provenance: Peale family; acquired by the American
Philosophical Society, Philadelphia, between 1945 and
present.

83. Baron Georges Cuvier
Grand Mastodonte, in Cuvier's *Recherches sur les Ossemens Fossiles des Quadrupedes*, 1812, pl. V
Engraving, 19.5 × 25.7 cm. (7¾ × 10 in.)
American Philosophical Society, Philadelphia

84. Titian Ramsay Peale II (1799–1885)
The Mammoth Skeleton
1821
Watercolor on paper, 37 × 48 cm. (14½ × 18⅞ in.)
Signed and dated at lower left: *T. Peale Jan: 1821.*

References: Sellers, *Mr. Peale's Museum* (1980), p. 144; John D. Godman, *American Natural History* (2nd. ed., 1831), ill. opp. p. 225 (engraved by G. B. Ellis); Theodore E. Stebbins, Jr., *American Master Drawings and Watercolors* (1976), p. 72.

American Philosophical Society, Philadelphia (B/P31, January 1821)

85. *Skeleton of the Mammoth Is Now To Be Seen*, printed by John Omrod, Philadelphia, c. 1790
Broadside, 30.5 × 22.5 cm. (12 × 8⅞ in.)
Inscribed at bottom: *H W Sellers with compliments of Chas Henry Hart 4/4/13.*

Provenance: Peale family; acquired by the American Philosophical Society, Philadelphia, between 1945 and present (973/C683/No. 583).

86. Ticket to the museum (engraved by Peale)
1788

Provenance: Peale family descent to Elise Peale Patterson de Gelpi-Toro.

87. Alexander Wilson (1766–1813)
Clark's Crow (now Clark's Nutcracker [*Nucifraga columbiana* (Wilson) or *Corvus columbianus* Wilson]) and Lewis's Woodpecker (*Asyndesmus lewis* [gray] or *Picus torquatus* Wilson)
1808
Pen and ink, pencil, and wash on paper; crow: 23.2 × 22.5 cm. (9⅛ × 8⅞ in.); woodpecker: 23.2 × 13 cm. (9⅛ × 5⅛ in.)

References (to the drawing and to Clark's Crow; for Lewis's Woodpecker, see No. 124): Alexander Wilson, *American Ornithology* III (1811), pl. xx, pp. 27–32; Coues, II, p. 530; III, p. 1028; Thwaites, III, p. 17; Robert Cantwell, *Alexander Wilson: Naturalist and Pioneer* (1961), pp. 141–42, opp. p. 192; Jackson, p. 298; Venia and Maurice Phillips, *Guide to the Manuscript Collections in the Academy of Natural Sciences of Philadelphia* (1963), p. 50; Cutright, *Lewis and Clark* (1969), pp. 187, 196, foll. p. 240, pp. 296–97, 384–87, 435, 448; Martina R. Norelli, *American Wildlife Painting* (1975), pp. 25, 88; Cutright, *History* (1976), pp. 45, 100, 188, 224, 230.

Provenance: Alexander Lawson, died 1846; his daughters, Malvina Lawson and Mary Lawson Birckhead, Philadelphia and West Chester, Pennsylvania; Academy of Natural Sciences of Philadelphia (Collection 79, vol. 2: 12A).

88. Alexander Lawson (1773–1846) after a drawing by Alexander Wilson (1766–1813)
1. Louisiana Tanager. 2. Clark's Crow. 3. Lewis's Woodpecker
1811
Hand-colored engraving and etching on paper, 36.2 × 26.7 cm. (14¼ × 10½ in.)
Signed and inscribed in the plate at lower left: *Drawn from Nature by A. Wilson*; at lower center: *1. Louisiana Tanager. 2. Clark's Crow. 3. Lewis's Woodpecker/ 20*; at lower right: *Engraved by A. Lawson.*

References: Alexander Wilson, *American Ornithology* III (1811), pl. xx, pp. 27–32; Robert Cantwell, *Alexander Wilson: Naturalist and Pioneer* (1961), pp. 141–42, opp. p. 192; Venia and Maurice Phillips, *Guide to the Manuscript Collections in the Academy of Natural Sciences of Philadelphia* (1963), p. 50; Cutright, *Lewis and Clark* (1969), foll. p. 240, p. 385.

Provenance: Alexander Lawson, died 1846; his daughters, Malvina Lawson and Mary Lawson Birckhead, Philadelphia and West Chester, Pennsylvania; Academy of Natural Sciences of Philadelphia (Collection 79, vol. 2: 12).

89. Crossbows

References: Sellers, *Mr. Peale's Museum* (1980), pp. 205–7, 349 fn. 52; James Mease, *Picture of Philadelphia* (1811), p. 314.

Peabody Museum of Archaeology and Ethnology, Harvard University, Cambridge, Massachusetts (HU 58295 and 58296)

90. Thomas Say (1787–1834)
1819
Oil on canvas, 61 × 50.8 cm. (24 × 20 in.)

References: Sellers, *Portraits & Miniatures*, No. 773; J.I. Merritt III, "Thomas Say: Explorer-Naturalist," in *Frontiers: Annual of the Academy of Natural Sciences of Philadelphia* III (1981–82), pp. 25–33.

Provenance: Peale's Museum until 1854; Sale No. 74; purchase, Mr. Harrington, 1854; Mrs. Joseph E. Mitchell; to the Academy of Natural Sciences of Philadelphia, 1887 (Collection 286).

91. George B. Ellis (active 1821–38) after a drawing by Charles A. Lesueur (1778–1846) in John D. Godman's *American Natural History* II, 1826
Pronghorn Antilope
Engraving on paper, bound in book, 21.8 × 12.9 cm. (8⁹⁄₁₆ × 5¹⁄₁₆ in.)
Signed and inscribed in plate at lower left: *Drawn by C. A. Lesueur*; at lower right: *Engᵈ by G. B. Ellis.*

Reference (for the species and the mounted specimen, see No. 133): John D. Godman, *American Natural History* II (1826), ill. opp. p. 321, pp. 321–26.

American Philosophical Society, Philadelphia

92. Entomological collection: moth and butterfly mounts arranged by Titian Ramsay Peale II (1799–1885)

References: *Proceedings of the Academy of Natural Sciences* 41 (1889), p. 435; Poesch, pp. 113–17; Venia and Maurice Phillips, *Guide to the Manuscript Collections in the Academy of Natural Sciences of Philadelphia* (1963), p. 173.

Provenance: Titian Ramsay Peale, died 1885; his heirs, 1885–89; gift to the Academy of Natural Sciences of Philadelphia, 1889 (Collection 320).

93. Titian Ramsay Peale II (1799–1885)
Sketchbook containing drawings and watercolors of animals
1821–22
A. BAT
Watercolor, 18.2 × 24.3 cm. (7⅛ × 9½ in.)
Inscribed at upper left: *Pteropus Edulis/Geoff =* ; at lower right: *From Batavia/Living in Philᵃ Museum/1822.*
B. MOOSE
Pencil and watercolor, 18.2 × 24.3 cm. (7⅛ × 9½ in.)
Inscribed at upper left: *15 months old Exhibited in Phila.*
C. TARTARIAN MONKEY
Pencil and watercolor, 18.2 × 24.3 cm. (7⅛ × 9½ in.)
Inscribed at lower left: *Simia Hamadryas/Museum/Aug: 1821;* at lower right: *Living in Philᵃ Museum/1821.*

Provenance: Peale family; acquired by the American Philosophical Society, Philadelphia, between 1945 and present (B/P31.15c).

94. *The Famous Grisly Bear*
1804
Broadside (enclosed in a letter from Charles Willson Peale to Thomas Jefferson, March 18, 1804), 21.4 × 15.5 cm. (8⁷⁄₁₆ × 6⅛ in.)
Reference: Sellers, *Mr. Peale's Museum* (1980), pp. 206–9.
Library of Congress, Washington, D.C., Manuscripts Department (Thomas Jefferson Papers, 24013)

95. Titian Ramsay Peale II (1799–1885)
MISSOURI BEARS
Watercolor and ink on paper, 18.2 × 24 cm. (7⅛ × 9⁷⁄₁₆ in.)
Signed at lower left: *T.R. Peale delin:*; inscribed at lower center: *Missouri Bear./Ursus horribilis: Ord*; at lower right: *Specimens col'd by Lt. Pike./presented to C.W. Peale.*
BEAR CLAWS
Pencil on paper, 8.2 × 5.5 cm. (3¼ × 2³⁄₁₆ in.), irregular; and 5.8 × 4.6 cm. (2⅜ × 1¹³⁄₁₆ in.), irregular.
References: Sellers, *Portraits & Miniatures*, No. S48; Sellers, *Later Life* (1947), p. 228; Sellers, *Mr. Peale's Museum* (1980), pp. 206–7, 209, 349 fn. 54; Peale letter to Thomas Jefferson, January 29, 1808, Thomas Jefferson Papers, Library of Congress; "Memoranda of the Philadelphia Museum," entry for January 28, 1808, Peale Papers, Historical Society of Pennsylvania; Poesch, p. 60.

Provenance: Peale family; acquired by the American Philosophical Society, Philadelphia, between 1945 and present (B/P31/15a/No. 9).

96. A Group of Shells
PINNA NOBILIS
Mediterranean
Academy of Natural Sciences of Philadelphia (1946–A)
(Not illustrated)

ANOMIA PLACENTA
Philippine Islands
Academy of Natural Sciences of Philadelphia (229110)
(Not illustrated)

DRUPA MORUM
Hawaii
Provenance: collected for Titian Ramsay Peale II by Thomas Nuttall, 1836; Academy of Natural Sciences of Philadelphia (199550).

CHAROMIA TRITONIS
Samoa
Provenance: Titian Ramsay Peale, 1834; Academy of Natural Sciences of Philadelphia (199555).
(Not illustrated)

CONUS GENERALIS
Samoa
Provenance: Titian Ramsay Peale, 1834; Academy of Natural Sciences of Philadelphia (199545).
(Not illustrated)

HARPA MAJOR
Mauritius Islands
Provenance: unknown, but same species as one collected by Titian Ramsay Peale on the Wilkes Expedition; Academy of Natural Sciences of Philadelphia (180952).
(Not illustrated)

97. Ojibwa Man's Snowshoes
Woman's Snowshoe *(Not illustrated)*
Provenance: Col. John Bradley, New Jersey, 1835; Peale's Museum, 1835 until 1850; Peabody Museum of Archaeology and Ethnology, Harvard University, Cambridge, Massachusetts (HU 52981 and HU 52982).

98. Algonquin (Southern Illinois) Beaver Bowl
Wood
Inscribed in Charles Willson Peale's hand: *Indian Sculpture of a Beaver/presented by Judge Turner.*
Reference: Sellers, *Mr. Peale's Museum* (1980), pp. 327–28.
Provenance: Judge George Turner; Peale's Museum until 1850; Peabody Museum of Archaeology and Ethnology, Harvard University, Cambridge, Massachusetts (HU 52998).

99. Grizzly Bear Ornaments
Peabody Museum of Archaeology and Ethnology, Harvard University, Cambridge, Massachusetts (HU 53007)

100. Choctaw Necklace
References: Sellers, *Mr. Peale's Museum* (1980), p. 120; "Memoranda of the Philadelphia Museum," entry for

January 9, 1828, Peale Papers, Historical Society of Pennsylvania.

Provenance: Miss E.M. Burn, 1828; Peale's Museum, 1828 until 1850; Peabody Museum of Archaeology and Ethnology, Harvard University, Cambridge, Massachusetts (HU 53026).

101. Model of a Chinese Lady's Foot and Leg with Silk Shoe

References: Sellers, *Mr. Peale's Museum* (1980), pp. 35, 70; "Memoranda of the Philadelphia Museum," entry for June 21, 1813 (may refer to this object), Peale Papers, Historical Society of Pennsylvania.

Provenance: Peale's Museum until 1850; Peabody Museum of Archaeology and Ethnology, Harvard University, Cambridge, Massachusetts (HU 53793).

102. Chinese Abacus or Counting Board

Peabody Museum of Archaeology and Ethnology, Harvard University, Cambridge, Massachusetts (HU 53321)

103. Horn Canteen and Ivory Canteen

References: Sellers, *Mr. Peale's Museum* (1980), pp. 166–67; "Memoranda of the Philadelphia Museum," entry for 1804 (following "02. Dec. 3"), Peale Papers, Historical Society of Pennsylvania.

Provenance: George Harrison, 1804; Peale's Museum, 1804–1850; Peabody Museum of Archaeology and Ethnology, Harvard University, Cambridge, Massachusetts (HU 53261 and HU 53262).

104. Fiji Headrest
Wood

References: Sellers, *Mr. Peale's Museum* (1980), p. 198; "Memoranda of the Philadelphia Museum," entry for June 6, 1808, Peale Papers, Historical Society of Pennsylvania.

Provenance: Mr. Coles and Edmund Fanning, by 1808; Peale's Museum, 1808 until 1850; Peabody Museum of Archaeology and Ethnology, Harvard University, Cambridge, Massachusetts (HU 53535).

105. Hawaiian Crested Helmet
Before 1841
Red, yellow, black, and white feathers on wickerwork, 56 × 39 cm. (22 1/16 × 15 3/8 in.)

References: Sellers, *Mr. Peale's Museum* (1980), pp. 40–42; William Howells, *Masterpieces from the Peabody Museum* (1978), pp. 48–49.

Provenance: Possibly deposited by George Washington at Peale's Museum in 1792; Boston Museum; to Peabody Museum of Archaeology and Ethnology, Harvard University, Cambridge, Massachusetts, 1899 (99-12-70).

106. A selection of minerals from the collection of Adam Seybert (1773–1825), arranged in the order specified by Parker Cleaveland, *Elementary Treatise on Mineralogy and Geology* (1816): rock crystal in carbonate of lime (Seybert no. 349); the pyramid of a large rock crystal from the Alps (Seybert no. 363); green clay from the farm of a Dr. Lawrence in Monmouth County, New Jersey (Seybert no. 1095); red chalk from Germany (Seybert no. 1104); yellow clay from Georgia (Seybert no. 1105); native sulfur from an unspecified locality (Seybert no. 1126); pale-colored amber (Seybert no. 1151) (*illustrated*); irised anthracite from Schuylkill County, Pennsylvania (Seybert no. 1160); native copper from Cornwall (Seybert no. 1251); crystallized chromate of iron from a locality near Baltimore, Maryland (Seybert no. 1448); lava from Mount Vesuvius, Italy (Seybert no. 1758); and volcanic ashes from the sides and base of Mount Vesuvius, Italy (Seybert no. 1783).

References: "Catalogue of Minerals in the Adam Seybert Collection," 1825, Academy of Natural Sciences of Philadelphia (Collection 141); John C. Greene and John G. Burke, *The Science of Minerals in the Age of Jefferson* (1978), pp. 29–30, 38–39, 44.

Provenance: Adam Seybert, Philadelphia, until 1812; John Speakman, 1812; to the Academy of Natural Sciences of Philadelphia, 1812.

107. A Fossilized or "Petrified" Bird's Nest and a Selection of Fossils (*not illustrated*) from the collection of Adam Seybert (1773–1825): Clay slate with fern impressions from Col de Balme in the Chamonix valley (Seybert no. 1070) and a fossilized shell, described as "Cornu ammonis" (Seybert no. 1803).

References: "Catalogue of Minerals in the Adam Seybert Collection," 1825, Academy of Natural Sciences of Philadelphia (Collection 141); John C. Greene and John G. Burke, *The Science of Minerals in the Age of Jefferson* (1978), pp. 29–30, 38–39, 44.

Provenance (for the fossils only): Adam Seybert, Philadelphia, 1812; John Speakman, 1812; to the Academy of Natural Sciences of Philadelphia, 1812.

108. *To the Citizens of the United States of America*
[The announcement of the formation of Peale's Natural History Museum, with an appeal for assistance, dated at Philadelphia, February 1, 1790]
1790
Broadside, 20.5 × 25 cm. (8 1/16 × 9 7/8 in.)

References: Sellers, *Peale* (1969), p. 257; Sellers, *Mr. Peale's Museum* (1980), pp. 45–47.

Massachusetts Historical Society, Boston (Sedgwick Papers, Vol. A, 238)

109. Museum Annual Subscription
1794 (list of subscribers headed by George Washington) [in bound volume]

Reference: Sellers, *Mr. Peale's Museum* (1980), pp. 71–73.

Historical Society of Pennsylvania, Philadelphia (Peale Papers)

(*Not in exhibition*)

110. Museum Gift Acknowledgment, hand-painted by Elizabeth Peale (1802–1857)
c. 1805
Engraving, 24.5 × 19.7 cm. (9¾ × 7¾ in.)
Signed, bottom center: *yours/Ruben/March 17ᵗʰ 1805*; inscribed: *Mrs. Morrison, of Tennessee*.

Provenance: Peale family; acquired by the American Philosophical Society, Philadelphia, between 1945 and present (B/P31, 50, Sellers family papers).

111. Unidentified artist
CHARLES WILLSON PEALE'S HOME AT THIRD AND LOMBARD, SITE OF HIS FIRST MUSEUM
Oil on panel, 19 × 13.3 cm. (7½ × 5¼ in.)
Reference: Sellers, *Mr. Peale's Museum* (1980), pp. 22–24, 69.

Provenance: Peale family; acquired by the American Philosophical Society, Philadelphia, between 1945 and present (Cat. 100, Box 81).

112. Letter from Charles Willson Peale to his daughter Angelica Peale Robinson, with drawing of museum's gas works, May 5, 1816
References: Sellers, *Portraits & Miniatures*, No. S136 [52]; Sellers, *Mr. Peale's Museum* (1980), pp. 228–30.

Provenance: Peale family; acquired by the American Philosophical Society, Philadelphia, between 1945 and present (C. W. Peale Letterbooks, Vol. 14, pp. 37–41, 1816).

113. Charles Willson Peale and Raphaelle Peale
FIVE MODELS FOR IMPROVEMENTS IN THE COMMON FIREPLACE
Painted wood and paper with brass and steel parts
Reference: "Description of some Improvements in the common Fire-places accompanied with Models, offered to the consideration of The American Philosophical Society By C. W. Peale and his son Raphaelle," *Transactions of the American Philosophical Society* V (1802), pp. 320–24.

Provenance: American Philosophical Society, Philadelphia, since 1797.

114. Smoke-Eater
Engraving after unlocated drawing by Charles Willson Peale, in *Weekly Magazine* II (July 21, 1798), opp. p. 353
Plate, 19.4 × 12.2 cm. (7⅝ × 5 in.); engraved surface, 18.4 × 8.9 cm. (7¼ × 3½ in.); page, 21.6 × 13 cm. (8½ × 5⅛ in.)
References: Sellers, *Portraits & Miniatures*, No. S81; Sellers, *Later Life* (1947), p. 101.
American Philosophical Society, Philadelphia

115. John I. Hawkins's Polygraph
Wood and metal, 43.2 × 25.4 × 12.7 cm. (17 × 10 × 5 in.)
University of Virginia, Charlottesville, Alderman Library, Manuscripts Department; on loan to Monticello, Home of Thomas Jefferson, Charlottesville

(*Not in exhibition*)

116. Drawing and explanation of John I. Hawkins's Physiognotrace, enclosed in a letter to Thomas Jefferson, January 10, 1803
Pencil and watercolor on paper
Library of Congress, Washington, D.C., Manuscripts Department (Thomas Jefferson Papers, 22193)

117. BARON FRIEDRICH HEINRICH ALEXANDER VON HUMBOLDT
Silhouette made with the physiognotrace
References: Sellers, *Peale* (1969), p. 315; Sellers, *Mr. Peale's Museum* (1980), pp. 160–66.

Provenance: Peale family descent; to Charles Coleman Sellers; to private collection, 1981.

118. *An Essay on Building Wooden Bridges*, printed by Francis Bailey, Philadelphia, 1797
Inscribed in pen at top center: *Charles Willson Peale/ March 15ᵗʰ 1797*.
Reference: Sellers, *Mr. Peale's Museum* (1980), pp. 94–95.
American Philosophical Society, Philadelphia

119. *Guide to the Philadelphia Museum*, printed at the Museum Press, Philadelphia, 1805
Reference: Sellers, *Mr. Peale's Museum* (1980), p. 200.
American Philosophical Society, Philadelphia

120. GERARD TROOST (1776–1850)
1823–24
Oil on canvas, 58.4 × 48.2 cm. (23 × 19 in.)
References: Sellers, *Portraits & Miniatures*, No. 879; Sellers, *Mr. Peale's Museum* (1980), p. 245; Academy of Natural Sciences of Philadelphia *Proceedings* VII (1854–55), p. 26.

Provenance: Peale's Museum until 1854; Sale No. 140; purchase, William S. Vaux, 1854; to the Academy of Natural Sciences of Philadelphia, 1855 (20).

121. Charles-Balthazar-Julien Fevret de Saint-Mémin (1770–1852)
CAPTAIN MERIWETHER LEWIS (1774–1809)
1807
Watercolor on paper, 15.9 × 9.5 cm. (6¼ × 3¾ in.)
References (to the drawing and to Peale's wax figure of the sitter in the museum): Sellers, *Later Life* (1947), pp. 240–41; Sellers, *Peale* (1969), pp. 344–45; Sellers, *Mr. Peale's Museum* (1980), pp. 187–88, 190–91, 348; "Memoranda of the Philadelphia Museum," entry for December 25, 1807, Peale Papers, Historical Society of Pennsylvania; Peale letter to Thomas Jefferson, January 29, 1808, Thomas Jefferson Papers, Library of Congress; J. Hall Pleasants, *The Walpole Society Notebook* (1947), pp. 37–38; Cutright, *Lewis and Clark* (1969), foll. p. 240, pp. 353–54; *Catalogue of American Portraits in The New-York Historical Society* I (1974), p. 456; National Gallery of Art, Washington, D.C., *The Eye of Jefferson*, entry by G[ilbert] V[incent]

(1976), pp. 74–75; Cutright, *History* (1976), pp. 45, 48, 224.

Provenance: William Clark; with C. W. Lyon, Inc., New York, c. 1947; The New-York Historical Society, New York City, Gift of the heirs of Hall Park McCullough, 1971 (1971.125).

122. PLAINS HORNED TOAD, actually a HORNED LIZARD (*Phrynosoma cornutum* [Harlan] or *Agama cornuta* Harlan)
c. 1806
Black and yellow watercolor on paper, 19 × 14.7 cm. (6¼ × 4¹⁵⁄₁₆ in.), irregular
Inscribed by Titian Ramsay Peale II at bottom: *Drawn by CWPeale/from a specimen brought by Lewis & Clark.*

References: Sellers, *Portraits & Miniatures*, No. S97 [3]; Sellers, *Mr. Peale's Museum* (1980), pp. 175, 186; Peale letter to Thomas Jefferson, July 24, 1804, Peale-Sellers Papers, American Philosophical Society; Thwaites, VII, p. 300; Jackson, pp. 192, 195 fn. 3, 277 fns. 2 and 3, 291, 302–3, 411 fn. 1, 490, 491 fn. 1; Cutright, *Lewis and Clark* (1969), pp. 61, 350, 385, 428, 450; Cutright, *History* (1976), p. 44.

Provenance: Peale family; acquired by the American Philosophical Society, Philadelphia, between 1945 and present (B/P31.15a).

123. LOUISIANA (now Western) TANAGER (*Piranga ludoviciana* [Wilson] or *Tanagra ludoviciana* Wilson)
1806(?)
Pencil and watercolor on paper, 21.3 × 17.9 cm. (8⁷⁄₁₆ × 7 in.)
Inscribed by Titian Ramsay Peale II at lower left: *C.W.P. del:*; at lower center: *Louisiana Tanager/From a specimen obtained on Lewis & Clark Exped᷒/Drawn for Captⁿ M Lewis (1806?).*

References (to the drawing and to the Louisiana or Western Tanager): Sellers, *Portraits & Miniatures*, No. S97 [2]; Sellers, *Mr. Peale's Museum* (1980), pp. 176, 186; Coues, III, pp. 1035–36; Thwaites, V, p. 111; Jackson, pp. 298, 411, 491 fn. 1; Cutright, *Lewis and Clark* (1969), pp. 296–97, 306, 384, 386, 450; Cutright, *History* (1976), pp. 45, 100, 230.

Provenance: Peale family; acquired by the American Philosophical Society, Philadelphia, between 1945 and present (B/P31.15a).

124. MOUNTAIN QUAIL (*Oreortyx pictus pictus* [Douglas] or *Ortyx picta* Douglas) AND LEWIS'S WOODPECKER (*Asyndesmus lewis* [gray] or *Picus torquatus* Wilson)
c. 1806
Pencil and watercolor, 21 × 18.6 cm. (8 × 7 in.)
Inscribed by Titian Ramsay Peale II at lower left: *CWP del:*; at lower right: *Drawn for Capt. M. Lewis/ (1806?)/by CWPeale.*

References (to the drawing, the mountain quail, and Lewis's Woodpecker): Sellers, *Portraits & Miniatures*, No. S97 [1]; Sellers, *Mr. Peale's Museum* (1980), pp. 176–77; Coues, II, p. 428; III, p. 936; Thwaites, IV, p. 252; Faxon, p. 136; Jackson, foll. p. 106, pp. 297, 298,

411, 490, 491 fn. 1; Cutright, *Lewis and Clark* (1969), p. 182, foll. p. 240, pp. 281, 288, 296–97, 384–85, 388, 391–92, 430, 435–36, 450, 453; Carl E. Bock, *The Ecology and Behavior of the Lewis Woodpecker (Asyndesmus Lewis)* (1970), pp. 1–2; Cutright, *History* (1976), pp. 44–45, 100, 230.

Provenance: Peale family; acquired by the American Philosophical Society, Philadelphia, between 1945 and present (B/P31.15a/No. 1).

125. Mandan Indian Robe
1797
Painted bison skin
References: Sellers, *Mr. Peale's Museum* (1980), pp. 173, 258, 260, 353 fn. 8; Meriwether Lewis letter (with enclosure) to Thomas Jefferson, April 7, 1805, Thomas Jefferson Papers, Library of Congress; "Memoranda of the Philadelphia Museum," entry for June 18, 1828, Peale Papers, Historical Society of Pennsylvania; Coues, I, pp. 250–51; Charles C. Willoughby, *American Anthropologist* ns. 7 (October–December 1905), pp. 634, 638, opp. p. 640; Raymond Darwin Burroughs, ed., *The Natural History of the Lewis and Clark Expedition* (1961), p. 304; Jackson, foll. p. 106, pp. 235–36, 241; Cutright, *Lewis and Clark* (1969), pp. 350, 355, 454.

Provenance: Lewis and Clark Expedition, 1805; Thomas Jefferson, Monticello, 1805–died 1826; possibly Lt. George Christian Hutter; his father, Christian Jacob Hutter, Pennsylvania, 1828; Peale's Museum, 1828–50; Peabody Museum of Archaeology and Ethnology, Harvard University, Cambridge, Massachusetts (99–12–10/53121).

126. Peace Pipe
References: "Memoranda of the Philadelphia Museum," entry following December 28, 1809, Peale Papers, Historical Society of Pennsylvania; "Articles collected by Merriwether [sic] Lewis Esq. and William Clark Esq. in their Voyage of Discovery up the Missouri to its source and to the Pacific Ocean" lists a number of peace pipes collected by the expedition and now given to the Peale Museum, Peale Papers, Historical Society of Pennsylvania; *Poulson's American Daily Advertiser*, March 1, 1810 [p. 2], includes a list of peace pipes presented to the museum by Lewis and Clark; "Memoranda . . . ," (see above), entry for June 18, 1828, lists several pipes.

Provenance: possibly Meriwether Lewis and William Clark through Thomas Jefferson, 1809; Peale's Museum, possibly 1809 until 1850; Peabody Museum of Archaeology and Ethnology, Harvard University, Cambridge, Massachusetts (HU 53101).

127. Plains Hunting Shirt
1806–7
References: Sellers, *Mr. Peale's Museum* (1980), pp. 180–81; "Memoranda of the Philadelphia Museum," entry following December 28, 1809, Peale Papers, Historical Society of Pennsylvania; "Articles collected by Merriwether [sic] Lewis Esq. and William Clark Esq. in their Voyage of Discovery up the Missouri to

its source and to the Pacific Ocean" lists "A Dress worn by Capt. Lewis & C," (possibly this hunting shirt), Peale Papers, Historical Society of Pennsylvania.

Provenance: Possibly Meriwether Lewis and William Clark through Thomas Jefferson, 1809; Peale's Museum, possibly 1809 until 1850; Peabody Museum of Archaeology and Ethnology, Harvard University, Cambridge, Massachusetts (HU 53041).

128. Ojibwa Feather Flag
Peabody Museum of Archaeology and Ethnology, Harvard University, Cambridge, Massachusetts (HU 53048).

129. MAJOR STEPHEN H. LONG (1784–1864)
1819
Oil on canvas, 61.6 × 51.4 cm. (24¼ × 20¼ in.)
Reference: Sellers, *Portraits & Miniatures*, No. 492.

Provenance: Peale's Museum until 1854; Sale No. 72; purchase, city of Philadelphia, 1854; on permanent loan to Independence National Historical Park Collection, 1854 (13.167).

130. TITIAN RAMSAY PEALE II (1799–1885)
1819
Oil on canvas, 62.2 × 51.4 cm. (24½ × 20¼ in.)
References: Sellers, *Portraits & Miniatures*, No. 679; Poesch.

Provenance: Peale's Museum until 1854; Sale No. 251; private collection, Pittsburgh; to Kennedy Galleries; to private collection.

131. Titian Ramsay Peale II (1799–1885)
DUSKY WOLF DEVOURING A MULE DEER HEAD
1820
Watercolor on paper, 19 × 23.5 cm. (7½ x 9¼ in.)
Inscribed at the lower right: *Dusky Wolf & Nubilus ·Say/Type spec.ᵐ killed & drawn at/Engineer cantonment by T R Peale/1820*; at lower right: *Female.*

References: "Memoranda of the Philadelphia Museum," entry for March 20, 1821, Peale Papers, Historical Society of Pennsylvania; James, I, pp. 167–73; II, pp. 276, 354 fn. 39; American Philosophical Society, Philadelphia, *Titian Ramsay Peale (1799–1885): An Exhibition of His Sketches, Watercolors and Oils*, catalogue by Stephen Catlett and Charlotte M. Porter (1981), p. 4, no. 2.

Provenance: Peale family; acquired by the American Philosophical Society, Philadelphia, between 1945 and present.

132. Titian Ramsay Peale II (1799–1885)
TWO GRAY SQUIRRELS
c. 1820
Brown and gray watercolor and pencil, 20.8 × 16 cm. (8³⁄₁₆ × 6⁵⁄₁₆ in.)
References (to the specimen and the drawing): "Memoranda of the Philadelphia Museum," entry for March

20, 1821 (possibly this drawing), Peale Papers, Historical Society of Pennsylvania; James, I, p. 370.

Provenance: Peale family; acquired by the American Philosophical Society, Philadelphia, between 1945 and present.

133. Titian Ramsay Peale II (1799–1885)
AMERICAN ANTELOPE
c. 1820
Pencil and watercolor on paper, 28 x 34.1 cm. (11¹⁄₁₆ × 13⁷⁄₁₆ in.)
Signed at lower left: *by T. R. Peale*; inscribed at lower center: AMERICAN ANTELOPE./*Antilocapra Americana Ord.*

References (to the drawing, the species, and the mounted specimen in Peale's Museum): Sellers, *Portraits & Miniatures*, No. S94; Sellers, *Mr. Peale's Museum* (1980), pp. 176–77, 186, 347 fn. 21; Meriwether Lewis letter to Thomas Jefferson, April 7, 1805; Jefferson letters to Peale, October 5 and 21, 1805; Peale letters to Jefferson, October 22, 1805, and April 5, 1806, all Thomas Jefferson Papers, Library of Congress; Peale letter to Jefferson, July 4, 1806, Peale-Sellers Papers, American Philosophical Society; William Clark letter to William D. Meriwether, January 26, 1810, Historical Society of Philadelphia; James, I, pp. 456, 462, 485; Coues, I, pp. 109, 120–21; *A Reprint of the North American Zoology, by George Ord. . . .* (1894), p. 24 (comments in original edition are on p. 292); Thwaites, I, p. 147; Poesch, p. 42; Raymond Darwin Burroughs, ed., *The Natural History of the Lewis and Clark Expedition* (1961), pp. 140–46; Jackson, pp. 235, 238, 261, 264, 267–68, 291–92, 297, 301–3, 490, 491 fn. 12; Cutright, *Lewis and Clark* (1969), pp. 81–82, 87, foll. p. 240, pp. 353, 375, 380, 385, 387, 389, 439; Cutright, *History* (1976), pp. 44, 49, 100.

Provenance: Peale family; acquired by the American Philosophical Society, Philadelphia, between 1945 and present (B/P31.15 b–no. 80).

134. SELF-PORTRAIT IN UNIFORM
1777–78
Oil on canvas, 15.2 × 14 cm. (6 × 5½ in.)
References: Sellers, *Portraits & Miniatures*, No. 625; *A Catalogue of Portraits and Other Works of Art in the Possession of the American Philosophical Society* (1961), p. 72; Whitfield J. Bell, Jr., *Antiques* CIV (1973), p. 892.

Provenance: Peale family; Charles Coleman Sellers; to the American Philosophical Society, Philadelphia, 1951 (58.P.67).

135. GENERAL WASHINGTON OVERLOOKING THE RARITAN RIVER AND THE ADVANCE OF THE BRITISH ARMY, in diary of June 18, 1777–August 30, 1778
Pencil drawing, 9.8 × 14.8 cm. (3⅞ x 5¹⁵⁄₁₆ in.)
Reference: Sellers, *Portraits & Miniatures*, No. S135 [22] and "Sitting of 1777," pp. 221–22.

Provenance: Peale family; acquired by the American Philosophical Society, Philadelphia, between 1945 and present.

136. MAP OF NEW YORK
November 4, 1776
Brown ink on paper, 41.4 × 33.5 cm. (16¼ × 13¼ in.)

References: Sellers, *Portraits & Miniatures*, No. S28; American Philosophical Society, *A Rising People: The Founding of the United States 1765–1789* (1976), p. 36. This map may have made use of the preliminary surveys of Claude-Joseph Sauthier for "A Topographical Map of Hudson's River . . . Engraved by William Faden. Published in London, October 1, 1776," in which the island of Manhattan and its surroundings closely resemble Peale's copy in their proportions.

Provenance: Peale family; acquired by the American Philosophical Society, Philadelphia, between 1945 and present.

137. CANNON, in diary of October 16, 1778–April 12, 1779
Pencil drawing, 8.6 × 15.3 cm. (3⅜ × 6 in.)
Inscribed on verso: *22nd Feby. Set out on a journey to take perspective Views of Trent and Prince Towns.*

Reference: Sellers, *Portraits & Miniatures*, No. S135 [24].

Provenance: Peale family; acquired by the American Philosophical Society, Philadelphia, between 1945 and present (B:P31-2, #5).

138. BENEDICT ARNOLD AND THE DEVIL, published in Francis Bailey's *Continental Almanac* of 1781 with a description of the figures
1780
Woodcut, 20.3 × 30.5 cm. (8 × 12 in.)

References: Sellers, *Portraits & Miniatures*, No. S34 (1872 version); William Murrell, *A History of American Graphic Humor* I (1967), No. 25 (1872 version); Sinclair Hamilton, *Early American Book Illustrators and Wood Engravers* I (1968), p. 13, No. 1343.

Provenance: Charles Allen Munn; to The Metropolitan Museum of Art, New York City, 1924 (24.90.1867).

139. WASHINGTON AND HIS GENERALS AT YORKTOWN
c. 1781
Oil on canvas, 54.3 × 75 cm. (21⅛ × 29⁹⁄₁₆ in.)

References: See Sellers, *Portraits & Miniatures*, No. 919; Eugenia Calvert Holland et al., *Four Generations of Commissions: The Peale Collection of the Maryland Historical Society* (1975), No. 12.

Provenance: Peale to Baltimore collector Robert Gilmor, Jr.; to Maryland Historical Society, Baltimore, 1845 (1845.3.1).

140. BENJAMIN FRANKLIN (1706–1790)
1785
Oil on canvas, 58.4 × 47.6 cm. (23 × 18¾ in.)

Reference: Sellers, *Portraits & Miniatures*, No. 279.

Provenance: Peale's Museum until 1854; Sale No. 121; purchase, Joseph Harrison, 1854; to Mrs. Joseph Harrison, Jr. (Sarah Harrison); to The Pennsylvania Academy of the Fine Arts, Philadelphia, 1912 (1912.14.2); lent in commemoration of the Tricentennial of Philadelphia.

141. GEORGE WASHINGTON (1732–1799)
1795
Oil on canvas, 73.7 × 60.3 cm. (29 × 23¾ in.)

References: Sellers, *Portraits & Miniatures*, No. 942; Theodore Bolton, *Antiquarian* XVI (1931), pp. 24–27.

Provenance: Peale's Museum until 1854; Sale No. 81; purchase, Thomas J. Bryan; to The New-York Historical Society, New York City (1867.299).

(*Not in exhibition*)

142. THOMAS JEFFERSON (1743–1826)
1791
Oil on canvas, 61 × 50.8 cm. (24 × 20 in.)

References: Sellers, *Portraits & Miniatures*, No. 413, No. SP68; Clarence W. Bowen, ed., *The History of the Centennial Celebration of the Inauguration of George Washington* (1892), p. 487; Charles Henry Hart, *McClure's Magazine* XI (May 1898), pp. 47–55; Fiske Kimball, *Proceedings of the American Philosophical Society* LXXXVII (1944), pp. 497–534; Julian P. Boyd, ed., *The Papers of Thomas Jefferson* (1950–); Alfred L. Bush, *The Life Portraits of Thomas Jefferson* (1962), pp. 30–33.

Provenance: Peale's Museum until 1854; Sale No. 82; purchase, city of Philadelphia, 1854; on permanent loan to Independence National Historical Park Collection, Philadelphia, 1854 (13.131).

143. JOHN ADAMS (1735–1826)
1791–94
Oil on canvas, 58.4 × 48.3 cm. (23 × 19 in.)

References: Sellers, *Portraits & Miniatures*, No. 3; Andrew Oliver, *Portraits of John and Abigail Adams* (1967), p. 70.

Provenance: Peale's Museum until 1854; Sale No. 48; purchase, city of Philadelphia, 1854; on permanent loan to Independence National Historical Park Collection, Philadelphia, 1854 (13.003).

144. WILLIAM BARTRAM (1739–1823)
1808
Oil on canvas, 58.4 × 48.2 cm. (23 × 19 in.)

References: Sellers, *Portraits & Miniatures*, No. 26; National Gallery of Art, Washington, D.C., *The Eye of Thomas Jefferson* (1976), No. 599.

Provenance: Peale's Museum until 1854; Sale No. 175; purchase, city of Philadelphia, 1854; on permanent loan to Independence National Historical Park Collection, Philadelphia, 1854 (13.014).

145. Peale's draft for an introductory lecture on natural history, 1799, and his *Introduction to a Course of Lectures on Natural History Delivered in the University of Pennsylvania, November 16, 1799*, published by Francis and Robert Bailey, Philadelphia, 1800.

Reference: Sellers, *Mr. Peale's Museum* (1980), pp. 100–110.

Academy of Natural Sciences of Philadelphia

146. THE PEALE FAMILY
c. 1770–73 and 1808
Oil on canvas, 143.5 × 227.3 cm. (56½ × 89½ in.)
Signed, dated, and inscribed at right center: *C. W
Peale painted these Portraits of his family/in 1773./wishing
to finish every work he had undertaken/—compleated
This picture in 1809!*

References: Sellers, *Portraits & Miniatures*, No. 617;
Henry T. Tuckerman, *Book of the Artists* (1870),
p. 53; John Hill Morgan, *Early American Painters* (1921),
pp. 70–72; *Catalogue of American Portraits in the New-
York Historical Society* II (1974), No. 1576; Philadelphia
Museum of Art, *Three Centuries of American Art* (1976).

Provenance: Peale's Museum until 1854; Sale No. 145;
purchase, Thomas J. Bryan, 1854–67; to The New-
York Historical Society, New York City, 1867
(1867.298).

147. JAMES PEALE (1749–1831) PAINTING A MINIATURE
1795
Oil on canvas, 76.2 × 63.5 cm. (30 × 25 in.)

Reference: Sellers, *Portraits & Miniatures*, No. 658.

Provenance: Peale family descent to Mabel Peale Elder,
great-granddaughter of the sitter; to Herbert L. Pratt,
1919; to Mead Art Museum, Amherst College, Massachusetts, 1945 (1945.10).

148. Titian Ramsay Peale I (1780–1798)
PAPELIO [BUTTERFLY], in his "Drawings of American
Insects," 1796
Pen and watercolor on paper, 24.1 × 19 cm. (9½ × 7½ in.)

National Agricultural Library, Beltsville, Maryland

149. MR. AND MRS. JAMES GITTINGS AND
GRANDDAUGHTER
1791
Oil on canvas, 101.6 × 162.5 cm. (40 × 64 in.)
Signed at left on balustrade: *C. W. Peale 1791.*

Reference: Sellers, *Portraits & Miniatures*, No. 301.

Provenance: Gittings family descent to Mary Gittings
(Mrs. James Magee); to her sister, Mrs. Charlotte
Gittings Cross; to The Peale Museum, Baltimore, 1974
(MA8754).

150. THOMAS JOHNSON FAMILY
1772
Oil on canvas, 122 × 148.6 cm. (48 × 58½ in.)

References: Sellers, *Portraits & Miniatures*, No. 423;
Edward S. Delaplaine, *The Life of Thomas Johnson*
(1927).

Provenance: Johnson family descent to Mrs. Ann
Grahame Ross, until 1896; to private collection.

151. MRS. SAMUEL CHASE (ANNE BALDWIN) AND HER
DAUGHTERS MATILDA CHASE AND ANNE CHASE
1772–75
Oil on canvas, 126.7 × 93 cm. (49⅞ × 36⅝ in.)

References: Sellers, *Portraits & Miniatures*, No. 139;
Eugenia Calvert Holland et al., *Four Generations of
Commissions: The Peale Collection of the Maryland
Historical Society* (1975), No. 6.

Provenance: Chase family descent to Mrs. Samuel
Ridout (Hester Ann Chase) and Mrs. William Laird; to
Maryland Historical Society, Baltimore, 1892
(1892.2.2).

152. MRS. JAMES SMITH [MRS. PATRICK CAMPBELL]
AND GRANDSON
1776
Oil on canvas, 96.5 × 76.2 cm. (38 × 30 in.)

Reference: Sellers, *Portraits & Miniatures*, No. 802.

Provenance: Smith family descent to Wilson Levering
Smith; to Mr. and Mrs. Wilson Levering Smith, Jr.; to
National Museum of American Art, Smithsonian
Institution, Washington, D.C., 1980 (1980.93).

153. SELF-PORTRAIT WITH ANGELICA AND A PORTRAIT
OF RACHEL
c. 1782–85
Oil on canvas, 88.9 × 69.2 cm. (35 × 27¼ in.)

References: Sellers, *Portraits & Miniatures*, No. 626,
No. SP107; Joseph Breck, *Art in America* II (1914),
pp. 424–31.

Provenance: Peale's Museum until 1854 (not listed in
Sale catalogue); purchase, George Rowan Robinson, a
grandson of Angelica, 1854; later cleaned and repaired
by Rembrandt Peale, who identified it then as the work
of his father; Mrs. Richard P. Esty, by 1952; to Kennedy
Galleries, 1960; to The Museum of Fine Arts, Houston,
Bayou Bend Collection, 1960 (B.60.49).

(*Not in exhibition*)

154. THE ARTIST'S MOTHER, MRS. CHARLES PEALE,
WITH HER GRANDCHILDREN
c. 1783
Oil on canvas, 75.5 × 63.5 cm. (29¾ × 25 in.)

Reference: Sellers, *Portraits & Miniatures*, No. 619.

Provenance: Rubens Peale; Peale family descent to
Mrs. Sabin W. Colton, Jr., great-granddaughter of the
artist; to her daughter, Mrs. Robert P. Esty; to private
collection, Detroit; to Kennedy Galleries; to private
collection.

155. THOMAS McKEAN (1734–1817) AND HIS SON,
THOMAS, JR.
1787
Oil on canvas, 128.3 × 104.1 cm. (50½ × 41 in.)
Signed and dated near chair at right: *C.W Peale, 1787.*

Reference: Sellers, *Portraits & Miniatures*, No. 522.

Provenance: Family descent to Phebe Warren McKean
Downs (Mrs. Norton Downs); to Philadelphia Museum
of Art, 1968 (68.74.1).

156. WILLIAM SMITH (1728–1814) AND HIS
GRANDSON
1788
Oil on canvas, 103.2 × 102.5 cm. (51⅜ × 40¼ in.)
Signed and dated at lower right: *C.W. Peale painted
1788.*

References: Sellers, *Portraits & Miniatures*, No. 810;
Arts in Virginia XVI (Winter–Spring 1976), pp. 14–21.

Provenance: Family descent to Mrs. Anne von Kapff,
great-granddaughter of the sitter; Mrs. William D.
Poultney; with Hirschl and Adler Galleries, New York
City, as agent, 1975; to Virginia Museum, Richmond,
1975 (75.11).

157. ROBERT GOLDSBOROUGH FAMILY
1789
Oil on canvas, 103.5 × 160 cm. (40¾ × 63 in.)
Signed and dated at lower right: *C W Peale/painted
Dec. 8/1789.*

References: Sellers, *Portraits & Miniatures*, No. 308,
No. SP122; Sellers, *Later Life* (1947), p. 233; Sellers,
American Art Journal II (1970), pp. 5–12.

Provenance: Goldsborough family descent; to private
collection.

158. MRS. JOHN NICHOLSON AND SON JOHN, JR.
1790
Oil on canvas, 91.5 × 70.2 cm. (36 × 27⅝ in.)
Signed and dated at lower right: *C. W Peale/
Painted 1790.*

Reference: Sellers, *Portraits & Miniatures*, No. 595,
No. SP104.

Provenance: Mr. and Mrs. John Nicholson; to their
son, John Nicholson, Jr., to 1848; to his daughter,
Frances S.D. Nicholson Ogden; to her son, Robert
Nash Ogden; to his daughter and son-in-law, Mr. and
Mrs. Carter Harrison; to The Art Institute of Chicago,
1952 (52.1001).

159. ALEXANDER ROBINSON AND HIS WIFE, ANGELICA
PEALE
1795
Oil on canvas, 66.7 × 89.5 cm. (26¼ × 35¼ in.)

Reference: Sellers, *Portraits & Miniatures*, No. 742.

Provenance: George Rowan Robinson, great-grandson
of Charles Willson Peale; to his daughter, Mrs. William
C. Edgar; to her daughter, Miss Marjorie Edgar; to
Miss Page Robinson; to Kennedy Galleries, 1967; to
private collection, 1968.

160. MRS. ALEXANDER ROBINSON (1775–1853) AND
HER DAUGHTER (1805–1819)
1818
Oil on canvas, 76.2 × 63.2 cm. (30 × 24⅞ in.)

Reference: Sellers, *Portraits & Miniatures*, No. 747.

Provenance: Angelica Yeatman Carr, great-granddaughter of the artist; Carr family descent to Alfred C.
and C.Y. Carr; to Kennedy Galleries; to private
collection.

161. REMBRANDT PEALE (1778–1860)
1818
Oil on canvas, 68.6 × 52.7 cm. (27 × 20⅞ in.)

References: Sellers, *Portraits & Miniatures*, No. 666;
Sellers, *Peale* (1969), p. 385.

Provenance: By family tradition, given to John Workman
of Philadelphia (1774–1827); owned by his daughter,
Ann Eliza Workman (1819–1899); willed by her to her
grandnephew, Robert Aitken Workman, 1898; Workman
family descent to his great-nephew, Donald Hamilton
Workman; to the National Portrait Gallery, Smithsonian
Institution, Washington, D.C., 1982.

162. THE STEWART CHILDREN (ISABELLA AND
JAMES STEWART)
1770–75
Oil on canvas, 94 × 124.5 cm. (37 × 49 in.)
Signed lower left: *Cha^{W.} Peale Pinx/Marilandia.*

Provenance: Anthony Stewart, father of subjects;
Isabella Stewart (died 1817); to Frances Isabella
Stewart, Augusta Brenton Stewart Galton (died 1940),
the Galton family, London; Newhouse family, New
York; Andrew Crispo Gallery, New York; Thyssen-
Bornemisza Collection, Lugano, Switzerland.

163. THE STODDERT CHILDREN
1789
Oil on canvas, 101.6 × 129.5 cm. (40 × 51 in.)
Signed and dated at right, on base of column: *C. W Peale
painted 1789.*

Reference: Sellers, *Portraits & Miniatures*, No. 832.

Provenance: Elizabeth Stoddert Ewell; at her death to
her son, Col. Benjamin Stoddert Ewell; William and
Mary College, Williamsburg, Virginia; to Harriot
Stoddert Turner, granddaughter of Harriot Stoddert
Campbell, 1894–after 1932; to Mrs. Turner's children;
on loan to Corcoran Gallery of Art; to The National
Society of The Colonial Dames of America, Wash-
ington, D.C., 1935 (234/0.50).

164. *An Epistle to a Friend, on the Means of Preserving
Health, Promoting Happiness; and Prolonging the Life
of Man to its Natural Period*, published by Jane Aitken
for R. Aitken, Philadelphia, 1803.

Library of Congress, Washington, D.C., Rare Books
Division (RA776.P35 Office)

165. Drawing and description of the vapor bath, pub-
lished in Henry Wilson Lockette's *An Inaugural
Dissertation on the Warm Bath*, printed by Carr and
Smith, 1801

American Philosophical Society, Philadelphia

166. THE PEDESTRIAN'S HOBBY HORSE, after an aqua-
tint in *The Repository of Arts, Literature, Fashion,
Manufacturers &c.* of 1819
c. April 1819
Black ink and brown ink wash on paper, 9.2 × 15.5 cm.
(3⅝ × 6⅛ in.)

References: Sellers, *Portraits & Miniatures*, No. S112; Sellers, *Later Life* (1947), p. 327; *Analectic Magazine* XIV (1819), p. 517.

Provenance: Peale family; acquired by the American Philosophical Society, Philadelphia, between 1945 and present (B/P31 Sketches).

167. Fan Chair
July 1786
India ink over pencil on paper, 25.3 × 20.6 cm. (9¹³⁄₁₆ × 8⅛ in.)
Inscribed on back: *To be published*.
References: Sellers, *Portraits & Miniatures*, No. S49; Charles B. Wood III, *Antiques* LXXXIX (1966), pp. 262–64.
American Philosophical Society, Philadelphia, Manuscript Communications, No. 10

168. Letter from Charles Willson Peale to Thomas Jefferson, with drawing of the milk cart, September 9, 1811
References: Sellers, *Portraits & Miniatures*, No. S136 [35]; Sellers, *Later Life* (1947), p. 256.
Provenance: Peale family; acquired by the American Philosophical Society, Philadelphia, between 1945 and present (C. W. Peale Letterbooks, Vol. 12, pp. 27–30, 1811).

169. Letter from Charles Willson Peale to Rembrandt Peale, with nine sketches of Belfield Farm, July 22, 1810
Reference: Sellers, *Portraits & Miniatures*, No. S136 [24–32].
Provenance: Peale family; acquired by the American Philosophical Society, Philadelphia, between 1945 and present (C. W. Peale Letterbooks, Vol. 11, pp. 36–39, 1810).

170. Letter from Charles Willson Peale to Robert Fulton, with drawing of Peale's plan for an exhibition at the Pennsylvania Academy, 1807
Reference: Sellers, *Portraits & Miniatures*, No. S136 [17].

Provenance: Peale family; acquired by the American Philosophical Society, Philadelphia, between 1945 and present (C. W. Peale Letterbooks, Vol. 8, p. 77, 1807).

171. Copperplate for ticket to the museum
1788
Provenance: Peale family descent to Elise Peale Patterson de Gelpi-Toro.
(*Not illustrated*)

172. Token of admission to Peale's Museum
Copper, diameter 3.3 cm. (1⁵⁄₁₆ in.)
Obverse: CHARLES WILLSON PEALE FOUNDER 1784; reverse: PHILADELPHIA MUSEUM/INCORPORATED 1821/ADMIT THE BEARER.
National Portrait Gallery, Smithsonian Institution, Washington, D.C., Peale Papers Collection
(*Not illustrated*)

173. Letter made with a polygraph, Charles Willson Peale to Raphaelle Peale, April 26, 1804
Provenance: Peale family; acquired by the American Philosophical Society, Philadelphia, between 1945 and present (C.W. Peale Letterbooks, Vol. 5, p. 51, 1804).
(*Not illustrated*)

174. Working model of the Hawkins Physiognotrace
Wood and brass, 57.2 × 40.6 × 28 cm. (22½ × 16 × 11 in.); in case, 59.7 × 52.1 × 30.5 cm. (23½ × 20½ × 12 in.)
National Portrait Gallery, Smithsonian Institution, Washington, D.C.
(*Not illustrated*)

175. *The Exhibition of the Columbianum or American Academy of Painting, Sculpture, Architecture*, printed by Francis and Robert Bailey, Philadelphia, 1795
Reference: Sellers, *Peale* (1969), pp. 268–73.
Historical Society of Pennsylvania, Philadelphia
(*Not illustrated*)

INDEX

PHOTOGRAPHIC CREDITS

The authors and publisher wish to thank the museums, libraries, and private collectors for permitting the reproduction of works of art or artifacts in their collections. Photographs have been supplied by the following: Will Brown: frontispiece, 1, 19, 21, 23, 24, 39, 40, 64, 65, 69–71, 130, 134, 154, 157, 160, Fig. j.; Hillel Burger: 78, 89, 98, 103, 104, 125–27; George M. Cushing: 108; James L. Dillon & Co., Inc.: 76, 79, 87, 88, 90, 92, 96, 106, 107, 120, 145; Rick Echelmeyer: 43, 44; Helga Studios: 148; Gene Mantie/Rolland White: 3, 18, 20, 63, 77, 81–85, 91, 93, 95, 110–13, 118, 119, 122–24, 131–33, 135, 150, 163, 166–70, Fig. e.; Michael Marsland: Fig. f.; Otto E. Nelson: 73; Joseph Szaszfai: Fig. c.; Taylor and Dull, Inc.: Fig. h.; Jeremy Whitaker: Fig. d.

LENDERS
TO THE EXHIBITION

Academy of Natural Sciences of Philadelphia

American Philosophical Society, Philadelphia

The Art Institute of Chicago

The Barra Foundation, Inc.

Bowdoin College Library, Brunswick, Maine

John Cadwalader, U.S.N.R. (Ret.)

Colonial Williamsburg Foundation, Virginia

The Connecticut Historical Society, Hartford

The Detroit Institute of Arts

Elise Peale Patterson de Gelpi-Toro

Historical Society of Pennsylvania, Philadelphia

Independence National Historical Park Collection, Philadelphia

The Library Company of Philadelphia

Library of Congress, Washington, D.C.

Maryland Historical Society, Baltimore

Massachusetts Historical Society, Boston

Robert L. McNeil, Jr.

Mead Art Museum, Amherst College, Massachusetts

The Metropolitan Museum of Art, New York City

Museum of Comparative Zoology, Harvard University, Cambridge, Massachusetts

Museum of Fine Arts, Boston

National Agricultural Library, Beltsville, Maryland

National Gallery of Art, Washington, D.C.

National Museum of American Art, Smithsonian Institution, Washington, D.C.

National Portrait Gallery, Smithsonian Institution, Washington, D.C.

The National Society of The Colonial Dames of America, Dumbarton House,
    Washington, D.C.

The New-York Historical Society, New York City

Peabody Museum of Archaeology and Ethnology, Harvard University, Cambridge,
    Massachusetts

The Peale Museum, Baltimore

The Pennsylvania Academy of the Fine Arts, Philadelphia

Philadelphia Museum of Art

Private collections

The Fine Arts Museums of San Francisco

The Society of the Cincinnati, Washington, D.C.

Robert Stewart

Allan Sussel

Thyssen-Bornemisza Collection, Lugano, Switzerland

Virginia Museum of Fine Arts, Richmond

Washington-Custis-Lee Collection, Washington and Lee University, Lexington, Virginia

The Henry Francis du Pont Winterthur Museum, Delaware

Worcester Art Museum, Massachusetts

Yale University Art Gallery, New Haven, Connecticut

ABOUT THE AUTHORS

CHARLES COLEMAN SELLERS was the author of *Charles Willson Peale*, the definitive biography of his ancestor, for which Sellers won the Bancroft Prize in History in 1970. Sellers was descended from Peale through Peale's daughter, Sophonisba Peale Sellers, and has been one of the major interpreters of Peale and his work. His other books on Peale include *Mr. Peale's Museum, Portraits and Miniatures by Charles Willson Peale*, and *Charles Willson Peale with Patron and Populace: A Supplement to Portraits and Miniatures by Charles Willson Peale*. He also wrote biographies of such other early American figures as Benedict Arnold, Lorenzo Dow, and Patience Wright.

Dr. Sellers was born in Overbrook, Pennsylvania, in 1903. He received his B.A. from Haverford College and his M.S. from Harvard University. He served as librarian of Dickinson College for many years. From 1956 to 1959 he was also the librarian of the Waldron Phoenix Belknap Library of American Painting at the Winterthur Museum, where he edited *American Colonial Painting*. Dr. Sellers died in 1980.

―――

EDGAR P. RICHARDSON is the author of a number of books on American art, including *Painting in America, American Romantic Painting, American Paintings in the Collection of Mr. and Mrs. John D. Rockefeller 3rd*, and *Washington Allston: A Study of the Romantic Artist in America*. He is also the author of *The Way of Western Art*.

Dr. Richardson was born in Glens Falls, New York, in 1902 and received his B.A. degree from Williams College. He was associated for over thirty years with the Detroit Institute of Arts, serving as Assistant Director from 1932 to 1945, and then as Director from 1945 to 1962. He then became Director of the Henry Francis du Pont Winterthur Museum from 1962 to 1966. He has been a trustee of Winterthur, Commissioner of the National Portrait Gallery, President of the Pennsylvania Academy of the Fine Arts, and a founder and for twenty-five years a trustee of the Archives of American Art. In addition, he served as editor of the *Art Quarterly* for nearly thirty years. During the course of his career he has received honorary degrees from Wayne State University, Union College, the University of Laval, the University of Delaware, and the University of Pennsylvania. He lives and works in Philadelphia.

―――

BROOKE HINDLE is the author of numerous books on American science and technology, including *Technology in Early America, The Pursuit of Science in Revolutionary America, David Rittenhouse*, and *Emulation and Invention*. In addition, he has been the editor of many other books, among them *America's Wooden Age, Early American Science, The Scientific Writings of David Rittenhouse*, and *Material Culture of the Wooden Age*.

Dr. Hindle was born in Philadelphia, Pennsylvania, in 1918. He attended the Massachusetts Institute of Technology, receiving his B.A. degree from Brown University, and his M.A. and Ph.D. degrees from the University of Pennsylvania. He was a member of the Department of History at

New York University for many years, becoming Dean of the University College of Arts and Science from 1967 to 1969 and head of the Department of History from 1970 to 1974. In 1974 he became Director of the Smithsonian Institution's National Museum of History and Technology, a post which he held until 1978, when he was appointed Senior Historian of the same institution, now called the National Museum of American History. He lives in Bethesda, Maryland.

———

LILLIAN B. MILLER is the author of *Patrons and Patriotism: The Encouragement of the Fine Arts in the United States, 1790–1860*, *In the Minds and Hearts of the People: Prologue to the American Revolution, 1760–1774*, and *The Dye Is Now Cast: The Road to American Independence, 1774–1776*. She is the editor of *The Collected Papers of Charles Willson Peale and His Family*, a microfiche publication with a detailed *Guide and Index*.

Dr. Miller was born in Boston, Massachusetts. She received her B.A. degree from Radcliffe College and her M.A. and Ph.D. degrees from Columbia University. She was formerly Associate Professor at the University of Wisconsin–Milwaukee and in 1981–82 Gannett Professor of the Humanities at the Rochester Institute of Technology. She is Historian of American Culture at the National Portrait Gallery, Smithsonian Institution, and Editor of the Charles Willson Peale Papers. She lives in Bethesda, Maryland.

THE TEXT OF THIS BOOK WAS PHOTOSET IN JANSON BY U.S. LITHOGRAPH, INC., NEW YORK. THIS TYPEFACE WAS DESIGNED BY ANTON JANSON, A SEVENTEENTH-CENTURY TYPEFOUNDER, WHOSE FIRST SPECIMEN SHEET APPEARED ABOUT 1675.

THE PAPER FOR THIS BOOK IS FUKIAGE MATTE COATED 128 GRAM, WHICH WAS MANUFACTURED BY THE DAISHOWA PULP COMPANY, IWANUMA, JAPAN. THE BOOK WAS PRINTED IN FOUR-COLOR OFFSET AND BOUND BY THE TOPPAN PRINTING COMPANY, TOKYO.